CHRIST

HIS CHURCH, HIS CROSS, HIS CROWN

The final work of
ROBERT P. LIGHTNER
with Pearl Lightner

DISPENSATIONAL
PUBLISHING HOUSE, INC.

Copyright © 2018 Robert P. Lightner
Cover and Illustration: Leonardo Costa
Cover and Illustrations © 2018 Dispensational Publishing House, Inc.

All rights reserved. This book or any portion thereof may not be reproduced or used in any manner whatsoever without the express written permission of the publisher except for the use of brief quotations in a book review.

"Scripture quotations taken from the New American Standard Bible® (NASB),
Copyright © 1960, 1962, 1963, 1968, 1971, 1972, 1973,
1975, 1977, 1995 by The Lockman Foundation
Used by permission. www.Lockman.org"

Printed in United States of America

First Edition, First Printing, 2018

ISBN: 978-1-945774-27-0

Dispensational Publishing House, Inc.
PO Box 3181
Taos, NM 87571

www.dispensationalpublishing.com

Ordering Information:
Quantity sales. Special discounts are available on quantity purchases by churches, associations, and others. For details, contact the publisher at the address above.

Orders by U.S. trade bookstores and wholesalers. Please contact the publisher:
Tel: (844) 321-4202

2 3 4 5 6 7 8 9 10 1

To Hoyle and Lucille Bowman with gratitude for your friendship and fellowship over the years from the trailer park in Dallas, Texas to Piedmont University in Winston-Salem, North Carolina.

Dr. Robert P. Lightner
1931 - 2018

A PERSONAL NOTE FROM THE PUBLISHER

On August 3, 2018, Dr. Robert P. Lightner went to be with his Savior. He had spent his last days writing the manuscript for the book you hold in your hands. It was his last work, and it is a work that is so needed in our day. Even in death, Dr. Lightner continues to teach.

Dr. Lightner joined the Dallas Theological Seminary faculty in 1968 after teaching for seven years at Baptist Bible College/Seminary in Johnson City, NY (now in Clarks Summit, PA). He has taught all the doctrines of Systematic Theology. Most of the 24 books he has written are about these doctrines. He began teaching at the seminary's extensions when the Extensions Program started. Since the 1950s he served as Interim Pastor 33 times at 24 different churches in Pennsylvania, New York, Arkansas, Oklahoma, Louisiana, and Texas, helping struggling churches and/or churches that were seeking a pastor. His longest interim lasted five years. His overseas ministry experience included Venezuela, Peru, Paraguay, the Philippines, and London (Spurgeon's Tabernacle). He continued teaching at seminary as needed and in Bible conferences and teaching modules at colleges and seminaries until 2015. His total time teaching at DTS was 47 years.

Pearl Lightner was invaluable in assisting Dr. Lightner in his ministry and in his writing. She typed his handwritten manuscripts, edited the typed work, served as his communications secretary, and so much more. She was a wife "whose price is far above rubies" (Prov. 31:10). Particularly for this book, as Dr. Lightner's health rapidly declined, Pearl was his chief editor. For this reason we have chosen to put her name on the cover along with the distinguished name of Robert P. Lightner, to honor the behind-the-scenes assistance of his loving wife of 66 years.

Each generation has only a few men of long-lasting integrity and wisdom in theological matters, and Robert Lightner was such a man for our generation. He was a gentleman in all respects, a churchman with extraordinary faithfulness, a teacher of the Word with the skill of a precision jeweler, and a theologian whose impact will last for many generations to come.

As you read this volume, you read about the One Dr. Lightner loved, lived for, and longed for.

> *Blessed be the God and Father of our Lord Jesus Christ, which according to his abundant mercy hath begotten us again unto a lively hope by the resurrection of Jesus Christ from the dead, To an inheritance incorruptible, and undefiled, and that fadeth not away, reserved in heaven for you, Who are kept by the power of God through faith unto salvation ready to be revealed in the last time. (1 Peter 1:3–5)*

GRANDPA'S TRIBUTE

It's difficult to know what to say about our grandfather. How do you sum up a lifetime like his? Grandpa Lightner's whole life was characterized by incredible care for God's Word, for his family, and for God's creation. The intense care that Grandpa poured out on his family was deep and real. He enjoyed a loving marriage with our grandma that lasted 66 years, which will be an inspiration to all of his children and grandchildren for the rest of our lives.

We knew our grandpa was highly educated, successful, and a "big name," especially among the Dallas Theological Seminary community. When his name was mentioned, we couldn't help but smile from ear to ear out of our intense pride for who he was. But to us, he wasn't an author, theologian, officiant, pastor, or professor. Dr. Robert Lightner was not his only name. To us, he was just Grandpa. We were proud to belong to him not just because of his accomplishments and service, but because of who he was to us. For the rest of time, no one will be able to take up the mantle of Grandpa to his grandchildren, or Daddy to his three daughters. Our grandpa understood that the highest and most unique calling God had given him was to his family. He put his family first and loved us with Christ-like humility his entire life, never putting us second to his work. We are sure he loved being Dr. Lightner, but he always showed his grandchildren that he loved being Grandpa even more. That is why while the world is missing Dr. Lightner, we are missing Grandpa.

Although he had 15 grandchildren, he managed to develop a personal relationship with each of us, making us feel like his most prized possessions. He poured himself into setting the example of God's love through the love he lavished unconditionally. Being his grandchild felt like being royalty. He took the time to call each of us on a regular basis and did everything he could to be there for each milestone in our lives, whether big or small. Even as he aged and his mobility became limited, he would still go to the greatest lengths to be present and let us know that we had his constant love and support. He would welcome us with big hugs, humor us with silly nicknames, attend school events, and take us on our ritual trips to McDonalds for ice cream on the way home from his farm in Forney, Texas. Grandpa Lightner even mowed lawns and collected cans in the Texas heat in order to send us the money.

Grandpa also loved helping his family experience his deep care for God's creation. On his farm he loved gardening, raising animals and tinkering with his 1940 Case tractor. We have many fond memories of times at the farm with him, from riding the horses, feeding the goats, collecting eggs from the chickens, picking vegetables in the garden, grilling hotdogs outside, and playing pool in the little farmhouse he built. Most importantly, we remember being with Grandpa and doing things that he cared about. He taught us the fulfillment that comes from being outside and from good, honest, hard work. Afterwards, we would sit in the shade of the porch of the farmhouse as we sipped a cold drink and swatted away flies, talking about anything with Grandpa because he was the best listener. Those experiences were formative for all of us. We each felt like we had 100% of Grandpa's care and attention. He was our biggest supporter and our best source of advice. We could not have been given a better role model.

Grandpa brought warmth wherever he went and he truly lived up to his nickname "Lightning Bob." He had a complete love of life and love for his family, his students and his colleagues. He never squandered opportunities for relationships and became a mentor to many, young and old. He knew that his calling was to love people, so he woke up each day with purpose. He loved people with Christ's love and demonstrated the existence of a good God to everyone around him. He was far from perfect, and he proved that God uses broken people to do great things.

Grandpa Lightner was truly irreplaceable. He was a man who was constantly filled with the joy of the Lord and knew how powerful that joy was. His laugh was one of those hearty, belly laughs that are genuine and infectious. His sneezes were surprising and unnecessarily loud with the intention of making his grandkids chuckle. His jokes were iconic; he always said that certain foods were "musty" because you "must" have another one!

Most important, and we know that Grandpa would want us to mention this aspect of his life, are the ways in which he was used by God to bring Him ultimate glory. Grandpa spent his life cultivating an extreme love and care for God's Word. He dedicated decades to studying, teaching, and preaching the Word of God. Much of his preaching and teaching came from the pulpit and in the classroom, but his teaching went far beyond that. While the voice that was heard loudly from pulpits and stages is now silent, his Savior will continue to speak to many through his words and through the life he lived. We will never know what kind of ripple effect his life will have on the Lord's work. But from his grandchildren's perspective, we know how he has impacted us and we will hold on to that forever.

We will always carry the lessons he taught us and the love he had for all of us. He never ceased to let us know how proud of us he was, how often he prayed for us, and how much joy he had in knowing that we walked with Jesus Christ our Savior. Our grandpa's example inspires us to live lives bigger than ourselves and to influence the world around us through our love for others and our knowledge of the Word of God. He desperately wanted his family to experience the joy that comes from knowing and living a life characterized by the truths of Scripture. Even though he is now out of our sight and in the presence of the Father, his legacy will live on in each of our lives. Our grandpa's character has helped us see that in the midst of our grief, this is a celebration. We will strive to imitate his love for family, his humility toward others, and his faithful pursuit of Jesus Christ until the day we see him again. Praise the Lord that now he is enjoying the sweetest of reunions with his family who have gone before him, running around in his completely healed body, and seeing his Savior face to face after devoting an entire lifetime to His glory. We are rejoicing that his faith has now become sight! Our prayer is that those who read this book will know more of the love and amazing grace of God, as our grandpa intended to convey.

Grandpa, thank you for never losing sight of what truly matters in this life. Thank you for living out what a good and faithful servant is. Thank you for raising your three daughters – our moms. We love and miss you, but know we will see you again in paradise. Until then, have a root beer with all who've gone before. We're sure it will taste pretty "musty!"

–This tribute was compiled by Amanda Shotts on behalf of those who called Dr. Robert Lightner, "Grandpa"

> Nathan Shotts
> Austin Bracy
> Jonathan Shotts
> Andy Steitz
> Conner Bracy
> Tim Steitz
> Taryn Bracy
> Ben Steitz
> Amanda Shotts
> Caleb Steitz
> Joshua Steitz
> Philip Steitz
> David Steitz
> Gisell Steitz
> Serenity Steitz

Table of Contents

Introduction 1

Part 1: The Biblical and Historical Christ 6

Part 2: Christ's Church 40

Part 3: Christ's Cross 78

Part 4: Christ's Crown 146

Annotated Bibliography 221

ACKNOWLEDGEMENT OF PERMISSION GRANTED

In the writing of this book, I have used sections in some of my earlier books. The publishers of these books have given me permission to do this. I give thanks therefore to Wipf and Stock, Kregel Publishers, and Baptist Standard Bearer.

Robert P. Lightner

INTRODUCTION

My goal in writing this volume is to show how four great doctrines: Christ, His church, His cross, and His crown relate to each other. How one interprets the Biblical teaching of any one of the four should be consistently applied to each of the other three.[1]

Interestingly, there are several proper names given to the second member of the Holy Trinity in the Bible. Here are some of the most common ones: Jesus, Jesus Christ, Son of Man, Christ, Son of God, Master, Son of David, Lord, Lamb of God, Jesus of Nazareth, Jesus the Nazarene, Lord Jesus, The Lord Jesus Christ. I believe that the last one is especially significant. It is His fullest and most complete name. "Lord" describes Him as the master, the sovereign of and over everything. "Jesus" describes Him in His humility. And "Christ" assigns Him as the Anointed One, the Messiah. Thus, I have used this name in the title of this book.

Three primary names for God the Father in the Old Testament[2] are God (Elohim), LORD (Yahweh), and Lord (Adonai). These names reveal much about God's character, so too the New Testament names of God the Son do the same. In both cases, the names are revelations of the character of each. There is no doubt that names of persons in the Bible convey meaning. They are not mere titles.

Many good individual volumes have been written about the Christ of Scripture, His church, His cross, and His crown. Most of these, however,

---
[1] I recommend two volumes on Bible Interpretation: Roy B. Zuck, *Basic Bible Interpretation* (Wheaton, IL: Victor Books, 1991) and Elliott Johnson, *Expository Hermeneutics* (Grand Rapids: Zondervan, 1990).
[2] See my *God of the Bible and Other Gods* for a fuller treatment of these names.

deal with the themes of this book in isolation from each other. In this book, I have set forth not only the major Biblical teaching on each of the themes but also the vital importance of seeing how the truths of Christ, His church, His cross, and His crown relate to each other. I have tried to show the connections between the four and how each is dependent upon the others.

It is my desire that the readers will see how what one believes about any one of these marvelous biblical truths affects and reflects what one believes about each of the others. I have written with the firm conviction that it is impossible to consistently view the teaching of Scripture while viewing any one of these four in isolation from any one of the other three. This is because in Scripture they complement each other. They build on each other and need to be viewed as interrelated essential aspects of the sovereign purpose of God.

I write with the hope of helping believers to understand what the Bible says about Christ and His church, cross, and crown. I may not convince many scholars or would-be scholars by my presentation, but I trust that all believing, motivated, and searching lay people will come to a closer walk with Christ as a result of reading this book.

There has been a lot said lately against the Jesus revealed in the Bible.[3] Is He really all the Bible claims Him to be? Were the authority of the Bible, the genuine humanity and absolute deity of Jesus of Nazareth simply creations of the fourth century mentality foisted upon the early Christians? Was Jesus ever married? Was Mary Magdalene His wife? Did she have a leadership role in the church? Did the early church turn Mary into a prostitute in order to keep women out of leadership roles in the church?

It is not my intention in this volume to refute the false claims perpetuated in fanciful novels or by the so-called scholars of the Jesus Seminar. Rather, it is my goal to set forth what the Bible says about Christ, His church, His cross, and His future reign on planet earth and to show how these relate

---

3 See the lead article "In Search of the Real Jesus" in *U.S. News and World Report* (Dec. 18, 2006). In sharp contrast, I heartily recommend *The Historical Jews Ancient Evidence for the Life of Christ* by Gary R. Habermas (Joplin, MO: College Press).

to each other. These four form a unity of truths. They are indispensable to and inseparable from each other and to the entire purpose and program of God revealed in Scripture.

Scholarly contributions have recently been written in defense of the Christ of Scripture. These have refuted and debunked the liberal notion voiced by the Jesus Seminar: "The Jesus of the gospels is an imaginative theological construct into which has been woven traces of the enigmatic sage from Nazareth–traces that cry out for recognition and liberation from the firm grip of those whose faith overpowered their memories. The search for the authentic Jesus is a search for the forgotten Jesus."[4]

What this quotation is saying in brief is that the Jesus Christ of the Bible is not the Jesus Christ of history.

If the Jesus revealed so extensively in the Bible is not all He claimed to be, His work on the cross is merely a tragic end to the good life of a noble man. This would mean that His death on the cross, His church, and His promised kingdom reign have no significance to us today. I want to establish that Christ's death on the cross is the very foundation for His church and His future reign over His global kingdom. The church Jesus promised that He would build, and did build, has as one of its highest purposes the responsibility to share with the world the message of the cross. The future kingdom that Jesus will establish on the earth and reign over will bring true peace and righteousness to the whole world. Members of Christ's church are promised that they will rule and reign with Him in that kingdom (2 Tim. 2:12; Rev. 20:6). These are some of my reasons for calling Christ, His church, His cross, and His crown four quadrants of one truth that must never be divorced from each other.

We will learn about some essential facts of the Person of the Lord Jesus Christ in Part 1. He is both the Jesus of history and the Biblical Jesus.

---

4 Quoting from the Jesus Seminar in *Reinventing Jesus* by Ed Komoszewski, James Sawyer, and Daniel B. Wallace (Grand Rapids: Kregel, 2006), p. 21. These recent, sound scholarly books have been written showing the fallacy of all the attempts to dissociate the Christ of Scripture from the Christ of history: *Breaking the Da Vinci Code* by Darrell Bock and *The Historical Jesus* by Gary R. Habermas. I recommend these highly.

In Part 2, Christ's church will be discussed. We will distinguish between the church which is described in Scripture as His body and the local church in the New Testament. Attention will be given to the liberal ecumenical movement with its goal of a one-world church and one-world government. When did the church which is the body of Christ begin? When will it be terminated on earth? These are some of the questions we will seek to answer. In Part 3, we will look at the cross work of Christ: its anticipation, necessity, accomplishments, extent of its benefits and its relationship to the believer's life today.

Part 4 of this book will delve into what I call the Crown of Christ—His teaching about His coming kingdom. We will observe what the Old and New Testaments say about the coming physical kingdom on earth. What precedes the kingdom and follows it will also be discussed.

I enlist my readers to think biblically and theologically with me through these pages. Please join me in the journey. Come along as we see how clearly Scripture presents our Lord Jesus Christ, His church, His cross, and His crown and how firm and indispensable a foundation has been laid for us in God's Word. We live in days in which the presentation of Christ to our society is needed more than ever before. With the recent passing of the famed world-wide evangelist Billy Graham, the world does not have a Christ-proclaiming leader of that stature, and perhaps never will again. It is incumbent upon each believer, serving faithfully in their local church, to have a firm grasp on the identity of Christ to present Him, His cross, His church and His crown to the world that surrounds them.

Our primary textbook for all four of these doctrines will be the Bible, primarily the New Testament. We will be interested in what the human penmen, directed and protected by the Spirit of God, had to say about the subjects discussed in that volume.

In short, this book is an attempt to illustrate the need to see relationships between what the Bible says about Christ, His cross, His church and

His crown. All of these are very closely related to each other. In fact, they are each only fully understood in light of each other. When they are seen together, a more complete picture emerges. Without Christ, there would have been no cross, no church and no future crown. Without the promised church, Christ's prophecy about establishing His church would have been proven false. Without the coming kingdom reign of Christ on and over planet earth, all the predictions of the coming kingdom in the Old and New Testaments would be proven to be false. The Biblical teaching of these four–Christ, His church, His cross and His crown–forms a beautiful mosaic of God's plan.

PART 1

THE BIBLICAL AND HISTORICAL CHRIST

OUTLINE

I. Christ's Extensive Use of the Old Testament Scriptures

II. Christ's View of the Divine Origin of the Old Testament

III. Christ's View of the Inspiration of the Old Testament

IV. Christ's View of the Authority of the Old Testament

V. The Person of Christ
- A. Christ, the Word of God Incarnate
- B. Christ's Eternal Existence
- C. Christ's Eternal Sonship
- D. Christ's Virgin Birth
- E. Christ's Sinless Humanity
- F. Christ's Undiminished Deity
- G. Christ the God-Man
- H. Christ's Sinless Life on Earth

THE BIBLICAL AND HISTORICAL CHRIST

Before we discuss the Person and work of Christ, it is essential that we understand how He viewed and used the Old Testament Scriptures. You may ask, why is that essential? It is because everything evangelicals believe about Christ, His cross, and His crown is based upon the Scriptures. Therefore, we need to know as we begin our study of these foundational issues not only how they relate to each other but also upon what authority we rest our case concerning Christ, His church, His cross, and His crown. Surely we would not want to embrace and build our faith on anything less than what Jesus Himself viewed as divinely inspired and, therefore, authoritative.

Christ's Extensive Use of the Old Testament Scriptures

To begin, it cannot be denied that Christ used the Old Testament Scripture extensively in His ministry.

> Our Lord not only believed the truth of Old Testament history and used the Scriptures as final authority in matters of faith and conduct, He also regarded the writings themselves as inspired. To Him, Moses, the prophets, David, and the other Scripture writers were given their messages by the Spirit of God. There is no trace of the modern idea that the men were inspired but not their writings. The writings are authoritative

not because of the human author but because God is regarded as the ultimate author.[5]

Christ used the Hebrew canon of Scripture only. He repeatedly rejected Jewish traditions which often contradicted Scripture. He considered the "traditions of men" as inferior to Scripture even though these traditions were often associated with Scripture, especially by the elders of Israel. Frequently, Christ spoke of the striking contrast between the "traditions" with "the commandment of God." Christ also clearly condemned the traditions of the elders when these were contrary to the commandments of God.

Christ did not use or even refer to the apocryphal writings which were available to Him. These non-inspired books were written sometime between 300 B.C. and A.D. 100. He used only the Hebrew canon of Scripture in His ministry, which did not include the apocryphal writings.

Christ did use the Septuagint in His ministry. This was a Greek translation of the Old Testament with dates ranging from 250 to 160 years before Christ. He used this translation often when He quoted and referred to the Old Testament. Christ's canon of Scripture, or list of books, was exactly the same as the Hebrew canon of Scripture. He even referred to the same three-part division that the Jews had, as He referred to the Law, Prophets, and Psalms (Luke 24:44).

Christ described the Old Testament as the very commandment and word of God (Mark 7:8, 9, 13) and contrasted it with "the tradition of men." He spoke of the enduring character of Scripture and its durability and eternality. The Scripture, Christ said, "cannot be broken" (John 10:35) which described its indisputable, indefectible, and inviolable character.

For Christ, Scripture was prophetic in character. That is, all that was prophesied would be fulfilled. The phrase "that the Scripture might be

---

[5] John W. Wenham, "Christ's View of Scripture" *Inerrancy* edited by Norman L. Geisler (Grand Rapids: Zondervan Publishing House, 1980), pp. 16-17.

fulfilled" was said by Him often. In this way, the certainty of Scripture was confirmed by Him.

We might reverently ask, why did Christ appeal so often, so extensively and exclusively to the Old Testament Scripture? To be sure, He did not come to earth to put Himself in the place of Scripture, to set it aside, or to supersede it in any way. Rather, Christ clearly and forcefully endorsed the divine authority of Scripture. It was not to be worshipped but to be obeyed as the very word of God.

Every time Christ appealed to Scripture directly or indirectly, He was expressing complete faith and trust in It. There are times when He quoted Scripture to express His own faith and feelings. He did this, for example, on the cross. While giving His life for sinners, He quoted from Psalm 31:5 when He said to God the Father, "Into thy hands I commend my spirit" (Luke 23:46). And again, while on the cross, He quoted from Psalm 22:1 (cf. Matthew 27:46) and demonstrated His complete trust and reliance upon the words of the Old Testament. He did this throughout His life on earth.

Christ also used Scripture to defend His views. Our Lord spoke with divine authority. He called upon the people to set aside the traditions of the fathers and replace them with the authority of God. To defend His view regarding marriage and divorce, Christ quoted from Genesis 2:23-24 (cf. Matthew 19:5). Again, in defense of His view of the resurrection of the dead, He quoted from Exodus 3:6, 15 (cf. Matthew 22:32). There are many other examples of this, but these should suffice for us to see how Christ defended His views and sustained His claims by appealing to the Old Testament as the written Word of God.

Christ also used Scripture often with His disciples. When He did so, He of course had a different reason than when He used the Old Testament in response to the Scribes and Pharisees. He had a very special and intimate relation to those He had chosen to be His disciples. Luke records how, in the latter part of His life on earth, Christ told them about His part in the fulfillment of the prophetic word (Luke 18:31-33) to encourage them in their faith.

In summary of Christ's extensive use of the Old Testament as God's Word, here is a list of the books to which He directly referred: Genesis (Matthew 19:4-5), Exodus (Mark 12:26), Leviticus (Luke 10:27), Numbers (John 3:14), Deuteronomy (Matthew 23:37). Five of the prophets were quoted by Christ: Isaiah, Jeremiah, Hosea, Zechariah, and Malachi. Christ quoted at least eight times from the Psalms: Matthew 21:16, 42; 22:44; 27:46; Mark 15:34; Luke 23:46; John 13:18; 10:34. It is beyond any shadow of doubt that Christ gave full endorsement to the entire Old Testament as the Word of God.

Christ's View of the Divine Origin of the Old Testament

There certainly is no room for doubt that Christ used the Old Testament Scriptures freely and accepted them as that which came from God. Beyond this reality, Christ also made a number of very specific pronouncements indicating His own view of Scripture's origin.

I am not at this point referring to Christ's view of the inspiration of Scripture. The truth of the inspiration of Scripture is certainly related to the truth of the revelation, or the making known, of Scripture. But the two works of God are not synonymous. The inspiration of Scripture pertains primarily to the recording of Scripture while the revelation of Scripture pertains to the imparting, or making known, of truth. We will deal later with Christ's view of Scripture's inspiration. At this point we want to discover what Christ believed and taught about the source of the inspired Word of God, of the origin of Scripture.

I want to provide proof from general consideration that Christ believed the Old Testament Scriptures came from God Himself. He is the source of the revelation. First, He used names and titles to designate His belief that Scripture originated with God. In John 10:34-35, He referred to the Scripture, Law, and Word of God as one and the same. Christ accepted the Old Testament as a communication from God when He called it the Word. The term Scripture reminds us that He accepted it in its written form. When He referred to the Old Testament as "Law," He was emphasizing its authority and trustworthiness.

Christ knew the prevailing Jewish belief in the divine origin of Scripture, and He never questioned that reality. The Jews of Christ's day accepted the Old Testament as the divine deposit of truth for man. Christ did criticize other things the Jews believed and practiced but never their high regard for the Old Testament. He never did, however, accept the additions and false interpretations which the Jewish leaders often placed upon the Old Testament. Christ's fiercest Jewish critics, the religious leaders among the people, rejected the Christ of the Scriptures. It was not the Jewish belief in the divine origin of Scripture that was wrong but their stubborn refusal to accept the One whom the Holy Spirit spoke of in their Old Testament.

Christ also accepted the miraculous in Israel's history which verified that God was the giver of the revelation. These historical events include the creation of the world and man (Matthew 19:4), the flood (Matthew 24:37-39), the burning bush Moses saw (Mark 12:26), the supply of manna for the Israelites (John 6:32), the serpent in the wilderness (John 3:14), and the famine of Elijah's day (Luke 4:25).

Christ constantly appealed to the Scriptures for Himself and others. All throughout His life on earth this was true, and it argues for His belief that the Scriptures were God's revelation to man.

Added to the above evidences of Christ's view of the origin of Scripture is the prophetic element in that revelation. Frequently during His earthly ministry He said the phrase "that it might be fulfilled" or its equivalent when relating to people. These statements referred either to prophecy that had already been fulfilled at the time or that was to be fulfilled in the future. This means He believed and taught that prophecy in the Old Testament had already received fulfillment or was to be fulfilled in the future. Christ, in other words, had complete confidence in the divine origin of Scripture.

There are many passages which give support in the strongest language possible to the fact that Scripture originated with God. He is the One who gave it. The revelation is His. Two among many such passages deserve special attention. Both passages record Christ responding to questions from the Sadducees, the Scribes, and the Pharisees.

The argument which the Sadducees raised involved the resurrection (Matthew 22:23-28), a truth in which they did not believe. Christ responded to their trick question by appealing to the words of Moses recorded in Exodus 3:6 which Christ said were given to them by God. Moses was simply the human penman of God's revelation. In other words, the real source of the words Moses wrote came from God Himself. Needless to say, Christ's answer caused great astonishment among the people. Do not miss the critical point here. The objection the Sadducees raised was based on what Moses had written. Christ's response to their question proceeded on the basis of what God had said, which Moses had received directly from God and recorded.

The Pharisees and Scribes on another occasion asked Jesus why His disciples did not keep the tradition of the elders among them because they ate food without first washing their hands. Here again, Christ's answer to representatives of these two groups astounded them because in His reply He accused them of transgressing "the commandment of God" and also making void "the Word of God." They had done this because they had failed to remember that what Moses recorded in Exodus 20:12 and Deuteronomy 5:16 God Himself had said (Matthew 15:3-6; Mark 7:8-13). God was the source of the revelation to Moses.

In conclusion of Christ's view of the divine source of the Old Testament, we will touch briefly on the means by which God gave the revelation, the character of it, and the purpose of it.

First, let's examine the *means* God used to give His revelation. Christ Himself was the means by which God revealed Himself. John the apostle put it this way, "No man hath seen God at any time, the only begotten Son, which is in the bosom of the Father, he hath declared him" (John 1:18). Christ taught the same truth to His disciples (John 14:9; 24; 17:6, 8, 14; Matthew 11:27). The revelation of God in Christ is not a continuous process. It was completed at the Incarnation.

The divine revelation was given to humans. On different occasions, Christ referred to the Scripture by naming the *human penman* of the revelation. Moses, David, Isaiah the prophet, and Daniel the prophet are named. This is significant because it demonstrates that the incomprehensible God condescended to make His will known to sinful man. Also, the writings of these men encompass the three divisions of the Old Testament Scriptures. How marvelous and amazing it is that God would use the ones He had created to be vehicles through whom He would reveal Himself. First to the writers and then through them.

The revelation God gave to the human penmen of Scripture was often in specific *words*. Not always, but many times God gave the precise words to the human writers of Scripture. Mark 12:26 is a clear examples of God doing this.

Second, let's look at the *character* of the divine revelation. God's revelation to man was given progressively. By that, we do not mean it was progressively more and more inspired. Rather, it means truth was added to truth. God did not give His total revelation all at the same time. His revelation to man was given gradually, in keeping with God's timetable. As Christ said clearly, "The Law and the Prophets were [proclaimed] until John" (Luke 16:16). Statements such as this tell us that the revelation was given gradually, at God's discretion.

Another characteristic of God's revelation is that Christ recognized and taught the binding and authoritative nature of it. Often He referred to Scripture as Law. The word Law was one of the three designations given to the Scriptures. But Christ applied the same label to portions not in the Law division of the Old Testament. For example, on one occasion Christ told His disciples that the religious leaders among the Jews hated Him (John 15:24). And they did so "that the word might be fulfilled that is written in their law, They hated me without a cause" (v. 25). In this instance, Christ quoted from Psalm 35:19 and 69:4. These portions are not in the Law division of the Old Testament, yet here, they are called "law."

As Christ approached His death, He acknowledged the Word of God as truth. He did this in His high priestly prayer. He said, "Sanctify them [the disciples] through thy truth: thy word is truth" (John 17:17). He was referring, of course, to the Old Testament Scriptures. Most likely the disciples heard the words in Christ's prayer. Therefore, they were assured in their own hearts and minds that the same faith in the Scriptures which characterized Christ's entire life was still His. Christ's statement "Your word is truth" was an acknowledgment that He Himself was the embodiment of truth.

Third, let's investigate the *purpose* for the revelation. Christ made known four major purposes. First, the revelation from God was to reveal *the Person of God* to make Himself known to mankind. The Scriptures are a disclosure of God. He is the God of the living. And He made this truth known to the Sadducees when He quoted to them the words of Moses (Mark 12:26-27) that are recorded in Exodus 3:6.

Second, Christ taught that Scripture was given to bear testimony to *the power of God*. In the same passage quoted above, Christ accused the Sadducees of not knowing the power of God because they did not know the Person of God.

Third, the Scripture was given by God to reveal the *purposes of God* for both His followers and Christ. Throughout His life on planet earth,

Christ was always doing His Father's will. His life from birth to death was the fulfillment of Scripture. His Incarnation and birth were predicted in Scripture (Matthew 1:22-23; Isaiah 7:14). Joseph and Mary's flight into Egypt with the baby Jesus was the fulfillment of Scripture (Matthew 2:13-15; Hosea 11:1). His childhood as He grew up in Nazareth was predicted by Isaiah hundreds of years before He was born (Matthew 2:19-23; Isaiah 11:1). The same prophet wrote of Christ's ministry of miracles (Matthew 8:16-17; Isaiah 53:4). His ministry to Gentiles was also a subject of prophecy (Matthew 12:15-21; Isaiah 42:1f). Christ's arrest and death on the cross of Calvary were also specifics revealed by God even before He was born.

Fourth, the Scripture was given to reveal the *Person of Christ*. Luke wrote that beginning with Moses and throughout all the prophets Christ interpreted for the people the things concerning Himself. The Holy Spirit did not direct Luke to include the interpretation and exposition of those things. He simply led him to record that Christ was alive and ministering to the two on the road to Emmaus (Luke 24:27). Interestingly, in the same context, Luke made it clear that all three of the Jewish divisions of the Old Testament books–Law, Prophets, and Psalms–spoke of Christ (v. 44).

Up to this point, we have observed how frequently and extensively Christ used the Old Testament Scriptures and how He insisted that they came from God Himself and were penned by chosen men. Now it is time to note Christ's teaching of the inspiration of that revelation of God.

Christ's View of the Inspiration of the Old Testament

Gaussen's formal definition of the inspiration of Scripture has been accepted as a thorough and orthodox definition: "… that inexplicable power which the Divine Spirit, put forth of old on the authors of holy Scripture, in order to their guidance even in the employment of the words they used, and to preserve them alike from all error and from all omission."[6]

The Greek word from which the word "inspiration" comes is *theopneustos*. It appears only once in the New Testament, in 2 Timothy 3:16. In explaining that verse, Benjamin Breckenridge Warfield writes, "What it says of Scripture is, not that it is 'breathed into by God' or is the product of the Divine 'inbreathing' into its human authors, but that it is breathed out by God, 'God breathed,' the product of the creative breath of God."[7]

Christ taught that the Old Testament was fully and completely inspired by God. He even extended His view to each and every word and detail as well as to the entirety of the original manuscripts of Scripture.

Interestingly, He did not even have the original autographs available to Him. Neither did anyone else, for that matter. The original manuscripts have been lost though we have a large number of copies, versions, and translations available to us today. Christ relied heavily upon the Septuagint, a Greek translation of the Old Testament with dates ranging from about 250-160 B.C. He also made provision for the inspiration of the New Testament even though none of it had been written when He was on earth. How did He do this? He did it by promising the disciples there would be the coming of the Holy Spirit and His enabling work upon the human authors (John 16:13-14).

Even a casual reading of the Gospels—Matthew, Mark, Luke, and John—reveals Christ's high view of the Old Testament Scriptures. He not only demonstrated His vast knowledge of the Scriptures but also His view of the full and complete inspiration of the Old Testament.

There is no record of anyone asking Christ what He believed or thought about the Old Testament. He made His view, His acceptance of it, known widely among the people. He taught the inspiration of the entire Old Testament. He said, "Think not that I am come to destroy the law, or the

---

[6] L. Gaussen, *The Divine Inspiration of the Bible* (Grand Rapids: Kregel Publications, 1971), p. 34.
[7] Benjamin Breckenridge Warfield, *The Inspiration and Authority of the Bible* (Philadelphia: The Presbyterian and Reformed Publishing Co., 1948), p. 133.

prophets: I am not come to destroy, but to fulfil" (Matthew 5:17). The Law and the Prophets is a standard title referring to the entire Old Testament Scriptures. Christ could hardly have employed stronger words to declare His view of the entire Old Testament. Luke recorded Christ's sweeping reference to the threefold division as it existed in His day. He declared, "… that all things must be fulfilled, which were written in the law of Moses, and in the prophets, and in the psalms, concerning me" (Luke 24:44).

Christ's high regard for the Old Testament and His view that it was given by God to man extended to the inspiration of the very words of Scripture. There is no indication whatsoever that He believed or taught merely inspiration of concept or thought. Instead, His entire argument frequently rested upon one or two words which He quoted from the Old Testament.

One example from the many of Christ's view of the verbal inspiration of Scripture will suffice to illustrate the point. The Sadducees, who rejected the resurrection, came to Him with a complicated story by which they intended to trap Him regarding the resurrection. Matthew records the incident in 22:23-33. The astonishing answer Christ gave to them stands or falls on the inspiration of one word and even the tense of that word. Jesus quoted Exodus 3:6 to the Sadducees and chided them for not knowing it: "But as touching the resurrection of the dead, have ye not read that which was spoken unto you by God, saying, I am the God of Abraham, and the God of Isaac, and the God of Jacob? God is not the God of the dead, but of the living" (Matthew 22:31-32). These words were spoken by God to Moses 400 years after Abraham had died, yet God used the present tense verb, "I am" rather than, "I was." Jesus uses this Exodus passage to prove resurrection to the Sadducees, and the entire argument rests upon the present tense of the verb.

Christ's View of the Authority of the Old Testament

The source of Scripture and its inspiration are very clear in Christ's teaching. Now we need to ask, "What authority did He place upon the divinely-originated and inspired Scripture which He used so extensively?"

First, it may be in order to demonstrate the authority of Christ Himself. Matthew, Mark, Luke, and John all recognized and affirmed His authority. Other human penmen of New Testament Scripture affirmed the same thing. Christ Himself testified to His own divine authority saying, "Heaven and earth shall pass away: but my words shall not pass away" (Mark 13:31). And again He said, "And every one that heareth these sayings of mine, and doeth them not, shall be likened unto a foolish man, which built his house upon the sand" (Matthew 7:26). Our Lord argued clearly for His own divine authority. And just as clearly, He submitted His own authority to the authority of God's Word. He appealed to no human authority but set forth His teaching as from God the Father. He said it this way: "My doctrine is not mine, but his that sent me" (John 7:16). Never did Christ impose His own personal authority over that of the Old Testament Scripture. Neither did Christ ever judge Scripture. Rather, He always endorsed it, obeyed it, and sometimes even fulfilled it. There is a unique relationship in Christ's teaching between His own authority and the authority of the Old Testament Scripture. The one does not abrogate the other in any way. The two confirm each other.

No discussion of Christ's teaching about the authority of Scripture is complete without reference to John 10:34-35. In the background of this passage, the Jewish leaders were about to stone Christ because He claimed to be God. His response to His accusers was: "Is it not written in your law, I said, Ye are gods? If he called them gods, unto whom the word of God came, and the scripture cannot be broken."

There are two phrases in John 10:34-35 which are pertinent to Christ's teaching of the authority of Scripture. The first phrase is in the form of a question: "Is it not written in your law, I said, Ye are gods?" (John 10:34). To those who were seeking to stone Him, Christ's defense was in the form of an appeal to Scripture. His appeal therefore was to what was "written," not mere oral traditions or concepts. Also, He refers to what was written as possessing legal and divine authority. It was "law." But significantly the passage Christ quoted to His critics (from Psalm 82:6) was not in the Law or Prophetic section of their Old Testament Scripture. In this way, He was ascribing legal, binding authority to the whole of Scripture. This means Christ was hanging the validity of His entire argument upon one word, "gods," which He called written in defense of His claim to be the Son of God.

The second phrase in Christ's response to His critics is, "And the Scripture cannot be broken" (John 10:35). With this phrase, He was responding to His own question, "Is it not written in your law, I said, Ye are gods?" In this way, He used "law" and "Scripture" as strict synonyms. Further, the word "cannot" expresses a divine and moral impossibility. Scripture, Christ taught, cannot be annulled, dissolved, abrogated, or rendered void, simply because it declares the will and purpose of God. To sum up Christ's words to His fiercest critics, what cannot happen to a single, minute part of Scripture cannot happen to the whole.

Despite Christ's teaching of the origin, inspiration and authority of the Old Testament presented above, an increasing number of individuals who view themselves as evangelical have come to embrace what is called Redaction Criticism. This is a variety of destructive Bible criticism.

Robert L. Thomas, a conservative New Testament scholar who rejects Redaction Criticism, has set forth the dangerous "characteristics" of it;

> (1) The redaction critic views the role of the gospel writers as that of theologians not historians.

(2) The philosophical basis used by redactionists to give respectability to their systems of falsification is similar to that behind the neo-orthodoxy of Karl Barth...and Rudolf Bultmann. That philosophy contends for two realms of reality, the obvious realm where space, time, and the physical senses prevail and a less obvious realm that they term the realm of faith.

(3) The philosophy system behind RC (Redaction Criticism) assigns so much of the Gospels to that nonhistorical realm of reality that it eliminates the Gospels as a possible basis for reconstructing a life of Jesus or determining a theology of Jesus. Just as FC (Form Criticism) says the events recorded in the Gospels are fabrications of the early church, RC (Redaction Criticism) says that the theological teachings in the Gospels are those of the individual writers, not of Jesus.[8]

Many of the evangelicals who embrace and teach Redaction Criticism are in evangelical churches, colleges, universities, and seminaries. This certainly does not bode well for the future of the historic Christian faith and, most importantly, for what Christ Himself taught.

The Person of Christ

Christ, the Word of God Incarnate

Christ is the supreme and final revealer and revelation of God. The human penman of the book of Hebrews put it this way: "God, who at sundry times and in divers manners spake in time past unto the fathers by the prophets, Hath in these last days spoken unto us by his Son, whom he hath appointed heir of all things, by whom also he made the worlds" (Hebrews 1:1-2). God's

---

[8] I heartily recommend this book: Robert L. Thomas and F. David Farnell, *The Jesus Crisis–The Inroads of Historical Criticism into Evangelical Scholarship* (Grand Rapids: Kregel Publications, 1998). I also heartily recommend Norman L. Geisler and William C. Roach, *Defending Inerrancy, Affirming the Accuracy of Scripture for a New Generation* (Grand Rapids: Baker Books, 2011). In this volume the authors give evidence that many of the same evangelicals referenced in the Jesus crisis do not believe in the *total* inerrancy of the original documents of Scripture.

Word written in the Old Testament was given, we might say, "piecemeal" and in anticipation of the coming of Christ. Before Christ's coming, God's revelation to man came through dreams, visions, laws, institutions, ceremonies, judges, kings, and prophets. But "in these last days," the messianic age, which began with the coming Christ, God sent His Son to bring to us His revelation in and through Him.

The Word of God written in the Old Testament and the Word of God incarnate through Christ, His Son, are not in conflict with each other. They do not contradict each other. The one is not more accurate than the other. Both Words came from God and both are completely accurate and reliable. They are both trustworthy. Yet it is true that God's incarnate Word complements and consummates God's inspired Word in Scripture.

Christ revealed the *Person* of God in ways that had never been made known before. For instance, Jesus unveiled the Father to mankind (see John 1:18; 1 Tim. 3:16). Christ also made known the *glory* of God (Isa. 40:5; John 1:14; 2 Cor. 4:6). Additionally, God the Son revealed the *power* of God the Father on many occasions and in many different ways (John 3:2; 1 Cor. 1:24).

The Person of Christ made known the *wisdom* of God (John 7:46; 1 Cor. 1:24). Jesus also declared the *life* of God (1 John 1:1-3). Further, the Savior disclosed and demonstrated the boundless *love* of God (John 3:16 ; Rom. 5:8; 1 John 3:16). Moreover, the Lord Jesus unveiled the *grace* of God, the undeserved favor He bestowed upon humanity (Luke 2:40; John 1:17; 2 Thess. 1:12).

The two Words from God, the Inspired Word and the Incarnate Word, or the Written Word and the Living Word, stand or fall together. They are two impregnable forces, pillars upon which biblical Christianity stands or falls. You simply cannot have the one without the other. They are the bedrock of the orthodox faith. When either one of these is spurned, Christianity is renounced. Again, neither one of these revelations can be held in isolation from the other.

In order to show how impossible and illogical it is to reject either one of these two Words from God and yet pretend to embrace or give credence to the other one, I want to show, in a limited way, the harmony between them.

First, both the Living Word and the Written Word came to us from God. He gave both of these Words to mankind.

Second, both the Living Word and the Written Word claim the same divine authority.

Third, both the Living Word and the Written Word complement each other. The Written Word bears testimony to the Living Word. Without the Written Word, we would know little about Christ. Only scant reference is made to Him in the non-canonical sources.

Fourth, both the Living Word and the Written Word have come to us involving the erring human element. By that I mean that the Living Incarnate Word was born of woman – Mary – and the Written Inspired Word was penned by humans.

Fifth, just as the Living Word was without sin, so the Written Word in the original manuscripts is without error. The two Words of God do not contradict each other at any point. There is perfect harmony between the two.

Christ's Eternal Existence

"Jesus Christ of Nazareth," as Peter called Him (Acts 3:6), lived before He was conceived miraculously in the womb of His mother Mary. He is the only One ever born of woman whose birth had absolutely nothing to do with His origin. According to Scripture, He is as eternal, without beginning or end of days, as is God the Father and God the Holy Spirit. He has an eternal existence which means, of course, that He never had a beginning. Before His conception and birth, and even before the creation of the world, He always was and ever will be.

Jesus was conscious of His eternal existence as the Son of God. He said He shared God the Father's glory before there ever was a world (John 17:5).

Before the foundation of the world, He was loved by God the Father (v. 23), according to His own testimony.

The prophets of old said of Christ long before He was born that He was the "mighty God" and "eternal Father" or Father of eternity (Isaiah 9:6). Micah the prophet said He would be ruler in Israel and "whose goings forth have been from of old, from everlasting" (Micah 5:2; c.f. Matthew 2:4-6).

In the opening words of the Gospel of John, the apostle affirmed the eternal existence of "the Word" who was "with God" and who "was God" (John 1:1). To whom does "the Word" refer here? John identified "the Word" as Jesus when he writes, "And the Word was made flesh, and dwelt among us, (and we beheld his glory, the glory as of the only begotten of the Father,) full of grace and truth" (v. 14).

The title "only begotten" is used of Christ five times (John 1:14, 18; 3:16, 18; 1 John 4:9). The Greek word translated "begotten" is derived from the roots *genos* which means kind or class, and *mono* which means only, or unique. With these terms, John stressed Christ's position as Son. He is the unique, one-of-a-kind Son of God.

Christ is referred to as the "Firstborn" seven times in the New Testament. This title highlights His priority, preeminence, dignity, rank, and position as the Son of God. Henry Alford, a Greek scholar, explained the title "firstborn" in this way: "'Firstborn of every creature' will then imply that Christ was not only firstborn of His mother in the world but first begotten of His Father before the world – and that He holds the rank, as compared with every created thing, of firstborn in dignity."[9]

One day when Christ's claim to be God was rejected, He said to the Pharisees who did not believe Him and who were determined to kill Him, "Your father Abraham rejoiced to see my day: and he saw it, and was glad" (John 8:56). They thought they had caught Him in a lie at last. Their response to His claim was, "Thou art not yet fifty years old, and hast thou

---
9 Henry Alford, *The Greek New Testament* (Chicago: Moody Press, 1958), 3: 203.

seen Abraham?" (v. 57). Quickly, Jesus went even further and responded by saying, "Verily, verily, I say unto you, Before Abraham was, I am" (v. 58). With that statement Jesus was not only claiming to have existed before Abraham lived, but He was at the same time claiming that He existed eternally. He took Jehovah's name, the "I Am" of Exodus 3:14; Deuteronomy 32:39; Isaiah 41:4 and 46:4. The Jewish elite got it at last. They understood exactly what He meant. That is why they picked up stones and tried to kill Him (John 8:59).

The above account represents a sampling of some of the direct Scriptural evidence that Jesus of Nazareth had an eternal existence. In addition to this direct teaching, there are also indirect theological evidences for His eternal existence. Here are three of those evidences.

First, every claim for His deity is at the same time a claim for His eternal existence. We will look at some of these below. Second, when the doctrine of the eternal Trinity is affirmed, so is the eternal existence of Christ the Son of God. No denial of the Trinity can be made without denying the eternality of Christ. And the reverse is just as true. No denial of the eternality of Christ can be made without denying the biblical doctrine of the Trinity. Third, Jesus Christ's heavenly origin argues for His eternality. He said, "I came out from God" (John 16:27). God the Father sent His Son from His presence into the world. Jesus the Son of God prayed for the restoration of the glory He had with the Father "before the world was" (John 17:5), which again clearly argues for Christ's eternal existence.

Christ's Eternal Sonship[10]

In the not-too-distant past, those who accepted Christ's eternal existence also embraced His eternal Sonship. The latter truth was viewed as an inclusion of the former truth. It was most unusual for any who believed Christ always existed to believe He was not eternally the Son of God.

---

10 For a full discussion of this subject see George W. Zeller and Renald E. Showers, *The Eternal Sonship of Christ* (Neptune, NJ: Loizeaux Brothers, 1993).

Eternal Sonship Denied

Denial of the eternal Sonship of Christ among evangelicals resurfaced some years ago. It has been advanced for some time by Dr. John MacArthur, a popular author, pastor, and Bible conference speaker. He explained his view in this way.

> He was always God but He became Son. He had not always had the title of Son. That is His incarnation title. Eternally He is God, but only from His incarnation has He been Son…Christ was not Son until His incarnation. Before that He was eternal God…His Sonship began in point of time, not in eternity. His life as Son began in this world… He was not a Son until He was born into this world through the virgin birth… The Sonship of Christ is inextricably connected with His incarnation… only after Christ's incarnation did God say, "This is My Son."[11]

The above view has been labeled "The Incarnational Sonship of Christ" as opposed to the eternal Sonship of Christ. MacArthur explained his view of incarnational Sonship further:

> Son does not refer to Jesus' divine essence… in eternity past, though there were always three persons in the trinity, there were not yet the roles of Father and Son. Those designations apparently came into being only at the incarnation… Son was a new name never before applied to the second person of the Godhead except prophetically, as in Psalm 2:7 which is interpreted in Hebrews 1:5-6 as referring to the event of the incarnation… only when "the Word became flesh and dwelt among us" as "the only begotten God" (John 1:4-18) did He take on the role and function of Son.[12]

---

11 John MacArthur, Jr., *Hebrews* (Chicago: Moody Press, n.d.), pp. 22-23.
12 Ibid., *Galatians* (Chicago: Moody Press, n.d.), pp. 107-8.

In his *Study Bible* published in 2005, MacArthur restated his view but did not give a clear defense for the eternal Sonship view: "We teach that, in the incarnation, the second person of the trinity laid aside His right to the full prerogatives of coexistence with God, assumed the place of a Son and took on an existence appropriate to a servant while never divesting Himself of His divine attributes (Phil. 2:5-8)."

Sadly, these and other statements in his *Bible Commentary* still raise serious questions about MacArthur's view on this critical issue.

While there is no verse of Scripture which states in so many words that Christ was always the Son of God, there is overwhelming biblical evidence that displays his eternal Sonship. John 20:28-31, 10:30-38, and 5:18, for example, encompass much more in the term "Son" than MacArthur would allow. Before presenting this evidence for the eternal Sonship of Christ, we need to understand the meaning of "son" as applied to Christ.

The title "Son of God" is used of men, angels, and Christ in Scripture. When used of Christ it has nothing do with His birth, with Mary being His mother. However, it has everything to do with His eternal relation to the Father. Christ is nowhere in Scripture called a child (*teknos*) of God. The Greek word *teknos* means a child born to parents. Instead the word *huios*, son, is always used of Him. This second term describes an heir destined to receive an inheritance. The following biblical facts must be taken into account to determine whether Christ was always the Son of God or became the Son when He was born of Mary:

- The Son of God existed at the time of creation. He had a part in it (Col. 1:13-17; Heb. 1:2).

- The Son of God is described as being in the Father's bosom (John 1:18; 1 John 1:1-2).

- The Son of God was sent by the Father (Isa. 9:6; John 3:16; 20:21; Rom. 8:32; Gal. 4:4; 1 John 4:10, 14).

- The Son of God returned to the Father (John 16:28; 17:5, 24).

The term "Son of God" describes the Savior's relationship to God the Father. His relationship to God is eternal and was not affected by the incarnation. "Son of God" is not less, but far more, than a name or title. It is another way of setting Christ forth as the only begotten. The second member of the Godhead did become the Son of man, the son of David, and the son of Mary when He became incarnate but He was the Son of God from all eternity. His eternal Sonship became apparent to us in the incarnation (Rom. 1:3, 4; Phil. 2:5-11).

John F. Walvoord's summary of the issues of Christ's Sonship is reflective of the biblical teaching;

> The scriptural view of the Sonship of Christ as recognized in many of the great creeds of the church is that Christ was always the Son of God by eternal generation and that He took upon Himself humanity through generation of the Holy Spirit; the human birth was not in order to become a Son of God but because He was the Son of God.[13]

In addition to "The Son of God" title used of Christ, two other titles are used which relate to His eternal Sonship. The first of these two is "firstborn." This title is used of Him seven times in the New Testament. Taken together, these references set forth three distinct meanings of "firstborn."

First, Paul described Christ as "the firstborn among many brethren" (Romans 8:29) and as "the firstborn of every creature" (Colossians 1:15). In the first passage, he is presented as the preeminent One, the Head of a new race. As such, He is to be acknowledged and glorified as the Son of God. In the second passage, there is no hint that Christ became the Son of God when he was born of Mary. Instead, it is His priority, preeminence, dignity and rank as the Son of God that are highlighted.

---

[13] John F. Walvoord, *Jesus Christ Our Lord* (Chicago: Moody Press, 1969), p. 44.

The second distinct meaning of the term "firstborn" when used of Christ describes Him as Mary's firstborn (Matthew 1:25 and Luke 2:7). He was indeed Mary's firstborn – first in time and in rank within the family.

The third distinct meaning of the term "firstborn" when used of Christ describes Him as the One raised from the dead (Colossians 1:18; cf. Revelation 1:5). Though others were raised from the dead before, He was the first to be raised with a resurrected body never to experience death again. Therefore, He is the only One with authority or preeminence over death (1 Corinthians 15:54-57).

The other descriptive term used of Christ which argues strongly for His eternal Sonship is the term "only begotten." This term is used of Him five times (John 1:14, 18; 3:16, 18; 1 John 4:9). The Greek term is *monogenes*. It is derived from the roots *genos* which means kind or class and *mono* meaning only or unique. Christ is the only, unique one-of-a-kind Son of God. Believers are sons and daughters of God and, therefore, are children of God. Christ is never referred to as a child of God but always as Son of God.

Christ's Virgin Birth

Evangelical theology has always included belief in the miraculous conception of Jesus Christ by the Virgin Mary.[14] At the turn of the twentieth century, the Virgin Birth was numbered among the five fundamentals of orthodoxy by the great stalwarts of the faith. Those who denied any one of the cardinal doctrines of the faith – the inspiration and authority of the Bible, the Virgin Birth of Christ, the deity of Christ, the substitutionary atonement of Christ, and the bodily resurrection and second coming of Christ – were not considered orthodox in faith.

Non-evangelical theologians today just as consistently reject the Virgin Birth of Christ. The rejection is in accord with the liberal refusal to accept the

---

14 See Robert Glenn Gromacki, *The Virgin Birth of Christ Doctrine of Deity* (Nashville: Thomas Nelson, 1974) for presentation of the doctrine from an evangelical perspective.

supernatural in biblical inspiration and all other areas of the historic Christian faith. In reality, liberal theology assumes a closed system of natural laws by its denial of supernaturalism. It is not coincidental that the same persons who deny the biblical teaching of the Virgin Birth also deny all other biblical teaching that involves the supernatural.

The Meaning of the Virgin Birth. The evangelical belief in the Virgin Birth of Christ is not the same as the Roman Catholic belief in the immaculate conception of Mary. The Bible does not teach that the mother of Jesus was herself without sin or that from the very beginning of her existence she was free from original sin.[15]

On the positive side, evangelicals believe that the Holy Spirit was the efficient cause–that is, He supernaturally produced the effect or result of Mary's conception. The Holy Spirit brought about conception in Mary's womb in a unique way. It was the Spirit who, through the miraculous conception, sanctified the human nature of Christ at its very inception, thus keeping it free from the pollution of sin.

Walvoord explains from the evangelical perspective:

> The whole tenor of Scripture as presented in both the Old Testament prophecies that he was to be God and Man and the New Testament fulfillment makes the virgin birth a divine explanation, insofar as it can be explained, of an otherwise insuperable problem. How could One who was both God and Man have perfectly human parents? The account of the virgin birth therefore, instead of being an unreasonable invention, becomes a fitting explanation of how in the supernatural power of God the incarnation was made a reality.[16]

The Importance of the Virgin Birth. Evangelicals believe the Virgin Birth is vitally important for a number of reasons. First, it is a teaching of Scripture,

---
15 For the original statement of the doctrine issued by Pope Pius IX on December 8, 1858, and a scriptural refutation, see Loraine Boettner, *Roman Catholicism* (Philadelphia: Presbyterian and Reformed Publishing Company, 1962), pp. 158-62.
16 John F. Walvoord, *Jesus Christ Our Lord* (Chicago: Moody, 1969), p. 104.

and since Scripture is authoritative, all its teachings are to be believed. Second, the Virgin Birth determines whether we have a naturalistic or super-naturalistic Christ. Only when His unique Person is divorced from the discussion does the Virgin Birth create difficulties. Third, by means of the Virgin Birth, God kept His Son from receiving a sin nature from either Joseph or Mary, and therefore He was qualified to be man's Redeemer.

Scriptural Support. Several lines of biblical evidence are used to substantiate Christ's Virgin Birth.

Early in the Old Testament, the Virgin Birth was implied in God's word to the serpent after the fall of man (Gen. 3:15). The reference to "her seed" is unparalleled. Normally, reference is to the seed of the male.

Matthew's quotation (1:23) of Isaiah 7:14 makes it very clear that "virgin" is the intended meaning of *almah*, which was used by the prophet. Also, Matthew's use of the feminine relative singular pronoun "by whom " (Matt. 1:16) provides strong support because Matthew thereby associated Christ's birth with Mary only. Joseph was completely eliminated. This is especially significant in contrast to the associations of male and female ancestors in the immediate context. Mary was with child "before" she and Joseph "came together" (Matt. 1:18). Joseph "knew her not till she had brought forth her firstborn son: and he called his name Jesus" (Matt. 1:25).

Luke, the physician, records the angel's explanation to Mary of her pregnancy. The Holy Spirit of God had come upon her to generate the child within her womb (Luke 1:34-35).

Christ's Sinless Humanity

Before giving a biblical defense for Christ's true but sinless humanity, a word about the seeds of Gnosticism which began to flourish in the early centuries of the Christian era is in order.

First, Gnosticism needs to be defined and described. The word Gnosticism, or Gnostic, comes from the Greek word *ginosko*. This word means "know" or "understand." The Gnostics claimed superior knowledge and that salvation came through knowledge.

Darrell L. Bock in his book, *Breaking the Da Vinci Code,* gives this definition of the Gnostics and Gnosticism:

> A Christian sect of the second and third centuries that believed in dualism, namely, a distinction between the purity of the immaterial world and corruptibility of the material world. They also believed the God of creation was not the pure God, that there was a distinction between Jesus who suffered on the cross and the Christ who was the transcendent Savior. They held that the revelation they received gave them unique insight over any other writings. This revelation provided them with access to *gnosis* or knowledge about God.[17]

Prior to the discovery of the Dead Sea Scrolls at Qumran, our knowledge and understanding of Gnosticism was primarily restricted to the writings of the early church fathers. They wrote of the Gnostics in scathing denunciations. These early writers rightly regarded Gnosticism as the product of the combination of Greek philosophy and Christianity.

The Gnostics believed and embraced a dualistic philosophy of life which said spirit, or the unseen, was good or light, and matter was evil or darkness. The Gnostic documents discovered in 1945 in Egypt and catalogued in the Nag Hammadi library have provided firsthand information about Gnostics and their beliefs. As noted earlier, Bock's book, *Breaking the Da Vinci Code*, responds directly and specifically to all the major differences between historic and biblical Christianity. There were a number of varieties of Gnosticism in the history of the early church, yet they all held to core issues which are far removed from biblical Christianity.

"Gnosticism" was an eclectic movement in which cosmological myths, the philosophical thoughts of the Greek and Oriental paganism, and truths

---

17 Darrell L. Bock, *Breaking the Da Vinci Code* (Nashville: Nelson Books, 2004), pp. 178-79.

of Christianity were represented. The religions of Babylonia, Syria, Asia Minor, Persia, and India, the Judaism of Philo and the message of Jesus and the apostles all were fused in the Gnostic crucible. As a rule, heathen features predominated.[18]

The dualistic philosophy with the belief that spirit is good and matter is evil is the most basic principle on which Gnosticism rests. From that platform, Gnostics developed what has been called the Emanation Theory. From the hidden spirit and good God there emanated a long series of divine essences the Gnostics called *aeons*. The inherent divine power in these aeons lessened as the distance from the original spirit God increased. Gnostics believe this process continued until there came a time when the spiritual immaterial element came into contact with matter and at that point was imprisoned in a material body. In this way, it was believed, man and the world were created. Needless to say, this is hardly in agreement and harmony with the Genesis account of creation.

The Demiurge occupied a sort of middle position between the world of spirit and the world of matter. (He was identified in Gnosticism with the Jehovah God of the Old Testament.) The Demiurge rather unwittingly brought the world and mankind into existence. He promised a world-conquering Messiah who would judge all the heathen. The good God would not allow this. Instead, he descended to Capernaum in an unreal body and called himself the Messiah.

The Messiah sent by the good God to conquer the world and judge the heathen disregarded the Demiurge's laws. The Demiurge prevailed and caused the Messiah to be crucified.

Since the "Messiah" sent by the good God did not have a real body, but a material evil body, the Demiurge was defeated and his power destroyed. "Messiah" then compelled the Demiurge to acknowledge him.

---

18 Otto W. Heick, *A History of Christian Thought*, Vol. I (Philadelphia: Fortress Press, 1965), p. 69. See also my *First, Second, & Third John & Jude* (Chattanooga, TN: AMG Publishers), pp. 175-177.

Heick's summary of this aspect of Gnostic belief is very much to the point.

> Gnosticism rejected the doctrine of the incarnation. It declared that Christ could not possibly have a body: (1) because the absolute cannot enter into a real union with the finite; and (2) because matter is evil, and the spiritual world is ever in conflict with it. It was thought that the Christ had joined himself for the time being with the body of a profoundly spiritual man called Jesus… This union was effected either at the birth or at the baptism of Jesus, and it was dissolved shortly before the crucifixion. It followed, therefore, that the Christ was not really crucified. The crucifixion of Christ was an optical illusion in which the man Jesus was the real sufferer. Thus Gnosticism, with its docetic conception, denuded the Redeemer of any real humanity, and destroyed the historic person of Christ. Gnosticism clearly derived its ideas of the Redeemer from pagan mythology. Hence it was never able to effect any genuine union between the Christ and Jesus of Nazareth.[19]

Christ's Undiminished Deity

Throughout the history of the church, the Savior's deity has been denied by what would now be called liberal theology. Evangelicals, on the other hand, while not denying Christ's humanity, have tended to neglect it. This has been true because one group wants to make certain that He is seen as fully human while the other group wishes to present Him as altogether God. The truth is, He is both. He is the God-man. Both Christ's perfect humanity and his undiminished deity are absolutely essential to His scriptural portrait.

By ascribing undiminished deity to Christ, evangelicals affirm that He is absolutely and truly God. Contemporary liberals speak of Him as Godlike and nearer to God than anyone else. While liberals fail to do justice

---

19 Ibid., p. 72

to biblical language concerning Christ's deity, evangelicals continue to affirm the historic, orthodox view that Christ, the Son of God, is as much God as the Father is God.

At least six lines of evidence of Christ's deity are delineated in Scripture. (1) Christ was called God (Isa. 9:6; John 1:1, 14; Heb. 1:8). (2) Christ possesses attributes of God. He is eternal (John 17:5), omnipresent (John 3:13), omniscient (John 2:25), omnipotent (Heb. 1:3), and immutable (Heb. 13:8). (3) Christ performed works of God: creation (Col. 1:16), preservation (Col. 1:17), providence (Heb. 1:2), forgiveness of sins (Luke 5:20-24), and judgment (John 5:22). (4) Christ demanded honor and worship that is due only to God (Matt. 14:33; John 5:23). (5) Christ Himself made divine claims: to hold authority over the laws and institutions of God (Matt. 12:6), to be the object of saving faith (John 17:3), and to have met in Himself all the spiritual and eternal needs of humanity (John 7:37; 14:6). (6) Christ affirmed unequivocally that He was equal with God (John 8:24, 58; 10:30).

"We confess that He is Very God and Very Man; Very God by His power to conquer death and Very man that He might die for us."[20] "He continueth to be God and man, in two distinct natures and one person forever."[21] To deny either the undiminished deity or the perfect humanity of Christ is to put oneself outside the pale of orthodoxy. Equally as essential to orthodox theology is the belief that these two are inseparable and will remain eternally united in the Person of Christ. The hypostatic union is the theological description of this and refers to the two hypostases, or natures, forming the one Person in Christ.

Apart from this union, Christ could not have been mediator between God and man. If He had been only man, His death could not have atoned for man's sin. If He had been only God, He could not have died, since God cannot die. If He had not been man, He would not have had a genuine link with humanity and would not have had perfect sympathy with man.

---

20 Belgic Confession, 1562
21 Westminster Shorter Catechism, 1647

Christ the God-Man

Nature and person are not synonymous. Persons have natures, yet personhood involves more than a nature. Person includes nature plus independent subsistence or reality embracing intellect, emotion, and will. The Son of God, who was one in Person and nature (divine), became two in nature (divine and human) while remaining one in Person through His Incarnation. The eternal Son of God did not join Himself with a human person, it must be remembered, but with a human nature.

In the union of the human and divine in Christ, each of the natures retained its own attributes. Deity did not permeate humanity, nor did humanity become absorbed into deity. The two natures retain their complete identity even though they have been joined together in a personal union. Christ is thus theanthropic (God-Man) in person. Embracing perfect humanity made Him no less God, and retaining His undiminished deity made Him no less human.

The Reality of the Union. Scriptural evidence for the unipersonality of Christ abounds. He always spoke of Himself as one. The Savior never distinguished between Himself as a divine Person and Himself as a human Person (John 8:18, 23, 58; 16:7). Both of the natures in Christ are seen in Scripture to be united in one Person. Of the many instances where Scripture teaches this, three central passages are especially helpful. Christ is said to be "of the seed of David" which stresses His humanity and, at the same time, "declared to be the Son of God" (Rom. 1:2-5). To the Galatian Christians, Paul declared Christ as God's Son who was also "made of a woman" (Gal. 4:4-5). In Philippians 2:5-11, Christ is seen as "equal with God" and at the same time in the "form of a servant."

The Mystery of the Union. Under the guidance of the Spirit, the apostle Paul said of the Person of Christ, who possessed two natures, "By common confession, great is the mystery of godliness: He who was revealed in the flesh" (1 Tim. 3:16 NASB). Again, the same writer wrote of the "mystery of God" as he referred to the Incarnation of Christ (Col. 2:2). Truly, the relation of the humanity and divinity of Christ will remain inscrutable to us. We do not have any analogies of it in our own natures or experiences. But the mystery must not deter us from accepting by faith the consistent biblical teaching.

Warfield wrote of this great mystery and warned of the dangers in attempting to solve the mystery completely: "We can never hope to comprehend how the infinite God and finite humanity can be united in one single person; and it is very easy to go fatally astray in attempting to explain the interactions in the unitary person of natures so diverse from one another."[22]

The Duration of the Union. Evangelical theology holds that the Incarnation of Christ is in perpetuity. That is, the act of Incarnation was not an arrangement just for the time of His life on earth. The fact is, His human nature continues forever. This is supported in several ways: Christ's resurrected body was glorified and suited for heaven. Presently, He is seated at the right hand of the Father and will return to earth as the Son of man (Matt. 26:64). The fact that He appeared in a visible body after His resurrection and was worshiped (John 20:17) also supports the contention. Christ ascended bodily to heaven (Mark 16:19; Acts 1:1-11; 7:56). At the present time, He is the "one mediator between God and men, the man Christ Jesus" (1 Tim. 2:5).

Christ's Sinless Life on Earth

Christ obeyed the Law of God perfectly and He suffered all of His adult life at the hands of those He came to redeem. Evangelicals agree with both realities. They do not all agree, however, on the purpose and the effects of these truths.

Theologians distinguish between what they call Christ's active obedience in His life and His passive obedience when He died on the cross. Some believe and teach that what Christ suffered during His life on earth before

---

22 Benjamin B. Warfield, *The Person and Work of Christ* (Philadelphia: Presbyterian and Reformed Publishing Company, 1970), p. 69.

He went to the cross was just as much substitution for sinners as was His death on the cross.

> The first Adam was by nature under the Law of God and the keeping of it as such gave him no claim to a reward. It was only when God graciously entered into a covenant with him and promised him life in the way of obedience that the keeping of the Law was made the condition of obtaining eternal life for himself and his descendants. And when Christ voluntarily entered into the federal relationship of the last Adam, the keeping of the Law naturally required the same significance for Him and for those whom the Father had given Him.[23]

Others believe, and I am one of these, that while Christ indeed suffered during His life on earth, that suffering and that obedience to the Law of God were not payment or substitution for man's sin. Only when He died in our place did He make substitution for us. How do these two realities relate to each other if one was in our place and the other was not in our place? Before I explain that relationship, I want to stress the reality of Christ's obedience and suffering in life.

Our Lord Jesus Christ obeyed every precept of the Law of God. He was, in fact, born under the Law (Galatians 4:4). He did not ever violate any of God's Law. He was "without sin" (Hebrews 4:15). The very fact that He embraced humanity means that He experienced suffering common to man.

Christ was led by the Spirit of God to be tempted by Satan (Matthew 4:1). Scripture teaches that Christ did not sin when tempted by the devil or at any other time.

The religious leaders of Christ's time rejected Him and even tried to kill Him before He could go to the cross. Surely the way the Sadducees, the Pharisees, the Herodians and the Scribes treated Christ caused Him suffering. After all, He had come to show them the true and only way to God.

---

23 L. Berkhof, *Systematic Theology* (Grand Rapids: William B. Eerdmans Publishing Co, 1968), pp. 380-81.

The religious elite were not the only ones who brought suffering and rejection to Christ. Even some of His friends and followers brought suffering to Him. When He needed them the most, Matthew tells us, "all the disciples forsook Him, and fled" (Matthew 26:56). Some disciples or followers showed apathy. Some abandoned Him (Mark 14:50). Even one of the twelve disciples officially rejected Christ and betrayed Him into the hands of His executioners (Matthew 26:47-56).

As I said earlier, I do not believe the life sufferings of Christ were substitutionary. Here are the major reasons why I am opposed to that view.

First, the view fails to take into account that before the Fall, Adam did not have a sin nature. Instead, it assumes that to be rightly related to God, Adam and his posterity were required to render perfect obedience to the commands of God. Boettner stated this view well when he said: "We believe that the requirement for salvation now, as originally, is perfect obedience."[24]

The whole concept of the vicarious nature of Christ's active obedience rests primarily on the idea of the covenant of works. The covenant promised eternal life for obedience, and, since Adam disobeyed and all his posterity in him, Christ, the last Adam, came to accomplish what the first Adam failed to do.

The fact that Adam came from the hands of the Creator sinless and perfect must not be overlooked. The command of God to obey Him was not designed to produce eternal life in him or to relate him rightly to God. He already enjoyed a state free of sin and a proper relation to his Creator. Human effort is never presented as a condition of salvation in Scripture. Rather, the command of God to Adam was designed to *demonstrate* his obedience to the authority of God.

Second, the view minimizes the work of Christ on the cross by making it insufficient. After portraying Adam as having a sin nature prior to the fall, it then regards Christ as having to fulfill a list of demands in order to become a worthy sacrifice. Just as Adam was not unworthy before God before the

---

24 Loraine Boettner, *The Atonement* (Nutley, NJ: Presbyterian Reformed Publishing, Co., n.d.), p. 59.

fall, so Jesus came into the world sinless. Christ's *life* was not substitutionary, His *death* was substitutionary, and sufficient in itself.

Third, no Scripture teaches that substitution for man's sin was made by Christ before He died on the cross. The Old Testament and the New Testament alike teach that Christ took the sinner's place and died in the sinner's stead on the cross.

In summary of Part 1, because Christ was the eternal Son of God, He could pay the debt we owed. Because He became the Son of Man, He could die for our sins in our place as our substitute. In other words, as the Son of God and the Son of Man, He was the only one qualified and able to die for sinners. The provision of redemption from our lost state could only be made by Him. The same is true of all the other provisions for salvation which must be received to be beneficial. Only the God-Man could reconcile the world to Himself. Likewise, the Lord Jesus Christ alone could be our satisfaction, our propitiation. Because of who He was and is, He could make the world of lost humanity redeemable.

Nothing more than physical death would have occurred had Jesus not been the God-Man. All of mankind would have been forever lost and without hope. No provision would have been made had He not been who He claimed to be: equal in essence with God the Father and yet fully human. Apart from the Person of Christ, there would have been no payment for sin and no salvation for lost humanity.

Since these things are true, it follows that what one believes about the Christ of Scripture affects greatly what is believed about the cross of Christ. It would be highly illogical and unscriptural to deny the absolute deity of Christ and His true sinless humanity and yet claim His death on the cross to be the only way of salvation. And it follows that the reverse would be just as illogical and unscriptural. Jesus Christ cannot be the savior of sinners if He was not absolute deity and perfect humanity. Both are essential to and indispensable from man's salvation. You cannot have the one without the other and be true to what the Bible claims about the Person of Christ.

PART 2

CHRIST'S CHURCH

OUTLINE

I. The Beginning of the Church

    A. An Historical Perspective

        1. The Ancient Period

        2. The Middle Ages

        3. The Reformation

        4. The Modern Period

    B. The Universal Church

        1. The meaning of *Ekklesia*

        2. The reality of the Universal Church

        3. The means of entrance and foundation

            a. Matthew 16:18-20

            b. 1 Corinthians 3:11

            c. Ephesians 2:19-20

            d. 1 Peter 2:4-8

    C. The Local Church

        1. Reality and identity

        2. Membership

        3. Organization and ordinances

        4. The mission in the world

        5. The exaltation of the Savior and the Scriptures

        6. The edification of the people of God

        7. The evangelization of the lost

II. Major Areas of Difference Among Evangelicals

A. Denials of the Universal Church
1. Matthew 16:18
2. 1 Corinthians 12:12-13
3. Ephesians 1:22-23
4. Ephesians 2:11-17
5. Ephesians 3
6. Ephesians 4:4-16
7. Ephesians 5:23-27
8. Hebrews 12:22-23

B. Views of the Beginning of the Church
1. Roman Catholicism
2. The Reformers
3. Covenant Theology
4. Landmark Baptist Views
5. Dispensational thought
6. The New Testament Qualifications

C. The Plurality of Elders

D. Deaconesses

E. The Mode of Believer's Baptism

F. The Lord's Table

G. The Government of the Church

III. The Church and the Church Member

CHRIST'S CHURCH

Having solidified our view of the identity of Christ, let us now proceed to understand the assembly of believers who gather together under Christ's banner, an assembly we call *the church* and understand to be *the body of Christ* on earth today.[25]

The Beginning of the Church

Ecclesiology is primarily a New Testament doctrine. The reference is both to the church and to the churches. The word "church" does appear in the Old Testament, but it simply refers to an assembly of people called together for a specific purpose. Only in the New Testament is the church identified as the body of Christ, a peculiar people especially gifted with a distinct program. Likewise, only in the New Testament are there references to local assemblies called churches. It must be admitted by all evangelicals that something new and unique began on the day of Pentecost. What a day that must have been for believers and unbelievers but for different reasons. What a wonderful day it will be when Christ returns for His own and they meet Him in the air.

The Savior also gave instruction concerning discipline and forgiveness of members of a local church (Matt. 18:15-17). A number of the New Testament epistles were addressed to local assemblies of believers (e.g., Phil. 1:1; 1 Thess. 1:1; 2 Thess. 1:1). Seven local churches are addressed by John in Revelation 2:3. The local church is called "the house of God… the church of

---

[25] This chapter was previously published by the author in *Handbook of Evangelical Theology*, Grand Rapids, MI: Kregel, 1995. Used by permission.

the living God, the pillar and ground of the truth" (1 Tim. 3:15).

An Historical Perspective

In the history of doctrinal development, the doctrine of the church entered the discussion rather late. This does not mean that the early Christians were uninterested in the church. On the contrary, they were very interested and involved on the personal level.

Doctrinal formulations concerning a given truth grew out of controversy. Only when the scriptural teachings were challenged did the ancients bring forth definitive statements concerning the truth in question. The rise of heresies forced the early Christians to set forth precisely what they did believe in contrast to the opposing views. This is certainly true of the doctrine of the church.

The Ancient Period

Until around A.D. 600, the centers of doctrinal controversy were the Trinity, Christ, the Holy Spirit, man, and sin. The fathers of the church gave their first attention to these issues because the earliest heresies arose over these doctrines. Two rather obvious emphases related to the church ran through this period. There was the stress on external unity on the one hand and internal purity on the other. The latter was clearly an action to the former. Both these emphases have, to a certain extent, continued into the present time.

It must be kept in mind that the ancient writers wrote primarily devotional literature for the laity rather than theological treatises. Yet the emphasis on the external unity of the church is discernible in the writings of such men as Clement of Rome, Ignatius, and Polycarp. There is evidence in their writings that they believed in both a universal church and local churches. Frequently, the burden for the unity of all the local churches can be seen, and the concern was not at all unnatural. After all, Christianity did need to stand united in the face of the increasing number of religious views that were arising. With the attempts to unite Christians, there also came the necessity of some sort of centralization of authority and power.

The early development of ecclesiasticism can be traced through three stages:

> First was the appearance of the monarchial bishop to whom fellow elders were obedient... Secondly, there was the development of the ecumenical domination... The final step, then, was the development of Roman supremacy. The concept of the universal church, which began to find expression in Ignatius and was definitely advocated by Irenaeus, demanded a centralizing of authority and control.[26]

Three individuals in the ancient period deserve special attention because of their profound impact upon the doctrine of the church, especially as it relates to external unity.

Irenaeus, in *Against Heresies*, reveals a definite shift of emphasis. Instead of the stress being on Christ's relation to the local church, there is emphasis on the need for the organic unity of the visible universal church. Irenaeus also advocated the perpetual succession of bishops from Christ. He said, "We are in a position to reckon up those who were by the Apostles instituted bishops in the churches, and (to demonstrate) the succession of these men to our own times."[27] Seed was sown by Irenaeus for the establishment of a system that would recognize one head over the entire church.

Cyprian wrote a famous work on the doctrine of the church entitled *On the Unity of the Church*, which developed the doctrine of the episcopal church. Cyprian believed in the unity of the catholic, or universal, church and in the full authority of the bishop. He taught the priesthood of the clergy based on their sacrificial work. Rebellion against any bishop was viewed as rebellion against God. For Cyprian, the bishops made up an organization that

---

[26] Earl D. Radmacher, *What the Church Is All about* (Chicago: Moody Press, 1978), p. 50. This work is extremely helpful in its development of the history of the doctrine of the church.
[27] Irenaeus, *Against Heresies*, 3.3.1-2.

represented the entire church. Outside of the church, there was no salvation. He wrote, "If you abandon the church and join yourself to an adulteress, you are cut off from the promises of the church. If you then leave the church of Christ, you will not come to Christ's rewards, you will be an alien, an outcast, an enemy. You cannot have God as your Father unless you have the church for your mother."[28]

Augustine, in his *City of God*, gave added impetus to the stress on the unity of the visible church, enlarging on Cyprian's concept. The result was a confusion of the scriptural teaching on the church and the churches. As we will see later, this same confusion characterizes the modern ecumenical movement.

The ancient period saw, in addition to the stress on external unity, an accompanying stress on internal purity. In fact, the latter was a direct result of the former. As a result of the emphasis on external unity, there developed a gradual secularization and lessening of spiritual emphasis in the churches. This created the need for a renewal of internal purity.

Emphasis on internal purity was advocated most strongly by those not identified with the orthodox church. These individuals set forth their opposition to the prevailing view that there was no salvation outside the church. They also disagreed sharply with the notion that the true church was the visible Catholic Church, which was composed of both good and evil. Instead, they stressed that the true church was composed only of the redeemed.

Three individuals were of special importance in this regard—Marcion, Montanus, and Donatus. Though the adherents of Marcionism, Montanism, and Donatism held differing (and even widely considered heretical) points of view, they all agreed that the church needed reform, and all attempted to accomplish that reform.

---

[28] Cyprian, *On the Unity of the Church*, 6.

The Middle Ages

There was little doctrinal development during the Middle Ages, and the doctrine of the church fared no better than other doctrines. The theologians of the time, called schoolmen or scholastics, accepted the doctrine of the church as developed by such men as Irenaeus, Cyprian, and Augustine.

Students of the medieval period are in general agreement that there was virtually no development in ecclesiology. They also agree that despite this fact, there developed an almost absolute hierarchy within the church. This, of course, made the Reformation necessary.

The Reformation

The Lutheran Contribution. Martin Luther spoke out against the Roman Catholic concept of the church. Contrary to Rome, he believed the church consisted of all true believers in Christ everywhere. He wrote, "This community or assembly consists of all those who live in true faith, hope, and love; so that the essence, life and nature of the church is not a bodily assembly, but an assembly of hearts in one faith."[29] It is clear also from the scriptural proof Luther used to support has view (e.g., Luke 17:20-21; John 18:36) that he, like Augustine before him, equated the church and the kingdom of God.

According to Luther, the term "church" was not to be used to describe the external organization, though he did believe in the local assembly. Luther never questioned the existence of two churches, but he chose to call the universal church "a spiritual inner Christendom." The local church he called "a bodily external Christendom."[30]

Luther did not develop the relation between the local church and the universal church; whatever may be said of his contribution, two things stand out clearly: (1) he did little to advance the New Testament teaching of the

---

29 Martin Luther, "The Papacy at Rome," *Works of Martin Luther* (Philadelphia: A. J. Holman, 1932), 1:349.
30 Ibid., p. 355.

local church; (2) the state did gain control of the church under his tutelage.

The Calvinistic Contribution. John Calvin was much more specific and definite in his views on the church than was Luther. He viewed the church in a threefold sense. First, he saw the invisible church as including all the elect. Second, Calvin said "church" referred to all who profess to know Christ: "Often, however, the name 'church' designates the whole multitude of men spread over the earth who profess to worship one God in Christ… In this church are mingled many hypocrites who have nothing of Christ but the name and outward appearance."[31] Third, Calvin did advance the close church-state relationship held by the church he left.

Cyprian's concept of the church is everywhere evident in Calvin's teaching. He simply restated and developed Cyprian's view, even to the point that he did not believe one could have God as his Father who did not have the church as his mother. This great Reformer did not believe the universal church existed beyond the sum of all the local churches.

The clarion calls of the Reformation were *sola scriptura*, scripture alone, and *sola fide*, faith alone. Everything else was secondary to the Reformers—even the doctrine of the church.

The Anglican Contribution. The Anglican Reformation in England did not have one outstanding leader as the Lutheran and Calvinistic movements did. Through the Act of Supremacy in 1534, the church in England separated from the Roman papacy. It separated organizationally at this time, but not theologically.

The Thirty-Nine Articles of Faith became the official creed of the Anglican Church; they remain so today, with little change from the original statements. No specific reference is made to the invisible or universal church in the Articles. Reference is made to "the visible church of Christ," which is where the emphasis rests. When Anglicans say, "invisible church," they refer to those members of the local church who have gone to be with the Lord.

---

31 Calvin, *Institutes of the Christian Religion*, 4.1.7.

There were both Lutheran and Calvinistic strands in the Anglican Church. There were also persons who felt too many Roman Catholic trappings remained in the church. Those who wanted to purify the church were called Puritans. At first, the Puritan movement was not Presbyterian or Congregational in polity. But it was not long until both these forms became apparent and developed into two parties within Puritanism. Both remained within the Anglican Church while stating their strong differences with it.

At the same time, there were those who advocated complete separation from the state church. These were known as Separatists, and two doctrines set them apart. In their churches only those who could demonstrate they were born again could be members. Also, each local church was completely independent from any other ecclesiastical control.

The Anabaptist Contribution. Technically, the Anabaptist Free Church movement was not really part of the Protestant Reformation. Unlike the Reformers, the leaders of the so-called sects were never a part of the Roman Catholic Church. Their protestations were from without, not from within. Also, unlike the Reformers, the Anabaptists were not interested in reforming the existing ecclesiastical system. Rather, they wanted to reconstruct the church according to the New Testament teaching as they understood it.

Reformers such as Luther, Calvin, and Zwingli had great respect for the church which mothered them. It was not their intent at the beginning to leave Rome and thus unchurch themselves. As far as they were concerned, the existing church was indeed the true church. It had fallen upon evil days, to be sure, but it was still the true church according to them.

The Anabaptists, however, set out to discard the territorial church pattern and replace it with the pattern they saw in the New Testament. Their objective was not to introduce something new, but to restore something old. "Restitution" was their slogan–a restitution of the early church. From the Anabaptist point of view, the difference between the Reformers and themselves was the difference between reform and restitution of the early church.[32]

A cursory reading of the Reformation literature might give the impression that the difference between the Reformers and the Anabaptists was over water baptism, but this was not the case. Totally divergent views of the church constituted the real difference. The issue of water baptism only served to bring the real difference out into the open.

The term "Anabaptist" was assigned to these people in a derogatory way by the Reformers themselves. The word means "re-baptize." But the ones to whom the name was given rejected it. They insisted that since infant baptism was not true baptism, they were not re-baptizing. They believed that the water baptism according to Scripture was only for those who had exercised faith in Christ as their Savior.

The Anabaptists stressed believer's baptism. They also repudiated the union of the church and state, a view that went hand in hand with infant baptism. For them, the church had fallen when Constantine made Christianity the state religion.

The Modern Period

It is no secret that there is a determined effort on the part of many to build a world church. The modern ecumenical movement is a reality. W. A. Visser't Hooft, the first general secretary of the World Council of Churches, surveyed the developments in the organization's history:

"The first had been the period of the pioneers... The second period was that of the architects who sought to give a more clearly defined shape to the ecumenical movement... The task was now to insure that the ecumenical movement should really become ecumenical, that it should become the ecumenical movement of the churches, and that it should develop adequate

---

32   Earl D. Radmacher, *What the Church Is All About*, (Chicago: Moody Press, 1972) p. 69.

structures... The story of the years since 1948 is essentially the story of the process through which the ecumenical movement became universalized. It is a story of ecumenical mobilization of practically all Christian churches."[33]

According to Visser't Hooft, the word "ecumenical" refers to "that quality or attitude which expresses the consciousness of and desire for Christian unity." Early in its usage, the word meant "pertaining to the whole earth." Later, it came to mean "pertaining to the whole church." Today, the term is used to describe the desire for the union of all Christian groups into one conglomerate called the church.

The drive for church union is without much regard for doctrinal agreement and did not begin in the church pew (no major heresy, in fact, ever began there). Instead, it began in academic centers, found its way to the pulpit, and then to the pew and, finally, out into the world.

Church unionism has made its mark in every major denomination. Great strides have already been made toward bringing all denominations together under one ecclesiastical umbrella without significant regard for doctrinal beliefs.

The Theological Background. The modern ecumenical movement can be traced to the rise of theological liberalism. This liberalism grew out of the man-centered philosophies of the Renaissance and the period that followed.

A profound interest in the world, along with faith in reason and man's own capabilities, characterized the Renaissance period. Widespread skepticism regarding the Bible and biblical Christianity prevailed. The attacks on Christianity became stronger and more direct as time passed. The philosophies of the period had a direct influence on the theologians of the day, many of whom in turn became the fathers of theological liberalism.

The liberal establishment which spearheads the mad drive for a monstrous world church is no more orthodox now than it has ever been.

---

33 W. A. Visser't Hooft, *The Ecumenical Advance: A History of the Ecumenical Movement*, 1948-1968, Vol. 2, ed. Harold E. Fey, pp. 3-4.

Through a deceitful game of semantic delusions, it is seeking to sell the public a thoroughly heterodox bill of goods, and what is sadly true is that multitudes of laymen are being persuaded to buy the product. Most of them are not aware of the fact that their purchase will ultimately involve the surrender of whatever remains of their church's liberties and will align them whether they like it or not with those men and movements which are diametrically opposed to the faith once delivered unto the saints–the faith of our fathers.

The basic problem of the rejection of the inspiration and authority of the Bible which plagued the founders of liberal theology and was embraced by the attempt of church union from the very beginning still characterizes the present ecumenical leadership. The doctrine that the Bible is the inspired and inerrant Word of God is rejected by them.[34]

The Historical Context. Without doubt, the rise and spread of theological liberalism paved the way for the church union movement. From the very beginning, the enthusiasts for church union rejected the cardinal doctrines of the Christian faith. Among these are the total inspiration of the Scriptures and the full deity of Christ the Savior.

Those who pioneered the church union movement did so through various organizations, which are described below. Except for the first, these were all started and promoted by theological liberals.

The World Evangelical Alliance. This organization was founded by evangelicals in 1845. From the very beginning, the WEA placed great stress on the Bible as the Word of God and Christ as the Son of God. Some of the members of the WEA were influenced by the higher critical view of the Scriptures. These were in the minority, however, and they withdrew in 1894 after they saw they could not win the movement to their liberal persuasions.

The Federal Council of Churches of Christ in America. Those who withdrew from the WEA organized the Open Church League, which later became

---

[34] Robert P. Lightner, *Church Union* (Des Plaines, IL: Regular Baptist Press, 1971), pp. 26-27. I recommend this work. I have used it throughout this section.

the National Federation of Churches and Christian Workers. In 1905, this organization became the Federal Council of Churches of Christ in America. The FCC had a very minimal doctrinal basis. The preamble stated it recognized Jesus Christ as "divine Lord and Savior." This brief statement was open to varied interpretations by the constituent bodies.

The World Council of Churches. The WCC had its beginning in several earlier organizations–the Conference on Faith and Order, the Conference on Life and Work, and the International Missionary Council. Theological liberals staffed each of these. Attempts were made in 1938 to form the WCC, but the outbreak of World War II made it necessary to delay the plans. The WCC was formed in 1948 in Amsterdam, Holland. From the start, theological liberals have occupied key places of leadership in the WCC. The basis for membership is concurrence with a very brief statement. "The World Council of Churches is a fellowship of churches which accept our Lord Jesus Christ as God and Savior according to the Scriptures and therefore seek to fulfill together their common calling to the glory of the one God, Father, Son, and Holy Spirit."[35] While this statement sounds good as far as it goes, there is no attempt made to determine how the members interpret it. This is apparent in view of the admission of groups like the Hicksite Quakers, who deny the deity of Christ.

The National Council of Churches of Christ in the U.S.A. In 1950, the old Federal Council of Churches became the National Council of Churches. Quite a few denominations are members today. Its brief doctrinal statement, "Jesus Christ as divine Lord and Savior," is also open to varied interpretations, as is evidenced by the membership. From the very beginning to the present, avowed and well-known deniers of the historic Christian faith have wielded tremendous influence in the NCC. The same efforts carried on by the WCC on a world level are performed by the NCC on a national level.

---

35 See ibid., pp. 34-39 for further documentation.

The Consultation on Church Union.[36] On December 4, 1960, Eugene Carson Blake, then the stated clerk of the United Presbyterian Church in the U.S.A., preached in the Grace (Episcopal) Cathedral of San Francisco, and proposed what became the Consultation on Church Union. COCU represents the largest single attempt toward a super-church. A perusal of the views of the leaders of this gigantic effort reveal quickly that they are not in harmony with the historic Christian faith. The initial proposals of COCU were not well received at first by the memberships of the consulting bodies. In response, the leaders retreated a bit and are making less bold attempts to accomplish the same goal–a super-church without regard for the faith once delivered to the saints.

What of the future? What the future holds with respect to the present church union efforts is difficult to predict. One thing is certain: God will one day judge any false world church that might be brought into existence. The liberal church union effort will collapse. Not only that, it will experience the judgment of God (Rev. 17:1-2).

The New Testament clearly teaches that false teachers would arise who would trouble the church (e.g., Acts 20:28-32; Gal. 1:6; 2 Peter 2:1). Equally clear is the scriptural teaching that the believer is to separate from false teachers and teaching (e.g., 2 Chron. 19:2; Amos 3:3; Eph. 5:11; Gal. 1:8-9; 2 Cor. 6:14-16; 1 Tim. 6:5; 2 Tim. 2:19; 3:5; 2 John 9-10; 2 Thess. 3:6).

The Universal Church

The meaning of *Ekklesia*

The word *ekklesia*, translated "church" throughout the New Testament, comes from two Greek words: *ek* and *kaleo*, "to call." The two words together

---

[36] A sampling of major denominations in the COCU include United Methodist, Episcopal, African Methodist Episcopal Zion, Christian Methodist Episcopal, African Methodist Episcopal, Presbyterian Church (U.S.A.), Christian Church (Disciples of Christ), United Church of Christ, and National Council of Community Churches.

mean "to call out." It follows, therefore, that *ekklesia* refers to a called-out assembly or a gathering of people. In the New Testament, there are several usages of *ekklesia*.[37]

An assembly of people. Israel in the wilderness was called "the church in the wilderness" (Acts 7:38). Even the heathen mob assembled at Ephesus was called a church (Acts 19:39). Likewise, *ekklesia* was used for a group of people assembled for a religious purpose (Heb. 2:12; cf. Ps. 22:22).

An assembly of Christians in a local church. Frequently, the New Testament speaks of the church which was in some particular place: "the church which was at Jerusalem" (Acts 8:1); "the church that was at Antioch" (Acts 13:1); "the church which is at Cenchrea" (Rom. 16:1); "the church of God which is at Corinth" (1 Cor. 1:2). *Ekklesia* is also used in the plural form for a group of local churches (1 Cor. 16:19, Gal. 1:2).

All professing Christians. In this sense, *ekklesia* takes on a meaning almost synonymous with Christendom. Paul said to the Romans, "The churches of Christ salute you" (Rom. 16:16). To the Galatians he wrote that he had "persecuted the church of God" (Gal. 1:13). In such instances, no particular church is in view, but rather all Christians being persecuted everywhere.

The body of Christ. Paul identified the church as Christ's body when writing to both the Ephesians (1:22-23) and the Colossians (1:18). All members of the church are vitally united with each other and with Christ, the head of the body and the Lord of the church. This union was consummated by the baptism of the Spirit.

The reality of the Universal Church

There are a number of usages of *ekklesia* that do not seem to refer to a local assembly of believers. Instead, they speak of that company of believers formed on the day of Pentecost into the body of Christ, which has been

---
37 See Earl D. Radmacher, *What the Church Is All About*, (Chicago: Moody Press, 1972) pp. 115-31, for an excellent summary of the usage of *ekklesia* in classical Greek and the Septuagint.

growing ever since as sinners trust Christ alone as Savior and are added to it. This company of the redeemed is called "the church" without consideration of whether or not those who are a part of it are members of local churches. However, there are some evangelicals who do not believe there is any so-called universal church that exists outside the local assembly. This difference of opinion will be addressed later.

The means of entrance and foundation

By the baptizing ministry of the Holy Spirit, the universal church was formed. At the time of salvation, each believing sinner is made a member of the body of Christ (1 Cor. 12:12-13). The Holy Spirit of God is the primary agent who identifies the believer with other believers. Each one is a member of the body, and each member is united with the other members and with Christ (Rom. 6:1-4).

In the Gospels, where the promise of Spirit baptism is first given, Christ is said to be the one who would baptize in the Spirit (Matt. 3:11; Mark 1:8; Luke 3:16). The same is true in the prophecy recorded in Acts 1:5. But in 1 Corinthians 12:12-13, Christ is not named as the one baptizing, but the Spirit is named. The believer is to be identified with the "body." This body is defined as the church in Ephesians 1:22-23 and Colossians 1:18. On the basis of this, we conclude that both the Holy Spirit and Christ are agents in the work of forming the body of Christ. The Spirit may be viewed as the primary agent and Christ the secondary agent in that he sent the Holy Spirit to begin his new work after his ascension.

Four passages of Scripture are of special significance to the teaching of Christ as the foundation of the church.

Matthew 16:18-20

In the history of the church, several views have been advanced as to the meaning of Christ's words: "Upon this rock I will build my church."

The view of the Roman Catholic Church is that Peter is the foundation of the church. The view is based on the Aramaic forms of the two English words "Peter" and "rock" in Matthew 16:18. However, there is no trace of Matthew's Gospel in Aramaic. In the Greek New Testament, the words are different and have different meanings. It is not too much to say that Rome's interpretation of Matthew 16:18 is indispensable to the whole theological superstructure of the Roman Catholic Church.

Peter's confession of faith is viewed by some as the foundation of the church. This view is closely related to the prominent evangelical belief that Christ is the foundation of the church. Though the views are not identical, they can hardly be separated from each other; together they constitute an evangelical consensus.

Peter in Greek is Petros. The word is masculine in gender and means rock. When Christ stated that He would build His church upon the rock, He used Petra, a different word, which is used sixteen times in the New Testament. Eleven of those times, it is used of a big boulder-type rock. Five times it is used metaphorically of Christ. Petros and Petra always seem to be used in a different sense, and that certainly appears to be the case in this passage. Very likely as Christ spoke, He pointed first to Peter when He said, "Thou art Peter." Then he pointed to Himself as He said, "And upon this rock I will build my church."

Several other considerations regarding Peter's subsequent behavior substantiate this interpretation.[38] Peter never claimed any authority over the other apostles; instead he denied it (see 1 Peter 1:1; 5:1-3; Acts 10:25-26). His actions, especially in relation to Christ, did not conform to his being

---
38 See Loraine Boettner, *Roman Catholicism* (Philadelphia: Presbyterian and Reformed Publishing Company, 1962), pp. 104-24

the one on whom the church was to be built. Just after Christ's promise to build the church, Peter denied that Christ should even die (Matt. 16:22). Furthermore, Peter slept in the garden while Christ prayed, and later he denied Him openly. If Peter was the foundation of the church, why was James the leader of the great Jerusalem council and not Peter (Acts 15)? Finally, in addition to the teaching in Matthew 16:18 that Christ is the foundation of the church, other passages contain supportive teaching (1 Cor. 3:11; Eph. 2:19-22; 1 Peter 2:4-8).

A word about the keys and the binding and loosing of Matthew 16:19 is in order. To Peter, Jesus said, "And I will give unto thee the keys of the kingdom of heaven: and whatsoever thou shalt bind on earth shall be bound in heaven: and whatsoever thou shalt loose on earth shall be loosed in heaven." To begin, it should be noted that Jesus gave the same word to the other apostles (cf. Matt. 18:18). This was not, therefore, the exclusive right of Peter. However, he was used in a special way to open the door of opportunity to the Gentiles (Acts 2, 8, 10). The figure of the keys in our Lord's words to Peter had to do with locking or unlocking, opening or closing, the gospel to the Gentiles. It was a declarative power given to Peter here, not a saving power. Peter himself made it abundantly clear that he had no saving power (see Acts 2:21; 10:43).

The binding and loosing in Christ's word to Peter relate to delivering the message of the gospel. When he gave the message, the people could be released from their sins. If he withheld the message, they would remain bound in their sin.

1 Corinthians 3:10-11

Here, Paul used the metaphor of a building as he wrote of the church. The local church at Corinth, and Paul's early work in starting it, was primarily in view. And yet, as he labored among the people, he built upon Christ by proclaiming Him and His finished work. It was not his own message he proclaimed, but that which he received from Christ. The foundation Paul laid as a wise master builder (Eph. 2:10) was that of Christ Himself and His teaching.

Ephesians 2:19-22

In this passage, the building metaphor is used differently than the way it is used in 1 Corinthians 3:10-11. There, the emphasis was on the truth of Christ, upon which the church was built. Here, the emphasis is on those individuals, Christ Himself and the apostles and prophets, who constitute the foundation of the church. In this passage, Jesus Christ Himself is said to be "the chief corner stone." The building referred to is the universal church, which is viewed as a "habitation of God through the Spirit." The fact that there is only one definite article with two nouns points to apostles and prophets constituting one class in their relation to the church. The apostles being placed before the prophets also supports this view.

1 Peter 2:4-8

It is highly significant that Peter considered himself not as the foundation of the church, but as having a role no different from the other apostles in the construction of the church. He made it clear by his quotation from Isaiah 28:16 that Christ alone is the "head of the corner." The specific meaning of the corner stone is open to some question. However, one thing is clear from the figure: Christ occupied an absolutely essential place in the church structure.

We may conclude from Christ's own words (Matt. 16:18) that He is the foundation of the church; in complete harmony with this are the other three passages discussed in this section.

The Local Church

Those who endeavor to base their views on the Scripture turn to the practices and precepts of the local church in the New Testament. Practice, here, is referring to the inspired record of the actions done by the New Testament church. On the other hand, precepts refers to the equally inspired record of the specific instruction declaring how the local church is to exist and function. In formulating doctrine, precepts take the priority. When there are no precepts, the practices are generally viewed as normative.

There is more in the New Testament about the practices of the early church, and practice must not be set aside as unimportant. Many biblical truths that we hold precious are not specific commands as to what we should believe or do but are simply what, in fact, New Testament Christians believed. We often believe and behave, in other words, because we are told what was believed by New Testament Christians and how they behaved as the people of God.

Reality and identity

The most common usage of *ekklesia* refers to an organized assembly of believers in a particular locality. The word is used at least ninety times with this meaning.

The ekklesia of the New Testament stated a time of meeting (Acts 20:7), leaders were chosen (Acts 20:17), corporate discipline was practiced (1 Cor. 5), and believers were united in raising money for the work of the gospel (2 Cor. 8-9). In the total teaching of the New Testament, certain things were true of the local church. Each assembly was made up of those who were regenerate and had banded together to observe the ordinances and engage in worship, Christian fellowship, and the spread of the gospel. They were organized and had chosen leaders to assist them in doing the will of God.

The local church is, in a real sense, a miniature of the universal church. To be a member of the universal, one must be divinely related to Christ. The most basic requirement of membership in the local church, if it is true to the New Testament pattern, is the same as the universal church–union with Christ. Christ is the living head of the church, which is His body. He desires to be the head of each local church as well. By means of Spirit baptism, believing sinners are identified with Christ and with other believers. Believer's baptism in water is an ordinance of the local church and is the means by which one's union with Christ in His death, burial, and resurrection is made public.

Membership

It seems certain that the local church of the New Testament had an accountable "membership." We can assume this for a number of reasons. First, the number of converts was known (Acts 2:41; 4:4). We also know that there were special requirements for widows (1 Tim. 5:9), and this could imply other requirements as well. The very fact that official leaders, such as elders and deacons, were chosen assumes responsibility and accountability on the part of the church (Acts 6:2-5; 20:17). The teaching of church discipline also assumes such responsibility and accountability (1 Cor. 5:13). How could an individual be disciplined unless he was a member of the assembly with certain privileges and responsibilities? Further, the office of elder or bishop seems to require membership. The one holding this office is to rule (Heb. 13:7). Evangelicals are in general agreement on these requirements, though there are differences over how they are to be implemented.

Organization and ordinances

The same arguments cited in support of membership requirements also argue for a measure of organization and structure in the church. The early church was marked by a very simple kind of structure, which arose to take the place of direct apostolic authority (Acts 4:35; 5:1-11; 6:2). The organization grew in response to the needs and problems that developed (e.g., Acts 6; 15:6, 22). Certainly, the organization of the New Testament church was definite in principle, yet it was not detailed nor specific in all areas. There was room for expansion and development as the churches grew.

Elder, bishop, and pastor refer to different ministries of the same person. Paul used the terms "elders," "overseers" and "bishop" when writing about the same people or person (Acts 20:17, 28; Titus 1:5-7). The terms were used interchangeably. Further, as he described the work of the pastor, he related it to shepherding (Eph. 4:11-12). From the references to elder, overseer and bishop we learn that theirs is the same kind of work. Pastor refers to a gift given by the Spirit of God. Elder, overseer and bishop refer more to the office than to the function of the office.

The qualifications for those who would be elder or bishop were carefully delineated by Paul (1 Tim. 3:1-7; Titus 1:5-9). These are high indeed. Unfortunately, they are not always taken into account today when the office is filled. Duties of the elder, bishop, or pastor are also quite specific (Acts 20:28; 2 Tim. 4:2; Titus 1:13; 2:15; 1 Peter 5:2). The local church itself has responsibilities toward the elder. These are also described in Scripture (1 Tim. 5:1, 17-19; 1 Thess. 5:13). A "crown of glory" (1 Peter 5:4) and "crown of righteousness" (2 Tim. 4:7-8) await the faithful leaders of God's people.

Deacons were also officers in the New Testament church. It is generally believed that their origin is to be found in the experience recorded in Acts 6. The word translated "deacon" means servant. It is used in an unofficial sense (e.g., Rom. 12:6-7) and in an official sense (e.g., 1 Tim. 3:8-13) with respect to special church officers. In the early church, the deacons assisted the apostles in caring for the needy in the assembly. The qualifications of these specially designated servants of God are essentially the same as those of elders. High standards of conduct are also given for deacons (1 Tim. 3:8-13).

Water baptism and Communion, or the Lord's Table, are two ordinances most practiced among evangelical churches. The terms "ordinance" and "sacrament" are both used among evangelicals. Ordinance seems more acceptable, since sacrament is generally understood to convey the idea of saving merit or grace. An ordinance refers to an outward rite appointed by Christ to be ministered by the church as a visible sign of the saving truth of the gospel. Most evangelicals observe two ordinances in their local churches. (Foot-washing is also observed as an ordinance by some churches, who look to John 13).[39]

Believer's baptism is a public testimony of one's union with Christ. The act symbolizes a believer's identification with Christ in his death, burial, and resurrection. The act is a solemn reminder to the individual and to all who observe that there is no turning back.

The Lord's Table, or Communion as it is commonly called, is generally observed more regularly and given more prominence than believer's baptism by many evangelicals. The number of times the ordinance is observed each year varies. Also, there are differences as to the kind of elements to be used. Some churches use wine and others use grape juice. The greatest difference among evangelicals over this ordinance concerns its meaning and significance, which will be discussed later in this chapter.

The Mission in the world

The universal church, the body of Christ, is manifested in the world through local churches; the invisible church is seen through the visible local assembly. In the New Testament, the local church is of divine appointment and charged with responsibilities under God. Paul made this clear when he told Timothy that the local church was the "pillar and ground of the truth" (1 Tim. 3:15).

It seems obvious that the mission of the church is vitally important. What is God's intended purpose for this divine institution? Surely he has a purpose for the church's existence, but what is that purpose? Why did Christ build the church? While the church has many responsibilities in the world, its primary mission centers in three duties: the exaltation of the Savior and the Scriptures, the edification of the people of God, and the evangelization

---

[39] See Herman A. Hoyt, *This Do in Remembrance of Me* (Winona Lake, IN) for arguments supporting footwashing as an ordinance of the church).

of the lost. Evangelicals are in general agreement that the church's mission is threefold, but divergence of practice prevails in attempting to accomplish this mission.

The exaltation of the Savior and the Scriptures

When Christ (the Incarnate Word) and the Bible (the Written Word) are honored, exalted, and obeyed, God is worshiped. To glorify God is truly the highest privilege and responsibility ever afforded man. Paul's repeated exhortations to Timothy and Titus demonstrate the importance of these two Words of God (1 Tim. 4:13-16; 2 Tim. 3:14-17; 4:2; Titus 1:9). When the written Word is studied and obeyed, the Living Word is exalted. To love and obey the one is to love and obey the other. The apostle, who was such a student of Scripture and was used of God to bring it to us, preached Christ in all His fullness (1 Cor. 1:23; 2 Cor. 4:5).

First and foremost, the local church in all its activities has the responsibility of equipping the saints with the Word of God. All that it does must be anchored in the Word of God and performed for the glory of God.

The edification of the people of God

In broad outline, Christ's great commission sets forth the answer to the question, why does the church exist? The evangelization of the lost is a major responsibility of the church (Matt. 28:19). "Go ye therefore, and teach all nations" is better translated, "Go ye therefore and *make disciples of* all nations." This is the evangelization command of the commission. The edification command is in the baptizing and teaching which follow. The church exists in the world to evangelize it. The church exists as a gathered community of believers to edify or build up those who are a part of it.[40] The emphasis throughout the New Testament is evenly distributed between these two responsibilities.

---

40 Gene A. Getz, *Sharpening the Focus of the Church* (Chicago: Moody Press, 1974), pp. 21-28.

The Lord Jesus forcefully stated the responsibility to feed his lambs and sheep (John 21:15-17). Much of Paul's missionary travel was for the purpose of edifying or building up the saints (e.g., Acts 14:23; 15:41; 16:4-5). He exhorted the Ephesian elders to "feed the church of God" (Acts 20:28). There is no lack of biblical support for this charge.

Unfortunately, it is often thought that only the pastor or church leaders are to edify the saints. To be sure, this is one of the major responsibilities of the undershepherds of God's flock. But Scripture abounds in admonitions to individual believers to edify each other through prayer, exhortation, bearing of burdens, and sharing with those in need.

The evangelization of the lost

This is indeed a primary responsibility of the church (see Matt. 28:19-20; Luke 24:47, 49; Acts 1:8; 13:2-3, 38-39; Rom. 10:12-15). The church's mission is to make Christ known to the whole world. Evangelism of the lost is basic to the very nature of Christianity. To be true to the New Testament, each local church must be responsible for those in its immediate vicinity. The early Christians were to take the message first to Jerusalem and then beyond their borders (Acts 1:8).

As members of local churches, we must not wait for the unregenerate to come to our assemblies. Each believer is to be a light for Christ in his or her world, pointing men and women, boys and girls to Him. This is not to say people can't or shouldn't trust Christ as personal Savior in the church. But it is to say that evangelization is to be done by individual believers in the workaday world outside the church as well.

In summary, then, the threefold mission of the church is to exalt the Savior and the Scriptures, to edify the people of God, and to evangelize the lost. This means the primary function of the church is not to Christianize society. Local churches in the New Testament were not given a so-called "cultural mandate." They were never told to exert their influence in the world in such a way and to such an extent that all the social evils of the day would be corrected. As the pillar and ground of the truth, the church has as its primary task the solemn responsibility to declare the whole counsel of God to a lost and dying world.

Major Areas of Difference Among Evangelicals

Denials of the Universal Church

The *ekklesia*, or universal church, is identified as the body of Christ (Col. 1:18). The term "universal" is preferred to "invisible." The latter term is especially open to misunderstanding because to some it implies unreality.

The truth is that a significant number of Christians do not believe in the existence of a universal church as distinct from local churches.[41] Rarely is the term "universal church" used by these people. Occasionally, the body of Christ may be referred to, but it is used to describe the sum of all the New Testament local churches. In this view, when one becomes a Christian, he becomes a member of the family of God but not of the universal invisible church. In other words, no one is a member of the body of Christ who is not a member of a local church. To them, the local church is the body of Christ, and vice versa.

---

[41] This denial characterizes several independent fundamental Baptist groups such as Old Landmarkism, Bible Baptists, Missionary Baptists, and the North American Baptist Association. These organizations do not include statements on the universal church in their doctrinal statements. Some works which promote the denial of the universal church are S. W. Anderson, *Real Churches or a Fog* (Texarkana, TX: Boggard Press, 1975); B. H. Carroll, *Ekklesia–The Church* (Louisville: Baptist Book Concern); Richard V. Clearwaters, *The Local Church of the New Testament* (Conservative Baptist Association of America); Chester E. Tulga, *New Testament Baptists in the Nature of the Church* (Chicago: Conservative Baptist Association of America). The view of the above is not too dissimilar from Roman Catholicism, which also denies the universal church. It teaches that no one can be a part of Christ's mystical body who is not a member of the visible Roman Catholic Church.

If the above view is correct, the following Scripture passages are difficult to interpret.

Matthew 16:18

Here, Christ promised that He would build the church in the future. This meant it was not in existence at the time He spoke. No particular local church was in view here, because He used the singular noun and because He promised perpetuity for the church that He promised to build. No local church is eternal, but the body of Christ is eternal.

1 Corinthians 12:12-13

Here, Paul identifies the church with Christ, the name of the one whose body it is. In view of this, the question is, to how many local churches could that name apply without blasphemy? In this passage, all who believe are described as parts or members of the body of Christ, whether they are members of the local church or not. There can be no mistaking it; all believers are baptized by the Spirit and are, therefore, members of the body of Christ (see Rom. 6:1-4).

Ephesians 1:22-23

In this passage, the church is identified as the body (cf. Col. 1:18). Furthermore, it is said to be "the fullness of him that filleth all in all," which would seem to describe the universal church rather than a local assembly, or even a group of local assemblies.

Ephesians 2:11-17

The "one body" referred to here is made up of Jews and Gentiles, who are constituted "one new man" in Christ. If the body is interpreted to mean the local church, it would follow that each local church must have in it both Jews and Gentiles.

Ephesians 3

In this chapter, the "one new man" and the "one body" of 2:15-16 are described further. The union of Jews and Gentiles in one body, so that Gentiles are "fellowheirs, and of the same body" (v. 6) with the Jews, is called the mystery–that is, something not revealed before. The truth had been "hid in God" (v. 9). The reference to the church in verses 10 and 21 must be understood in view of this. It is through the church that "principalities and powers in heavenly *places* might be known," the very "wisdom of God." Also, through this church, glory comes to Christ "throughout all ages." It seems highly unlikely that all these references to the church refer to the local assembly.

Ephesians 4:4-16

Once again, the emphasis is on "one body," the "body of Christ," and "the whole body." The divinely given abilities for service are also described in this chapter. These gifts of the Spirit are given as means for the "perfecting of the saints, for the work of the ministry" (v. 12). The "body" referred to in this chapter must be seen as the "new man" referred to earlier (2:15) and cannot be the local church.

Ephesians 5:23-27

Several references to the church appear in these verses. Christ is said to be the church's head and also "the Saviour of the body." He loved the church, and proved it by His death. It is Christ's purpose to provide for Himself a spotless and holy church. How could these statements possibly refer to the local church? If they do, the question is, to which one do they refer?

Hebrews 12:22-23

The "church of the firstborn" is included here among the occupants of the heavenly Jerusalem. The church spoken of here could not in any sense be earthly.

Views of the Beginning of the Church

Roman Catholicism

The Roman Catholic Church regards itself as the continuation of Israel. Rome claims that spiritual power is higher and more important than political power, and therefore, the church claims authority over the state.

Roman Catholicism emphasizes the visible and external nature of the church but does not deny the mystical or invisible church. However, this church is defined as the fellowship of believers who are part of the visible church, that is, the Roman Catholic Church. Roman Catholic theology insists there is no church invisible or universal that is not a part of the visible or local church, as can be seen in the "Encyclical of the Mystical Body of Christ" by Pope Pius XII, given June 29, 1943.

The Reformers

The Reformers had little quarrel with Rome's doctrine of the church. They were far more concerned with defending the doctrine of salvation by faith alone and the authority of the Bible alone. And yet, the Reformers did recognize the true body of believers, even though they placed great stress on the visible organization. For them, the church had its roots in Judaism and included all the saints of all ages. The church was the inheritor of Israel's promises.

Luther believed the church was the assembly of all the believers in Christ upon earth.[42] Calvin said, "The church includes not only the saints

---

42   Luther, "The Papacy at Rome," p. 349.

presently living on earth, but all the elect from the beginning of the world."[43] Thus, it could be said that the Reformers, as represented by these two, believed the church began with Adam.

Covenant Theology[44]

This system generally sees the church beginning with God's covenant with Abraham and his seed. Therefore, covenant theologians do not distinguish between God's program with Israel and His program with the church. They also see the church as the inheritor of Israel's promises. Although the church did not come to maturity until the Spirit's ministry on the day of Pentecost, Covenant Theology sees the church in the Old Testament and the church in the New Testament as essentially the same. Covenant Theologian Charles Hodge said, "The church under the new dispensation is identical with that of the old. It is not a new church, but one and the same. It is the same olive tree (Rom. 11:17, 24). It is found in the same covenant, the covenant made with Abraham."[45]

Landmark Baptist views

Certain Baptist groups, especially in the south, insist the church began with Christ. Clearwaters is a spokesman for this viewpoint: "The church, therefore, was established in the days of Jesus' sojourn in the flesh. The work of its construction was begun with material prepared by John the Baptist, later the twelve apostles of our Lord."[46]

---

43 Calvin, *Institutes*, 4.1.7.
44 Covenant Theology may be defined as that system of theology which is based on the theological covenants of works and grace, with a minimizing of the biblical covenants, and has as the primary purpose of God the redemption of mankind.
45 Charles Hodge, *Systematic Theology* (Grand Rapids: Eerdmans, 1960), 3:549.
46 Clearwaters, *The Local Church of the New Testament*, p. 26.

Dispensational thought

Certain forms of dispensational theology,[47] commonly regarded as ultra or hyper by other dispensationalists,[48] see two churches. They believe there was first the Jewish (Acts 2) and later the Gentile church. A sharp distinction is made between the church begun on the Day of Pentecost and the one in the epistles of Paul. There is some disagreement among dispensationalists as to precisely when the church began. Some say it started in Acts 2, others in Acts 9 or Acts 13, and still others after Acts 28.

The New Testament qualifications

Since Christ promised to build the church (Matt. 16:18), it seems clear that it did not exist when He spoke. He provided teaching for the church when it would exist (John 13-17). Christ gave Himself for the church (Eph. 5:25). He purchased it with His own blood (Acts 20:28) and He is the resurrected head of the church (Col. 3:1-3). Therefore, the church depended not only on His death but also on His resurrection for its existence.

If the Holy Spirit formed the church by His baptizing work (1 Cor. 12:12-13), it could not have begun until that work was operative. There is no evidence of the baptism of the Spirit until Acts 2.

The bringing together of Jews and Gentiles in one body is called a mystery (Eph. 3:1-6) which means it was not revealed before. A biblical mystery is defined in Romans 16:25. Paul says the mystery was not made known in other ages "as it is now revealed unto his holy apostles and prophets" (Eph. 3:5). The "as" clause may be taken either in a restrictive sense, meaning the truth was partially revealed before, or it may be taken in a descriptive sense, indicating it was totally unrevealed before. Since the same truth was

---

[47] Dispensational theology may be defined as that system of theology which sees the Bible as the unfolding of the distinguishable economies in the outworking of God's purpose and which sees the ultimate purpose of God to bring glory to himself in all His relations with all His creatures.

[48] See Charles C. Ryrie, *Dispensationalism Today* (Chicago: Moody Press, 1965), pp. 192-205, for an excellent summary and critique.

declared by the same writer on another occasion (Col. 1:25-26) without the "as" clause, it seems best to understand the phrase in Ephesians 3:5 in the descriptive sense. Though this does not tell us precisely when the church began, it does mean it did not exist in the Old Testament.

The beginning of the church is definitely related to the Day of Pentecost (Acts 2). First, the Spirit's baptism is future from the ascension of Christ (Acts 1:5). Second, the Day of Pentecost is the time when the promise in Acts 1:5 was fulfilled. Third, we know this because of Peter's reference to prophecy and his discussion of what happened in the house of Cornelius (Acts 11:15-16). Fourth, Paul declared that as a result of the baptism of the Spirit, the body was formed (1 Cor. 12:12-13). Fifth, we are told that the body formed by the Spirit's baptism is the church (Eph. 1:22-23; Col. 1:18).

The Plurality of Elders

Must there always be a plurality of elders, bishops, or pastors–whichever they are called–in every local church if it is to be true to the New Testament pattern? I do not believe so. Though the term "elder" does appear consistently in the plural, there are strong reasons why plurality is not always demanded,[49] even though many evangelicals insist this is the case.

First, there were house churches rather than large public meeting places in New Testament times. Therefore, the use of the plural need not mean that each and every church had a plurality of elders. It may be understood to refer to one elder for each of the house churches in the city. Second, there is an interesting switch from the singular bishop to the plural deacons (1 Tim. 3:1-2, 8). This change lends some support to the validity of having only one elder or bishop in some instances. Third, the "angel," or messenger, in Revelation 2-3 most likely referred to the single elder of each of those churches since it would seem strange to give divine messages regarding

---

[49] See Manfred E. Kober, *The Case for the Singularity of Elders* (Ankeny, IA: Faith Baptist Bible College).

human conduct to angelic beings. There are other instances where the same word obviously refers to humans (e.g., Mark 1:2; Luke 7:24; 9:52; James 2:25).

Deaconesses

Some believe the New Testament supports the office of deaconess.[50] There is not much specific support for this, however. Only two references speak of women as deacons, and in each case the word may refer to an unofficial servant and need not be taken in an official sense (Rom. 16:1-2; 1 Tim. 3:11).

The Mode of Believer's Baptism

Water baptism is a public testimony of one's union with Christ. The act symbolizes the believer's identification with Christ in His death, burial, and resurrection. Two basic modes of baptism are practiced by evangelicals today–sprinkling and immersion.

Those who sprinkle believe their view is the correct one for the following reasons: (1) Sprinkling is a better practice than immersion to picture what the Holy Spirit does when He comes upon a believer; (2) The meaning of *baptizo* is to bring under the influence of, not simply to immerse; (3) Immersion seems impossible due to logistical or other considerations, in their interpretation of those who sprinkle, in a number of cases (e.g., Acts 2:41; 8:38; 9:18; 16:33); and (4) The water rituals related to baptism in the Old Testament included not only immersion but also sprinkling and pouring.

Arguments supporting immersion are as follows: (1) The primary meaning of *baptizo* is to immerse; the secondary meaning is to bring under the influence of; (2) Every instance of believer's baptism in the New Testament allows for immersion; (3) Immersion results from the natural meaning of preposition *ek*, "out," *en*, "in," and *eis*, "into;" (4) The Greek language has a word for sprinkle, *rontizo*, which is never used of believer's baptism; (5) The early church practiced immersion until the third century when pouring was

---

50 See Homer A. Kent, *The Pastoral Epistles* (Chicago: Moody Press, 1982), pp. 135-40 for arguments for deaconesses.

permitted in the case of illness; and (6) Immersion best pictures a believer's total identification with Christ in His death, burial, and resurrection.

The Lord's Table

The Lord's Table is also understood differently among evangelicals. Protestant evangelicals have held three principal views of the relation of the elements to Christ. All three of these views differ drastically from the Roman Catholic view, known as transubstantiation, which means the bread and the wine actually are changed to the body and blood of Christ as the priest prays.

The Lutheran view is called consubstantiation. In this view, the elements do not change, but there is a spiritual participation, a real presence of Christ, in the elements.

The Reformed position holds that the elements do constitute a means of grace through partaking of them. There is a spiritual presence of Christ in the bread and the cup, but there is no real presence of Christ in them.

The evangelical view, as argued by Zwingli, holds that there is no change in the elements, no participation of Christ in them and not even a spiritual presence. They are simply memorials, not means of grace. This is probably the most popular view among evangelical Christians today and finds the greatest support in the Scriptures.

The Government of the Church

Evangelicals all agree that the local church needs to be governed. All who name the name of Christ give assent to Christ as the head of the local church, just as He is the head of the universal church. But He is not there in the body, giving instructions to each local assembly. Human leaders must determine His will for the church from the pages of Scripture. But these Christians do not agree on how the local church should be governed.

There are basically four types of local church government: (1) The papal form is practiced by the Roman Catholic Church. In this approach, authority rests ultimately in the pope; (2) The episcopal form places authority in the bishops; (3) Presbyterianism practices the representative form, with final authority resting in the sessions and the synods; (4) The congregational form of church government places final authority with the congregation.

A number of modifications and combinations of these four types have developed through the years, especially among independent church groups. The elder-rule approach, where the elders are self-appointed, often for life, and rule without allowing for much congregational involvement is a relatively recent example of this.

The congregational form of government does not mean the congregation decides on every single matter. There is no such thing as pure congregationalism, any more than there is a pure democracy. The New Testament church appointed leaders who had specific responsibilities. They were responsible ultimately to the congregation, however, and of course the congregation was responsible to Christ.

Organization stopped at the local level in the New Testament church; there was no authority outside the local assemblies. Each one was autonomous and self-supporting, carrying on its own affairs without direction from a larger group.

Because of the following reasons, it seems certain that the congregation of believers in a local church has the responsibility of governing the church through chosen leaders. Instruction for dealing with an erring brother was to take the matter to the church (Matt. 18:16-17). Before elders or deacons were chosen, the emphasis was on group action (Acts 2:41-47). The whole church was involved in electing leaders (Acts 6; 15; Titus 1:5). Barnabas was sent to Antioch by the church (Acts 11:21-23). Likewise, Barnabas and Paul were also sent by the church (Acts 13:1-3). The church "ordained" men (Acts 14:23). In resolving the conflict in the Jerusalem council, the emphasis is clearly on the church, the "multitude," the "brethren" (Acts 15). It is highly significant that throughout the epistles the churches are addressed. Corporate discipline was enjoined upon the church (1 Cor. 5:4-5, 7, 11). In the same vein, the church was to restore the erring brother. The church is warned about accepting false teachers (e.g., 2 Cor. 11:4). This seems strange if in fact the church had nothing to do with their selection. Epaphroditus was sent by the church of Philippi as its messenger (Phil. 2:25). The church at Colossae was warned about false teaching (Col. 2:8, 18). Finally, the complaints were against the churches in Asia Minor (Rev. 2-3).

The Church and the Church Member

What can we learn from the development of the doctrine of the church in history, and what difference does that history make for us now? The need to distinguish between the church and the churches seems urgent. A proper biblical balance between the two is very important. We also need to keep the stress on external unity and internal purity in proper perspective.

We should ask ourselves, what can I do as a member of my local church to make it a truer representation of the universal church? How can I receive a broader vision of the church beyond my own local assembly? Is the Bible really opposed to the building of a super-church without regard to crucial doctrinal beliefs? Am I in any way contributing toward such a goal? These are some of the questions which should be answered.

Every member of the body of Christ is needed, even those with whom we disagree. Each has a part to play in the body of Christ; each member of the local church is needed to accomplish the task God has for it. The church is not the building, but the individuals who meet there for worship and service are the church.

PART 3

CHRIST'S CROSS

OUTLINE

I. The Importance of Christ's Cross

II. The Necessity of Christ's Cross
- A. Four Types of Sin
    1. Imputed Sin
    2. Inherited Sin
    3. Individual Sins
    4. Social Sins
        a. Social responsibility
        b. The decree of sin
- B. Why Evil?
- C. Can Man Save Himself?
    1. Man's Estimate of Himself
    2. God's Estimate of Man
- D. The Truth about Sin

III. The Divine Purpose of Christ's Death
- A. The Real Issue
- B. The Arminian Answer
- C. The Strict Calvinistic Answer
- D. The Moderate Calvinistic Answer
- E. Another Option
- E. Conclusion

IV. For Whom Did Christ Die?
- A. Scriptures Which Seem To Limit the Extent of the Atonement
- B. Scriptures Which Broaden the Extent of the Atonement to Include All Men
    1. Passages containing the word "world"
    2. Passages containing the word "whosoever"
    3. Passages containing the word "all" or its equivalent
    4. Limited redemptionist explanation of the unlimited passages

V. What Did Christ's Death Accomplish?
- A. Redemption
- B. Propitiation
- C. Reconciliation

VI. How Should We Then Live?
- A. In Harmony with Christ's Finished Work
- B. As Forgiven People
- C. Walking with Christ

CHRIST'S CROSS

The Importance of Christ's Cross

From His youth and even before His birth, Christ's cross work was planned by God the Father. Today the cross is still a symbol of His coming to earth. Virtually every religion has a visible sign and for Christianity it is the cross.

"Christianity then is no exception to having a visible symbol. The cross was not its earliest, however. Because of the wild accusations which were leveled against Christians and the persecutions to which they were exposed, they 'had to be very circumspect and to avoid flaunting their religion. Thus the cross, now the universal symbol of Christianity, was at first avoided, not only for its direct association with Christ, but for its shameful association with the execution of a common criminal also.'"[51]

For both believers and unbelievers, the cross of Christ is central. As we shall see, Christ suffered both in His life on earth and of course on the cross. We also will seek to answer the questions why did Christ die on the cross, and for whom did He die? What exactly did Christ's death on the cross accomplish? We want also to give serious attention to how believers should live their lives in view of the cross.

Many believe that crucifixion was first used by barbarians, with the Greeks and Romans adopting and perfecting the technique centuries later. It is believed to be the cruelest method of killing employed, with executioners often delaying death in order to prolong the victim's suffering.

---

51 John R. W. Stott, *The Cross of Christ*. (Downers Grove: IL. Intervarsity Press, 1986), p. 20.

So, what exactly did Jesus teach about His way of dying? The cross seems to have been uppermost in His mind. We are told that one day as He and His disciples were going through Galilee, He said to them, "The Son of man is delivered into the hands of men, and they shall kill him; and after that he is killed, he shall rise the third day" (Mark 9:31).

There are many other references in Scripture demonstrating that Jesus believed and taught that His crucifixion was why He came to earth. The Old Testament predicts Christ's crucifixion, His cross, a number of times. Perhaps Isaiah 53:5 is the most familiar passage: "But he *was* wounded for our transgressions, *he was* bruised for our iniquities: the chastisement of our peace *was* upon him; and with his stripes we are healed." The apostle Paul wrote, "For the preaching of the cross is to them that perish foolishness; but unto us which are saved it is the power of God "(1 Cor. 1:18). Because of Christ's cross work, believers are exhorted in Scripture to give spiritual sacrifices to God, not to *become* children of God but *because* we are children of God.

Stott lists several sacrifices believers are told to give to God.[52] I will list these and accompanying Scripture references:

1. Present our bodies to His service as living sacrifices (Rom. 12:1).

2. Offer to God our praise, worship, and thanksgiving (Heb. 13:15).

3. Prayer as a sacrifice which ascends to God like fragrant incense (Ps. 141:2)

4. A broken and contrite heart which God accepts and never despises (Ps. 51:17)

5. We are called to present both sacrifice and service (Phil. 2:17).

6. We are well-pleasing to God when we offer ourselves as sacrifices to God (Phil. 4:18).

---

52 Ibid., p. 263f.

7. Sacrifice is our life poured out like a drink offering in the Old Testament (Phil. 2:17; see Num. 6).

8. A special offering of service for God (2 Tim. 4:6).

> When I survey the wondrous cross
> On which the Prince of Glory died,
> My richest gain I count but loss,
> And pour contempt on all my pride.
>
> Forbid it, Lord, that I should boast
> Save in the death of Christ, my God!
> All the vain things that charm me most,
> I sacrifice them to His blood.[53]

The Necessity of Christ's Cross

Four Types of Sin

The Lord Jesus Christ came from heaven to die in the sinner's place. He paid the price for all mankind because all mankind sinned in Adam. The Bible says, "For as in Adam all die, even so in Christ shall all be made alive" (1 Cor. 15:22). The cross of Christ, therefore, was necessary because all have sinned and come short of God's glory. What kind of sin caused the necessity of the cross? Let's consider four types of sin, as well as general evil in our world.

Imputed Sin

The term "imputation" means adding to someone's account what may or may not be his. It's an accounting term. Lewis Sperry Chafer gave this helpful explanation of the theological meaning of imputation:

> In the matter of man's relation to God, the Bible presents three major imputations: (a) imputation of Adam's sin to the human

---
53 Isaac Watts, "When I Survey the Wondrous Cross." 1707.

race, (b) imputation of the sin of man to the substitute, Christ, and (c) an imputation of the righteousness of God to the believer. Imputation may be *real* or *judicial*. That which is real is the reckoning to one of that which is antecedently his, while judicial imputation if the reckoning to one of that which is not antecedently his.[54]

What is the relationship between Adam and the race of mankind? Does his sin affect the rest of the human race? The Bible's answer is "yes." Adam is viewed by God as the representative head as well as the natural head of the human race. The apostle Paul put it this way: "Wherefore, as by one man sin entered into the world, and death by sin; and so death passed upon all men, for that all have sinned" (Rom. 5:12). Sin entered the world by one man who committed one sin. The result was death not only upon the one man who committed the sin, but upon all he represented and who were to come from him. Paul explained why the penalty of death was imposed upon all. It is because "all sinned." The Greek is emphatic here.

Erickson's explanation of the "all have sinned" (Rom. 5:12) is very helpful:

> The last clause in verse 12 tells us that we were involved in some way in Adam's sin; it was in some sense also our sin. But what is meant by this? On the one hand it may be understood in terms of federal headship—Adam acted on behalf of all persons. There was a sort of contract between Adam and God as our representative so that what Adam did binds us. Our involvement in Adam's sin might better be understood in terms of natural headship, however… the entirety of our human nature, both physical and spiritual material and immaterial has been received from our parents and more distant ancestors by way of descent from the first pair of humans. On this basis we were actually present within Adam so that we all sinned in his act. There is no injustice then to our condemnation and death as a result of original sin.[55]

---

54 Lewis Sperry Chafer, *Systematic Theology* (Dallas: Dallas Theological Seminary Press, 1964), 2:296.
55 Millard J. Erickson, *Christian Theology* (Grand Rapids, MI: Baker Book House, 1985), 2:637.

The issue is not that each man commits deeds of sin in the course of his lifetime. That is true, but that is not what is being taught in Romans 5:12. What is being taught is that every member of the human family who has ever been born or will ever be born was related in some way to Adam. When he sinned, the race sinned in him. When Adam sinned, we sinned. He not only represented us, but we sinned in him. The potential of the entire human family was on him, so that what he did, all did in him and through him. Therefore, all are guilty and receive the same penalty–death. In another connection, Paul said essentially the same thing: "For as in Adam all die," he added, "even so in Christ shall all be made alive" (1 Cor. 15:22).

Inherited Sin

King David said, "In sin did my mother conceive me" (Ps. 51:5). That sinful heart, that corrupt nature which Adam and Eve received when they sinned, they passed on to their children, and they to theirs, and the process continues today. All who are born of woman, with the exception of Christ, are born with the bent toward sin. They are born with the sin nature. Jeremiah, the prophet, stated the human condition like this: "The heart *is* deceitful above all *things*, and desperately wicked: who can know it?" (Jer. 17:9).

Paul the apostle was as clear on the matter when he said we "were by nature the children of wrath" (Eph. 2:3). Or again, "There is none righteous, no, not one" (Rom. 3:10). All humans are born in a state of separation from God. They are spiritually dead, insensitive to the things of God. All are without God and without hope apart from the redemption provided at Calvary.

Individual Sins

There is a real sense in which the entire human race participated in the sin of Adam. Adam represented all mankind in his actions. More than that, he possessed in himself the potential of all who would ever be born in the human family. As a result, all have sin charged to their account, imputed to them.

As a result of imputed sin, all inherit a sin nature from their parents. All are inwardly committed to sin from the very start. No one needs to be educated to sin. It comes quite naturally.

Because we possess a sin nature from conception, all soon become guilty of committing individual sins. These sins, too, serve to condemn us. Outside of Christ, we stand condemned before God and in need of His salvation because we commit deeds of sin and because we have a sin nature inherited from our parents—imputed to us by virtue of our relation to Adam, who represented us and in whom we sinned.

As a result, man stands as a condemned sinner, guilty before God. As a result of this confluence of sin—the imputed sin, the inborn corruption, and the individual sin—no one is able to do anything to merit favor in the sight of God. No one is able to contribute anything for salvation, either at the time of salvation or by way of promise for the future. The sinner is spiritually bankrupt and can, therefore, do absolutely nothing to merit God's favor, His great salvation. God must provide all the resources if man is ever to be saved from sin. In eternity past, God planned the reconciliation for the sinner, accomplished in Christ in history.

Social Sins

Up to this point, we have talked primarily about individual sins. Adam and Eve sinned as individuals. Every member of the human family except Christ is born with sin already imputed to them because Adam represented all and all were in some sense in him when he sinned. In addition, each one is born with a sin nature inherited from his parents. Because all possess imputed sin, all commit their own acts of sin.

The Bible also refers to collective or group sin, sins of the human race without any particular individuals in view. Powers or influences do not commit sin; people do. Yet Scripture does refer to what might be called social sins. Isaiah, for example, wrote about group sin when he admonished the people as a whole to "Wash you, make you clean; put away the evil of your doings from before mine eyes; cease to do evil; Learn to do well; seek judgment, relieve the oppressed, judge the fatherless, plead for the widow" (1:16-17). "Clearly God is speaking of oppressive conditions for which He holds society responsible. No one individual is responsible for these situations. No single person can alter them. Failures in these areas are sins of society."[56]

A similar emphasis appears in Isaiah 6. The prophet wrote of "a people of unclean lips" (v. 5). He had no particular individual or individuals in mind, but the people of Israel as a whole. This was true of the people even though there were individual exceptions. God told Isaiah to go and warn the people of their sin and God's sure judgment apart from their repentance.

Social responsibility

We tend to ignore social sins and place responsibility for them upon others. It all seems so distant from us. Erickson reminds us that,

> …some persons who would never think of killing another human being, taking another's property, or cheating in a business deal may be part of a corporation, nation, or social class which in effect does these very things. Such persons contribute to these evils through financial involvement (by paying taxes or dues), direct approval (by voting), or tacit consent (by not disapproving or registering opposition).[57]

---

56 Erickson, 2:642.
57 Ibid.

What can be done about social sins or group sins? Erickson sets forth three different strategies for overcoming social sin: regeneration, reform, and revolution.[58]

Some view group sins as the composite of the sins of individuals. Social problems in this view will never be solved by dealing with society as a unit. Any change in society can only come about as the individuals in it are changed. From the Christian standpoint, only as individuals are regenerated will society be altered. Environmental changes are not what the world needs most but rather individual, internal changes, which in turn will affect the society.

Others insist that since society's problems are larger than individual human wills, the solution must include reforming or changing the structures of society. Those who hold this view usually work for change through the political structure.

Still another strategy for dealing with social sins is revolution. This is the most radical of the three approaches. Destruction and replacement of existing structures is necessary. Terrorism is often associated with this approach.

The first of these strategies combined with elements of the second find support in Scripture. Christians need an awakened concern for the social dimension of sin. They need to be actually involved in doing all they can to remove themselves from participation in society's sins. Christians also can become involved in opposing social sins by electing Christians in places of responsible leadership in local, state, and federal governments.

The decree of sin

Paul summed up social sin in his declaration that all are "under sin" (Rom. 3:9; Gal. 3:22). This implies that the entire human race is under a decree of sin. There is a judicial judgment of God upon the human race

---
58 Ibid., 2:655-658.

because of its relation to Adam and because of the sins of each member. There can be no mistaking, God's verdict is upon every member of the human race. The human family is *guilty*. God's condemnation justly rests upon all of Adam's descendants, even before any particular sins are committed.

Why Evil?

Why would God, who is all-powerful and good, allow the entrance and continuance of sin with its resulting consequences? The question applies equally to what may be called "natural evils," billed as acts of God and eliminated from most insurance policies, and "moral evils." Illustrations of the former include earthquakes, tornadoes, hurricanes, and diseases such as cancer.

Romans 8:22 reminds us that the creation is closely associated with the destiny of man. Adam was responsible for the garden before the Fall, and consequently the creation suffered at his fall. No wonder that the creation is now marred by sin, but also is eagerly anticipating our resurrection.

Because of the work of the cross, this world touched by calamity is not the world of eternity. God will make a new earth free from natural disaster for all time. One can explain natural calamity without resorting to manipulating Scripture, as do some forms of Calvinism,[59] or denying evil, as in Christian Science.[60]

God allowed sin's entrance into His universe, but He also took sin upon Himself, paying the utmost price for man's redemption from sin and the world's ultimate deliverance from it. Between now and the time we see our Lord face to face, we must be content to say our God chose the best possible plan, even though that plan included allowing for the entrance and continuance of sin until He ultimately banishes it.

---

[59] Gordon H. Clark, *Religion, Reason, and Revelation* (Philadelphia: Presbyterian Reformed Publishing Co., 1961), 221ff.

[60] For a helpful response to these, see Erickson, 1:414-432

Can Man Save Himself?

Man's Estimate of Himself

The words of the Pharisee as he prayed summarize how most people think of themselves: "God, I thank thee, that I am not as other men are, extortioners, unjust, adulterers, or even as this publican" (Luke 18:11). Every human effort toward reconciliation with God is unacceptable to Him and constitutes a rejection of the biblical teaching concerning man's total inability to assist in his own salvation.

Adam and Eve were the first people tempted to do something on their own to find favor with God. The fig leaves they covered themselves with represented an attempt to make themselves acceptable to God. We know from the biblical record that the fig leaves were unacceptable to God, not because they did not cover Adam and Eve's nakedness sufficiently, but because they were sinners attempting to placate God on their own. God rejected their act. They were already dead spiritually. They had lost their relationship with God. Only He could restore it.

From that day to this, man has sought to make himself acceptable to God in a thousand different ways, but it still cannot be done. The ladder of human works is well-worn but too short. No man has or ever will reach God's presence by climbing its rungs. Every such attempt, however small or large, is evidence that the condemned sinner does not really believe he stands condemned.

God's Estimate of Man

What is God's verdict against humanity? Scripture's answer to this question shows the necessity of Christ's death and of the necessity for the sinner to trust Christ alone for his complete salvation.

God has the only remedy for sinful man: "For the Son of Man is come to seek and to save that which was lost" (Luke 19:10). All people will "perish" apart from salvation (John 3:16). They are already judged by God and in their sinful condition they love darkness rather than light. They commit deeds against God and they hate the light (John 3:17-20). God's wrath abides on all (John 3:36). They are dead in trespasses and sins (Eph. 2:1) and are in the "power of darkness" (Col. 1:13), perishing (2 Cor. 4:16). Satan, the evil one, holds all people who are without Christ in his power (1 John 5:19).

God declares that, from His perspective, people without Christ are "filled with all unrighteousness, fornication, wickedness, covetousness, maliciousness; full of envy, murder, debate, deceit, malignity; whisperers, Backbiters, haters of God, despiteful, proud, boasters, inventors of evil things, disobedient to parents, Without understanding, covenantbreakers, without natural affection, implacable, unmerciful" (Rom. 1:29-31).

There are none who are righteous, none who seek for God, none who do good, none who are in awe of God's holiness (Rom. 3:10-18). For example, David confessed he was "shapen in iniquity; and in sin did my mother conceive me" (Ps. 51:5). The prophet Jeremiah said, "The heart is deceitful above all things, and desperately wicked: who can know it?" (Jer. 17:9).

God is not saying that each and every sinner is guilty of each and every sin that is named. Rather, such sins characterize the whole human race. Each sinner is, of course, guilty of more than enough personal sin to condemn him. Before anyone can be redeemed, he must accept God's estimate of his sinfulness. God's viewpoint of man as sinner must be received or there will be no salvation. No adjustment of one's behavior can alter this hopeless plight. No self-originating promise to enthrone Christ as Lord will do it either. Only the regenerating work of the Spirit of God can make saints out of sinners. This work of the Spirit is based upon the substitutionary death of Christ alone and is apart from all human effort or commitment. Not every sinner is as wicked as he might be. Not all commit the most wicked deeds possible. But all do sin and all fail God's standard, demonstrating the destitution of any life or merit before God. It is God's perspective, not man's, which matters and with which the sinner must be concerned.

The gospel is offensive because it strips people of all room for pride in human accomplishment. There is a reproach associated with the message of the cross because it removes every possibility of self-deliverance. No one can give God anything in exchange for salvation. Nothing the sinner can give is acceptable as a substitute for sin.

The Truth about Sin

Evangelical Christians are in common agreement on man's exceedingly sinful condition. However, most people who reject the Bible's authority reject this most unpleasant reality about man's sin and alienation from God.

New-age[61] enthusiasts, for example, believe man is himself divine, ultimately perfect, and, in fact, infinite. Man is good. Sin is an illusion. "Mankind and all life is basically good."[62] They reinterpret Christ's glory as the divine power innate in all people; "There is nothing else but God: That we are all part of a great being."[63] One New Age "Christ," Lord Maitreya, claimed, "My purpose is to show man that he need fear no more. That all of light and truth rests within his heart. That when this simple factor is known man will become God."[64]

No matter what sophisticated jargon is used or how much a New Ager or other unbeliever redefines biblical vocabulary, truth stands. The truth is

---

61 Evangelical Ministries to New Religions defines the New Age Movement as a "spiritual social and political movement to transform individuals and society through mystical enlightenment hoping to bring about a utopian era of a 'new age' of harmony and progress. While it has no central headquarters or agencies, it includes loosely affiliated individuals, activists groups, business and professional groups, and spiritual leaders and their followers. It produces countless books and magazines reflecting a shared-world view of vision. How that world view is expressed, what implications are drawn and what applications are made differ from group to group." See also "Experts on Nontraditional Religions Try to Pin Down the New Age Movement," *Christianity Today*, 17 May 1989, 68.
62 Shirley MacLaine, *Out on a Limb* (New York: Bantam Books, 1983), 204.
63 From Benjamin Crème, *The Reappearance of Christ and the Masters of Wisdom* (North Hollywood, CA: Tara Center, 1980), 134.
64 Benjamin Creme, *The Message from Maitreya, the Christ #98* (N. Hollywood: Tara Center, 1981), 204.

that we are all sinners before the holy God who created us and only that God can rescue us from the futility of life without Christ. Our Savior is the Lord Himself!

The Divine Purpose of Christ's Death

> Grace! 'tis a charming sound,
> Harmonious to the ear;
> Heav'n with the echo shall resound,
> And all the earth shall hear.
> Saved by grace alone!
> This is all my plea;
> Jesus died for all mankind,
> And Jesus died for me.[65]

The Real Issue

The task before us is to discover a biblical answer to the question, "Why did Christ die?" After settling that issue, we will then be in a position to ask a second question, "What is the extent of Christ's propitiation?" or "For whom did Christ die?" Admittedly, these are difficult questions to address. One who desires to be true to the revelation of Scripture must be careful not to become a slave of any man-made system of theology. The question is not, "What did the reformers believe and teach?" or "Shall I be a Calvinist or an Arminian?" nor even, "What is the historical view of the church?" As important and helpful as these matters are, the crux of the matter is, "What saith the Scriptures?"

There is no question about it, the issue between limited and unlimited atonement centers in the design or purpose of the redemptive work of Christ. Evangelicals on both sides agree that not all will be saved. Therefore,

---

65 Phillip Doddridge. "Grace! 'tis a charming sound." 1740.

the extent of the atonement or the answer to the question, "For whom did Christ die?" can be given only by understanding the divine intent of the Father in the death of His Son. Loraine Boettner put it succinctly when he said, "The nature of the atonement settles its extent."[66] This clear-cut issue is not always understood. Too often the determining of limited or unlimited atonement is pictured as a choice between Calvinism and Arminianism. It should be clearly understood that one need not be an Arminian simply because he rejects limited atonement. On the other hand, one is certainly not a Calvinist just because he accepts limited atonement. In other words, there are other and more serious differences between Calvinistic and Arminian theology, and even between these two systems and other systems, than simply the extent of the atonement.

The fact of the matter is that a good many today who are proud to embrace Calvinism fail to realize that Calvinism involves far more than the acceptance of the five famous points. This is especially true of premillennialists and dispensationalists who claim to be Calvinists. Christians of these persuasions must be aware of the fact that Calvinism is a system of theology which has come to embrace covenant theology and amillennialism and is, therefore, in direct opposition to both premillennialism and dispensationalism.

The same could be said for Arminianism. To say one is an Arminian means not only that he rejects the five points of Calvinism, but also that he accepts a "system" of theology, for that is what Arminianism is.

It seems far better to say that a person believes this tenet or that one as he may find agreement with it in the Bible rather than to imply acceptance of an entire system unless the individual is prepared to accept the whole theological structure. The desire and goal of the child of God must not be adherence to a humanly-constructed system simply for the sake of tradition or church relations. Let us be Biblicists above everything else and at all

---

66 Loraine Boettner, *The Reformed Doctrine of Predestination* (Philadelphia: The Presbyterian and Reformed Publishing Co., 1965), p. 152.

costs; and when and where this position conflicts with man-made systems of theology, let it be!

There is an increasing number of individuals who wholeheartedly accept four of the famous five points of Calvinism, although they reject limited atonement, or as it is sometimes called, particular redemption. These should probably be referred to as moderate Calvinists because while they believe in total depravity, unconditional election, irresistible grace and the perseverance of the saints, they do not hold to limited atonement.

Their refusal to believe that Christ died only for the elect does not make them Arminians any more than it makes them universalists. They differ drastically with both the Arminians and the universalists. These moderate Calvinists differ with the Arminians because they do not believe all men are born with sufficient grace or divine favor to believe in Christ but rather that all men are born totally dead in trespasses and sins, possessing no divine favor and incapable of doing anything to merit the favor of God. They differ with the universalists because they do not believe Christ's death for all means all will eventually and ultimately be saved. Instead, they believe that the only ones who will be saved are those who appropriate the death of Christ by personal faith because they have already been chosen by a sovereign God.

The Arminian Answer

James Arminius (1560-1609) was a noted professor of theology at the University of Leyden in Leyden, Holland. After his appointment to answer the attacks being made upon supralapsarianism, or hyper-Calvinism,[67] which

---

67 The "lapsarian" controversy concerns the logical order of the decrees of God. Actually, there is only one decree or plan of God with many parts. Scripture simply does not state the order in which God planned the various stages of His plan. In fact, it is even questionable whether God ever viewed them as separate items anyway. It would be more in keeping with the character of God to say that He conceived of each part and the whole of His sovereign decree at one time. At any rate, theologians have attempted to arrange a logical order for the various parts of God's plan. The word "lapsarian" comes from the Latin *lapsus* meaning "fall." When the prefix supra meaning "above," appears, it means placing the decree of God to elect men before His decree to allow the fall of man. At the time of Arminius supralapsarianism was being circulated by Dirck Coornhert (1522-1590). This extreme view has been modified by many who call themselves Calvinists today. Many

led him to accept a less severe type of Calvinism, he became the central figure in the theological controversy of his day in the Dutch Reformed Church. As is usually the case, the followers of Arminius have distorted his views. What passes today as Arminianism would hardly be identifiable with that which Arminius set forth in his Declaration of Sentiments delivered to the states of Holland in October of 1608.[68]

Just one year after the death of Arminius, a group of his followers drew up five articles of faith in the form of a protest commonly called the Remonstrance or the Five Arminian Articles. These articles were in opposition to those parts of the Belgic Confession of Faith and the Heidelberg Catechism which stressed what came to be known as the five points of Calvinism, which were later set forth at the Synod of Dort (1618-1619).

Though our purpose here is not to deal with each of the "five points" of Arminianism but only the one pertaining to the atonement, it will be well to summarize the five. Roger Nicole has done this very accurately for us: "I. God elects or reproves on the basis of foreseen faith or unbelief. II. Christ died for all men and for every man, although only believers are saved. III. Man is so depraved that divine grace is necessary unto faith or any good deed. IV. This grace may be resisted. V. Whether all who are truly regenerate will certainly persevere in the faith is a point which needs further investigation."[69]

It will be well now to see the full statement regarding the atonement set forth in the Remonstrance. This will help us understand the answer of

---

Calvinists adopt the infralapsarian view instead. This view places the decree to elect some from among the sinful race after the decree to permit the fall. Still others prefer the sublapsarian view which places the decree to elect not only after the fall but also after the decree to provide salvation for all. Calvinists are found among all three of these positions and these are all in opposition to the Arminian view which, though it is identical to the sublapsarian view, makes salvation depend on foreseen human virtue and faith. Though John Calvin does not directly discuss this particular issue, most of his followers believe he held to infralapsarianism and can find nothing to the contrary in his writings.

68 See *The Works of James Arminius*, D.D., Vol, I, trans. James Nichols (Buffalo: Derby, Miller and Orton, 1853).

69 Roger Nicole, "Arminianism," *Baker's Dictionary of Theology*, ed. Everett F. Harrison (Grand Rapids: Baker Book House, 1960), p. 64.

Arminianism to the question of the divine design of the atonement. Article II of the Remonstrance reads as follows:

> That… Jesus Christ, the Saviour of the world, died for all men and for every man, so that he has *obtained for them all, by his death on the cross, redemption and the forgiveness of sins* [italics mine]; yet that no one actually enjoys this forgiveness of sins except the believer, according to the word of the Gospel of John 3:16, "God so loved the world that he gave his only-begotten Son, that whosoever believeth in him should not perish, but have everlasting life." And in the First Epistle of John 2:2: "And he is the propitiation for our sins; and not for ours only, but also for the sins of the whole World."[70]

The crucial point of this statement regarding the purpose and extent of the atonement centers in the word "obtained." This is precisely the Arminian view, not only that Christ's death *provided* salvation for all but that His death *obtained* it for all. This explains, of course, why those who subscribe to Arminianism believe that each member of Adam's race possesses sufficient grace to be saved. In the Arminian concept, God has endowed every man with a grace or favor which enables him to repent and believe, if he will.

In the Arminian concept, this means of course that on the basis of Christ's death, because He *obtained* forgiveness of sins for all, every man now has a degree of grace sufficient to generate faith and repentance if the man yields to it. Viewing it from another perspective, this means the one who does not believe does not do so because he lacks some human efficiency or ability to cooperate with God. This places man in the position, then, in which he determines whether the sufficient grace he possesses will or will not become effectual.

In reality, then, Arminianism rejects the truth that every man is born totally incapable of doing anything to merit favor with God or even to

---

[70] Philip Schaff, *The Creeds of Christendom,* III (New York: Harper and Son Publishers, 1919).

move toward God, and, rather, gives man a measure of grace which makes him acceptable to God only if man will add his part and accept God's work. Boettner, a Calvinist, says, "According to the Arminian theory the atonement has simply made it possible for all men to cooperate with divine grace and thus save themselves if they will."[71]

In conclusion, the point to be made here is that these other ideas regarding man's natural condition and native ability to cooperate with God stem from the idea that Christ's death *obtained* salvation for all and made possible sufficient grace for all to cooperate with God in salvation. This means in reality that the decision to believe or not to believe is quite unrelated to the electing purposes of God or the effectual working of the Holy Spirit but rests ultimately and entirely with the individual.

The Strict Calvinistic Answer

The views of the Arminians set forth in the Remonstrance of 1610 were examined and rejected as heretical at a national Synod of Dort, meeting from November 13, 1618, to May 9, 1619. Not only did the Synod reject the Remonstrance position but it also set out to present the true Calvinistic teaching regarding the five matters called into question. They accomplished this by stating what we know today as the "five points of Calvinism." The term "Calvinism" was derived from the great reformer John Calvin (1509-1564), who along with many others expounded these views.

The "five points of Calvinism" presented at the Synod are as follows: (1) total depravity, (2) unconditional election, (3) limited atonement, or particular redemption, (4) irresistible grace, or the efficacious call of the Spirit, and (5) perseverance of the saints, or eternal security.

Concerning the third point, that of limited atonement, the Synod of Dort declared: "For this was the Sovereign counsel and most gracious will and purpose of God the Father, that the quickening and saving efficacy of the

---

71 Boettner, *The Reformed Doctrine of Predestination*, p. 152.

most precious death of His Son should extend to all the elect, for bestowing upon them alone, the gift of justifying faith, thereby to bring them infallibly to salvation…"[72]

From the day these words were uttered to the present day, followers of Calvinism have understood this statement to teach limited or particular atonement. The design of the atonement according to Calvinists was to secure the salvation of the elect. The Calvinistic doctrine differs from the Arminian teaching in that Calvinists confine the atonement to the elect and view all men in their natural state as totally depraved, thus lacking any ability to cooperate with God in anything. It is not difficult to prove from the writings of Calvinists that the design of the atonement was to save those for whom Christ died. Steele and Thomas state it bluntly: "Christ's redeeming work was intended to save the elect only and actually secured salvation for them… The gift of faith is infallibly applied by the Spirit to all for whom Christ died, thereby guaranteeing their salvation."[73]

John Murray asks and answers the questions at issue in typical Calvinistic fashion:

> Did Christ come to make the salvation of all men possible, to remove obstacles that stood in the way of salvation, and merely to make provision for salvation?… Did he come to put all men in a savable state? Or did he come to secure the salvation of all those who are ordained to eternal life? Did he come to make men redeemable? Or did he come effectually and infallibly to redeem? The doctrine of the atonement must be radically revised if, as atonement, it applies to those who finally perish as well as to those who are the heirs of eternal life… This we cannot do… If some of those for whom atonement was made and redemption wrought perish eternally, then the atonement is not itself efficacious… We shall have none of it. The doctrine of "limited

---

[72] Schaff, *The Creeds of Christendom*, III.
[73] David N. Steele and Curtis C. Thomas, *The Five Points of Calvinism Defined, Defended, Documented* (Philadelphia: The Presbyterian and Reformed Publishing Co., 1963), p.17.

atonement" which we maintain is the doctrine which limits the atonement to those who are heirs of eternal life, to the elect. That limitation insures its efficacy and conserved its essential character as efficient and effective redemption.[74]

The theologian Charles Hodge voices the same view when he says, "The righteousness of Christ did not make the salvation of men merely possible, it secured the actual salvation of those for whom He wrought."[75]

Speaking as a Calvinist and for Calvinism as opposed to Arminianism, R. B. Kuiper said: "Calvinism, on the contrary, insists that the atonement saves all whom it was intended to save."[76]

Thus, it should be clear that the answer of Calvinists as to the divine design and intent of Christ's sacrificial work was not merely to provide salvation but to actually secure it for the elect with no provision whatsoever for the non-elect. They view the work of Christ on the cross as efficacious in itself. In their view, the cross secures and applies its own benefits. The saving work of Christ on the cross saves.

It must be remembered that the extent of the saving work of Christ or the answer to the question, "For whom did Christ die?" is determined by the design of the cross. Some Calvinists limit the extent of the cross to the elect simply because they believe it was designed in itself, and quite apart from anything else, to save. In contrast, others who consider themselves moderate Calvinists reject limited atonement because they believe the design of the cross provided a basis of salvation for those who believe (the elect) and a basis of condemnation for those who refuse to believe (the non-elect).

Although the Calvinists who accept limited atonement thus confine the extent of the saving work of Christ to the elect, it should not be thought

---

[74] John Murray, *Redemption—Accomplished and Applied* (Grand Rapids: Wm. B. Eerdmans Publishing Co., 1955), pp. 73, 74.
[75] Cited by Boettner, *The Reformed Doctrine of Predestination*, p. 155.
[76] R. B. Kuiper, *For Whom Did Christ Die?* (Grand Rapids: Wm. B. Eerdmans Publishing Co., 1959), p. 73.

that they limit the sufficiency or value of Christ's death. This they do not do. The usual statement coming from them is to the effect that the death of Christ was *sufficient* for all men but *efficient* only for the elect. This statement is intended by limited redemptionists to satisfy those who object to their limited view. But does it really answer the difficulties raised by the scriptural passages which teach the universality of the atonement? What they really mean when they say Christ's death was sufficient for all is that His blood was of such infinite value that no more could have been required of the Father had He intended the Son's death to extend to all men.

Or again, as a strict Calvinist has put it, "Thus Christ's saving work was limited in that it was designed to save some and not others, but it was not limited in value for it was of infinite worth and would have secured salvation for everyone if that had been God's intention."[77]

Now this all sounds fine, but it does not mean, as some suppose, that God actually intended Christ's death to be all-encompassing in its scope. When this *sufficiency* of the death of Christ for all is admitted by the limited redemptionists, they are still insisting that Christ died only for the elect and merely admitting that had it been the desire of God, He could have extended Calvary's benefits to all without requiring any more or greater sacrifice from Christ. It is really a play on words to say that the death of Christ was *sufficient* for all but *efficient* only for those who believe if the sufficiency has already been prescribed in its extent by God. In the limited concept, the sufficiency cannot, because of divine decree, exceed or go beyond the efficiency of Christ's death. Moderate Calvinists, quite to the contrary, believe that the sufficiency of the work of Christ not only could have extended to all mankind, but that by the express design of God the Father it did extend to all mankind. The limited redemptionists will not admit that this is the teaching of Scripture; therefore, they should not obscure their view with the phrase "sufficient for all, efficient for those who believe," since it in no way alters the limited nature of their view.

---

77 Steele and Thomas, *The Five Points of Calvinism Defined, Defended, Documented*, p. 39.

There is another phrase used by strict Calvinists which is supposed to answer objections to their limited view of the atonement. It is found frequently in attempts to explain universal words such as "all," "whosoever," and "every man." When these words are used with reference to Christ's death, limited redemptionists often say, "Christ died for all without distinction but not for all without exception." Such a statement in no way relieves the difficulties of the limited view nor does it satisfy the biblical descriptions of the extent of the Savior's sacrifice on Calvary. Such an attempt is merely a play on words which camouflages the glaring contradiction produced when a restriction is placed on words which are naturally and normally universal in meaning.

A word of summation of the Arminian and Calvinistic views of the divine purpose of Christ's death is now in order.

The divine purpose, in the Arminian view, was to obtain redemption and the forgiveness of sins for all men by supplying sufficient grace to all men to believe if they will. The Calvinistic answer to the question, "Why did Christ die?" has been very much to the contrary. Calvinists who accept limited atonement believe the Savior died for the elect only and that by His death He not only provided salvation for that limited number but also infallibly secured their salvation.

The Moderate Calvinistic Answer

Isaac Watts clearly defines the conflict between the two opposing schools of interpretation regarding the divine design of the atonement:

> When the remonstrants assert that Christ died for all mankind merely to purchase conditional salvation for them; and when those who profess to be the strictest Calvinists assert [that] Christ died only to procure absolute and effectual salvation for the elect; it is not because the whole Scripture asserts the particular sentiments of either of these sects with an exclusion of the other. But the reason of these different assertions of men is this, that the holy writers in different texts pursuing different sub-

jects, and speaking to different persons, sometimes seem to favor each of those two opinions; and men, being at a loss to reconcile them by any medium, run into different extremes, and entirely follow one of these tracks of thought and neglect the others.[78]

On the basis of what we discovered previously concerning the purpose of Christ's death, it may be emphasized again that according to Scripture Christ's death was a complete and final substitute for sinners and was most certainly designed to secure the eternal salvation of the sinner who does nothing but believe in Jesus Christ as his Savior and Sin-bearer. We observed that Scripture broadens the design of the atonement to include all men in a provisional way. That is, the benefits of Calvary are realized and *applied* only to those who believe, but the *provision* reached to every member of Adam's race. This is the uniform testimony of Scripture and especially of those central passages—such as 2 Peter 2:1; 1 John 2:2; Romans 5; and 2 Corinthians 5—which deal respectively with the limited and unlimited sense of redemption, propitiation and reconciliation.

The Godhead will surely effect all that was designed in the atonement. The question, therefore, is not, "Will the divine design be realized?" for that question is answered in the affirmative by virtue of the fact that the design is God's. Rather, the question is, "What is the divine design?" Arminians see the design of God in the atonement as the *obtaining* or *purchasing* of redemption and sufficient grace for all men, leaving man with the decision to choose or not to choose this redemption. Calvinists, of the strict type, view the design of the atonement as that which *secures* the redemption, not of all men indiscriminately, but of the elect only. So while the Arminians and Calvinists view the design of the atonement similarly, they view the extent very differently.

The moderate Calvinist view lies between these two. Christ most certainly died to secure the salvation of those who believe and it is my

---

78 Isaac Watts, *Works*, VI, pp. 286, 287, cited by Jonathan Edwards and others, *The Atonement* (Boston: Congregational Board of Publication, 1859), pp. 251, 252.

conviction that the Bible teaches that Christ died to provide a basis of salvation for all men. To those who are the elect and who, in the Calvinistic system, therefore believe in Christ, this provision secures for them their eternal salvation when they believe. For those who do not believe and thus, in the Calvinistic system, evidence the fact that they are the non-elect, the provision exists as a basis of condemnation. The eternal destiny of men, according to the Bible, is not determined by the extent of the atonement or by man's relationship to Adam and his sin, but by man's relationship to Jesus Christ Who died for sin and sins–the root and the fruit (Rom. 6:10; 1 Cor. 15:3).

The moderate Calvinist, therefore, rejects the idea that Christ died to *secure* the salvation of all men or that He provided every man with sufficient grace to cooperate with God. If that be true, according to the moderate Calvinist, then God is defeated because all men will not be saved. The moderate Calvinist also rejects the idea that Christ died to secure the salvation of the elect only. If that be true, the cross can no longer be the basis of condemnation for those who do not believe (John 3:18). The moderate Calvinist believes that the twofold testimony of Scripture can be harmonized only in the view that believes Christ died to make possible the salvation of all men and to make certain the salvation of those who believe.

Strict Calvinists have not allowed for this mediating position (it is a mediating position not because it is partly biblical and partly non-biblical but because it is between the strict Calvinist and strict Arminian views). Usually Calvinists view the choice as either the Arminian view of providing salvation and sufficient grace for all and securing it for none or the strict Calvinistic view of securing salvation only for the elect.

Another Option

A. A. Hodge speaks as though there were only two choices: "Did Christ die with the design and effect of making the salvation of all men indifferently possible, and the salvation of none certain; or did He die in pursuance of an eternal covenant between the Father and Himself for the purpose as well as with the result of effecting the salvation of His own people?"[79] We must reject both views because neither one of them is altogether biblical. Christ did die for all men (John 3:16; 2 Cor. 5:19; 2 Pet. 2:1; 1 John 2:2), and He also died to secure and make certain the salvation of His own (John 10:15; Eph. 5:25).

The fact is, the Bible teaches very clearly that Adam's sin was imputed to the race (Rom. 5:12-20), that the sin of the race was imputed or reckoned over to Christ (Isa. 53:5, 6, 11; 1 Pet. 3:18; 1 Pet. 2:24, 25; 2 Cor. 5:21), and that the righteousness of Christ is imputed to the believing sinner (Rom. 3:21, 22; 2 Cor. 5:21; Heb. 10:14).

The Arminian solution to the problem is to ascribe to all men sufficient grace enabling them to believe, if they so choose. The Calvinistic solution is to restrict the extent of the atonement to the elect and make it the only saving instrumentality. Neither of these solutions is completely biblical.

Would it not be better to face Scripture objectively, accepting not only its clear teaching of man's native sinfulness and total inability to please God but also its equally clear emphasis upon the unlimited provisionary nature of the work of Christ on the cross and the necessary condition of faith for salvation?

The Bible is clear that man must believe to be saved. All men are lost until they individually and personally exercise faith in Christ as their own Savior. There simply is no distinction in the Bible between elect and non-elect sinners in their unregenerate state.

The insistence of the New Testament writers upon the necessity of faith demonstrates the provisionary nature of the atonement. At least 150 times, faith is made the single condition of salvation, thus stressing the fact that all the benefits of Calvary's completed work are withheld until men believe. Peter's use of one of the words for "redeem," translated as "bought" (2 Pet. 2:1), reveals that the price of redemption for all men was paid by Christ.

---

79 Archibald Alexander Hodge, *The Atonement* (Grand Rapids: Wm. B. Eerdmans Publishing Co, 1953), p. 363.

This, of course, does not imply the release of all men; this comes only at the moment of faith in Christ.

Lewis Sperry Chafer said,

> Certainly Christ's death of itself forgives no sinner, nor does it render unnecessary the regenerating work of the Holy Spirit. Any one of the elect whose salvation is predetermined, and for whom Christ died, may live the major portion of his life in open rebellion against God and, during that time, manifest every feature of depravity and spiritual death. This alone should prove that men are not severally saved by the act of Christ in dying, but rather that they are saved by the divine *application* of that value when they believe. The blood of the Passover lamb became efficacious only when applied to the door post.[80]

In all fairness, it should be said that most limited redemptionists do not rule out the necessity of faith. Nevertheless, their strong emphasis upon Christ securing the salvation and even saving the elect in His death and at the time of His death makes the condition of faith for salvation seem rather unnecessary. This difficulty is frequently answered by limited redemptionists by their further insistence that Christ not only died for the elect, securing their salvation and saving them, but that He also procured at the same time the means whereby this salvation would be applied. That is, He purchased the necessary faith of the elect also giving it to them as a gift which they in turn are to give back to Him at the point of salvation.

Careful examination will reveal that Ephesians 2:8-9 does not teach what some Calvinists would like it to teach. "For by grace are ye saved through faith; and that not of yourselves: it is the gift of God: Not of works, lest any man should boast." That which is "the gift of God" in the verse is not faith or grace but the entire act of salvation. This view has the support of the Greek text since the relative pronoun "that" is in the neuter gender while the word

---

80 Lewis Sperry Chafer, *Systematic Theology* (Dallas: Dallas Seminary Press, 1950), III, p. 193.

"faith" is feminine. Too, the context supports this view since the emphasis is upon salvation by grace and not by works.

John Eadie, the Greek exegete, rightfully points out that Calvin himself held to salvation as the gift from this passage. Eadie's own interpretation is very clear: "The phrase *ouk ex ergon* must have salvation and not faith as its reference."[81] Many other exegetes share this view and insist upon it. As another example, Sir Robert Anderson's word concerning Ephesians 2:8-9 will serve well: "'The gift of God' here is *salvation by grace through faith*. Not the faith itself. 'This is precluded,' as Alford remarks, 'by the manifestly parallel clauses "not of yourself," and "not of works," the latter of which would be irrelevant as asserted of faith.'"[82]

Some acknowledge that saving faith is not the special gift of God in this verse; yet they insist that it is said to be such elsewhere in Scripture. Aldrich cites the following verses as those usually used to prove the strict Calvinistic point of view: Acts 5:31; 11:18; Philippians 1:29; 3:9; Romans 12:3; 2 Peter 1:1; 2 Timothy 2:25 and John 6:44, 45. Since it is not our purpose here to refute the Calvinistic doctrine of the origin of faith, the reader is referred to the article cited above for Dr. Aldrich's very fine refutation of this unproven Calvinistic assumption. His conclusion is that while many New Testament passages and even whole books were written to prove that salvation is a gift, none of these passages or any others make faith itself the gift from God to the elect.

Calvinists believe so strongly in this that many of them arrive at a very logical conclusion if their premise be accepted. That is, faith becomes a product of regeneration and not an actual means of receiving it. Berkhof puts it this way: "This faith is not first of all an activity of man, but a potentiality wrought

---

81 John Eadie. *Commentary on the Epistle to the Ephesians* (Grand Rapids: Zondervan Publishing House, n.d.), p. 152.
82 Sir Robert Anderson cited by Roy L. Aldrich, "The Gift of God," *Bibliotheca Sacra*, CXXII (July-September, 1965), p. 249. This is an excellent article dealing with this issue. It is highly recommended.

by God in the heart of the sinner. The seed of faith is implanted in man in regeneration."[83] Shedd makes a similar observation: "The Calvinist maintains that faith is wholly from God, being one of the effects of regeneration."[84] Along this same line Arthur W. Pink, a staunch Calvinist, comes up with a rather strange solution. He begins by admitting that the non-elect are *unable* to believe and then proceeds to enumerate what they must do: "…Set to his seal that God is true… Cry unto God for His enabling power–to ask God in mercy to overcome his enmity, and 'draw' him to Christ; to bestow upon him the gifts of repentance and faith."[85] However one looks at this list of duties, it constitutes rather strenuous chores for a depraved man who it was said could not respond to the gospel in faith because he is dead in sin. As Aldrich so aptly stated it, "The extreme Calvinist deals with a rather lively spiritual corpse after all."[86]

What is the solution to this seemingly hopeless dilemma? Is there not some way to harmonize what the Bible says about the extent of the atonement, man's lost condition, God's electing purposes and the need to meet the God-ordained requirement of faith for salvation? A step in the right direction toward the understanding of these truths lies in the acceptance of certain guiding principles set forth in the Bible.

First, the Bible views all men as spiritually lost and sinners unable to do anything to please God. From God's perspective, "There is none righteous, no, not [so much as even] one" (Rom. 3:10). No distinction is made between lost sinners who are elect and those who are not elect. Elect people are just as depraved as the non-elect. This sinful condition brought forth the wrath of God. It was not just His wrath against the sin of the elect which made necessary Christ's death but rather His wrath against every member

---

83 L. Berkhof, *Systematic Theology* (Grand Rapids: Wm. B. Eerdmans Publishing Co., 1953), p. 503.
84 W. G. T. Shedd, *Systematic Theology* (Grand Rapids: Zondervan Publishing House, n.d.), II, p. 472.
85 Arthur W. Pink, *The Sovereignty of God* (Cleveland: Cleveland Bible Truth Depot, 1950), pp. 198, 199.
86 Roy L. Aldrich, *Bibliotheca Sacra*, CXXII (July-September, 1965), p. 248.

of Adam's race. It seems to follow then that the price paid to bring divine satisfaction must be as all-inclusive and extensive as the wrath of God and the sin of man which made the satisfaction necessary in the first place.

Second, Scripture makes personal faith the sole condition for the appropriation of Calvary's benefits to the individual. Faith is commanded of all men without any distinction. Also, the consequences of failing to believe or of rejecting God's provision in Christ are clearly revealed. Men are condemned for not believing in the name of the only begotten Son of God. It is true not only of those who have heard the gospel of Christ but also of those who have not heard. God makes no difference as far as eternal destiny is concerned between those who have heard and rejected and those who have not heard of Christ but have rejected the knowledge God gave to all men of Himself in nature and the conscience (Ps. 19; Rom. 1). To reject the lesser revelation of God in nature and conscience is to reject the greater, saving revelation of God in Christ. God commands faith and repentance of all men indiscriminately (i.e., Acts 17:30), and every universal offer of the gospel and exhortation to believe must be viewed as God's genuine offer.

The Bible views faith or belief as separate from salvation. Scripture does not teach that faith follows regeneration as some Calvinists would have it. In the Bible, men are always exhorted to believe in order that they might receive life. It is never the other way around. The message of the gospel is not to regenerate people to believe in something they already have. Rather, the message is to believe so that they might receive what they do not have but so desperately need.

Murray, who accepts and defends limited atonement and also believes regeneration precedes faith, seems to present a contradiction when explaining the relation of faith to salvation. Beginning his chapter on faith and repentance he says, "Without regeneration it is morally and spiritually impossible for a person to believe in Christ, but when a person is regenerated it is morally and spiritually impossible for that person not to believe."[87] In words which are almost diametrically opposed to these Murray adds, "We entrust ourselves to him not because we believe we have been saved but as lost sinners in order that we may be saved."[88] How it is possible to be regenerated, to possess divine life, before the exercise of faith and yet not be saved is not explained by Murray.

It is better to view the aspects of the salvation process as simultaneous rather than to force the Scripture into a preconceived theological mold which in reality makes faith virtually unnecessary. Walvoord states,

> The normal pattern for regeneration is that salvation occurs at the moment of saving faith. No appeal is ever addressed to men that they should believe because they are already regenerated. It is rather that they should believe and receive eternal life. Christians are definitely told that before they accepted Christ, they were "dead in trespasses and sin" (Eph. 2:1, A.V.).[89]

Here, in clear and simple words, we have the twofold truth concerning salvation in Christ–the sinner must come; yet he will not come unless drawn by the Father. To come to Christ is the same as to believe on Him.

It is true that common grace, or the Spirit's general work of restraining sin (Gen. 6:3; 2 Thess. 2:7) and convicting the world (John 16:8-11), reveals man's need of salvation; yet it falls short of the actual salvation of the individual man in his lost condition and requires more than an understanding of his need. The lost man needs divine enablement and this comes through efficacious, or special, grace at the precise, simultaneous moment of faith. The Bible related these two very closely–the Spirit's work of giving life and the individual's reception of it by faith. The one is never seen without the other.

Third, this faith in Christ as Savior which is necessary for salvation does not add anything to the full and complete redemption procured by Christ.

---

87 Murray, *Redemption–Accomplished and Applied*, p. 133.
88 Ibid, pp. 136, 137.
89 John F. Walvoord, *The Holy Spirit* (Findlay, Ohio: Dunham Publishing Company, 1958), p. 135.

Faith does not save; Christ saves and Christ alone. Faith must be viewed as the means through which the grace of God comes to the needy heart. The salvation received is not improved upon nor is its nature altered in any way by the reception of it by faith.

Fourth, Scripture declares that faith is not a work. "But to him that worketh not, but believeth on Him that justifieth the ungodly, his faith is counted for righteousness" (Rom. 4:5). Faith in the Scriptures is never spoken of as God's faith, but it is always associated with man. Men are required to exercise faith, and this in no sense implies gaining merit or earning salvation since the Bible itself makes faith the condition of receiving the free, undeserved and unearned grace–salvation. Long ago, Gresham Machen said "… Faith consists not in doing something but in receiving something."[90] Another Calvinist joins in distinguishing faith from any good work: "Faith is no more than an activity of reception contributing nothing to that which it receives."[91]

Conclusion

What a sovereign God is ours Who could devise a plan of salvation so infinite and complete! This divine plan, formulated before the foundations of the world, included the death of Christ as a substitute for all, the Spirit's work of conviction, and the necessity of faith for the application and appropriation of that completed work.

For Whom Did Christ Die?

God the Father, in the death of His Son, provided a means of salvation for all. Considering the biblical evidence for man's total inability, the

---

[90] J. Gresham Machen, *What Is Faith?* (Grand Rapids: Wm. B. Eerdmans Publishing Co., 1925), p. 172

[91] J. I. Packer, *Fundamentalism and the Word of God* (Grand Rapids: Wm. B. Eerdmans Publishing Co., 1960), p. 172.

need of the Holy Spirit's work in the sinner's heart and the necessity of personal faith in Christ for the appropriation of salvation, this is a scriptural conclusion.

We now come to the question, "For whom did Christ die?" As was indicated earlier, the nature and purpose of His death determines the extent of His death. Since we have said He died as a final and complete substitute providing salvation for Adam's race, the case would seem to be closed. However, our purpose here is to examine the scriptural evidence on both sides of the question. In this process, it will be necessary for us to divorce ourselves as much as possible from any preconceived viewpoints.

Scriptures Which Seem to Limit the Extent of the Atonement[92]

Isaiah 53:5: "But He was wounded for *our* transgressions, He was bruised for *our* iniquities: the chastisement of *our* peace was upon Him; and with His stripes we are healed." Without question, Christ the Messiah is the One in view here who was to be wounded and bruised for men. It is equally clear that Isaiah is speaking about his own people, the Jews, in the personal pronouns. Thus, the most ardent limited redemptionist must admit that this limited passage is too limited since some Gentiles were saved, although Isaiah speaks only of the Jews nationally.

Matthew 1:21: "...For He shall save *His people* from their sins." It is clear that Christ would relate His salvation to "His people." It seems equally clear in the context that Christ was coming to save His own race–the Jewish race. The recorded genealogy, Christ's association with David, and the fulfillment of Hebrew prophecy all point to the Jews. However, even the most ardent limited redemptionist surely would not want to extend the benefits of Christ's death to the Jews only. Even this "limited" passage must then be broadened to include at least some Gentiles.

---

[92] Various italicized words found in the verses are mine.

Matthew 20:28: "Even as the Son of man came not to be ministered unto, but to minister, and to give His life a ransom *for many*." The preposition translated "for" clearly teaches substitution–one in the place of another.

Matthew 26:28: "For this is my blood of the new testament, which is shed *for many* for the remission of sins." Though a different preposition is used here which sometimes means "for the benefit of," substitution is nevertheless plainly in view.

John 10:15: "…I lay down my life *for the sheep.*"

Galatians 3:13: "Christ hath redeemed *us* from the curse of the law, being made a curse *for us*…" Obviously, Paul is speaking in the context to believers; and since he includes himself here, he is relating the redemption to the redeemed. The question here, as in many other instances where writers of Scripture include themselves when speaking of the death of Christ, is, "Does this mean the writer is excluding all others except believers?" How else could Paul have related Christ's death to himself without saying He died for "us"? If references such as this, in which the writer includes himself in the death of Christ, may be used to prove limited atonement, then when writers of Scripture use similar phraseology in speaking of man's sin, it could be said that they teach limited depravity or sin. For example, in such passages as, "the LORD hath laid on him the iniquity of *us* all" or "all *our* righteousnesses are as filthy rags," are we to understand by the writer's inclusion of himself that thereby only believers are sinners? On the basis of such an argument, it could also be said that God loves only believers since John says, "We love Him, because He first loved *us*" (1 John 4:19). Surely John's inclusion of himself and other believers in God's love does not mean God does not love unbelievers, though many limited redemptionists affirm that to be the case.

The curse spoken of in the Galatians 3 context extends to "every one that continueth not in all things which are written in the book of the law to do them" (Gal. 3:10). The curse is as far-reaching as the Fall since no one is justified by keeping the law (v. 11). Now the point of verse 13 is that Christ's death reached to those under the curse (all men) and delivered them from it by becoming a curse in their stead. Of course, that deliverance was a living reality for the apostle because he had personally appropriated it by faith, but does the fact that he says it is true of himself and other believers mean the same deliverance was not provided for all the others who were under the curse?

Ephesians 5:25: "… Christ also loved the *church*, and gave himself *for it*." Unless the church is made to refer to the saints of all ages (which cannot be done without departing from a literal interpretation; cf. Matt. 16:18; 1 Cor. 10:32; Heb. 12:22, 23), this passage must also be extended beyond the borders of that new entity established on the day of Pentecost (Acts 2). No one who believes Israel and the church are distinct and entirely separate can appeal to this passage in Ephesians 5 to support the limited redemptionist view. Certainly, Christ died for others outside of the body of Christ.

Hebrews 9:28: "So Christ was once offered to bear the *sins of many*…"

Acts 20:28: "Take heed therefore unto yourselves, and to all the flock… to feed *the church of God, which He hath purchased with His own blood.*" The word translated "purchased" in this text means to preserve one's life, as in Luke 17:33. "In contrast to the use of agorazo, which would emphasize the idea of purchase, the verb used here has more the thought of the result of the action, that the church has been 'acquired.' The idea is therefore one of possession rather than emphasis on the act of purchase."[93]

These selected passages serve to illustrate the fact that the Bible does speak of the atonement in relation to specific individuals and groups. According to these and other passages, Christ came to redeem His own, to provide a ransom for many, to die for the sheep, and to give Himself for the church. The unlimited redemptionist has absolutely no problem reconciling all such references with his view. It should be understood, however, that none of the passages which speak of Christ's death for specific groups or individuals can be used to exclude others.

---

93 John F. Walvoord, "Redemption," *Bibliotheca Sacra*, CXIX (January-March, 1962), pp. 6, 7.

Scriptures Which Broaden the Extent of the Atonement to Include All Men[94]

Passages containing the word "world"

Although many passages fall into this category, only a few will be cited here.

John 1:29: "… Behold the Lamb of God, which taketh away the sin of *the world*."

John 3:16: "For God so loved *the world*…" "In this passage, as almost no other, a restricted use of the term *cosmos* is presented; not restricted, as the Limited Redemptionist demands, to the elect of this age, but restricted to humanity itself apart from its evil institutions, practices, and relationships. God loved the lost people who make up the *cosmos* and this love was great enough to move Him to give His only begotten Son, in providing a way of salvation through Him so complete that by believing on the Son as Savior the lost of this *cosmos* might not perish but have everlasting life."[95]

John 3:17: "For God sent not his Son in the world to condemn the world; but that *the world through Him might be saved*."

John 4:42: "… This is indeed the Christ, the Saviour of *the world*."

Second Corinthians 5:19: "To wit, that God was in Christ, reconciling *the world* unto Himself…"

First John 4:14: "…The Father sent the Son to be the *Saviour of the world*."

---

94 Various italicized words found in the verses are mine.
95 Chafer, *Systematic Theology*, II, p. 78.

Passages containing the word "whosoever"

Chafer observes that "the word *whosoever* is used at least 110 times in the New Testament, and always with the unrestricted meaning."[96] This being the case, the following have been selected as examples.

John 3:16: "…That *whosoever believeth* in Him should not perish, but have everlasting life."

Acts 2:21: "…*Whosoever shall call* on the name of Lord shall be saved."

Acts 10:43: "…Through His name *whosoever believeth in Him* shall receive remission of sins."

Rom. 10:13: "For *whosoever shall call* upon the name of the Lord shall be saved."

Revelation 22:17: "…And *whosoever will*, let him take the water of life freely."

Passages containing the word "all" or its equivalent

Again, only a few of the many passages will be cited.

Luke 19:10: "For the Son of man is come to seek and to save *that which was lost*."

Romans 5:6: "… Christ died for the *ungodly*."

First Timothy 2:6: "Who gave Himself a *ransom for all*, to be testified in due time." This verse contains a word translated here as "ransom" which does not occur anywhere else in the New Testament. The word was formed by the prefixed preposition *anti-*, which clearly teaches substitution, to the simple word *lutron*, which means "ransom" or "release." Concerning the use of this rare word formed by these two other words, Morris says, "Such a term well suits the context, for we read of Christ 'who gave himself on behalf of all.'"[97]

---

96 Ibid., III, p. 204.
97 Morris, *The Apostolic Preaching of the Cross*, p. 48.

Second Corinthians 5:14-15: "...That if one died *for all*, then were *all dead*: And that He died *for all*, that they which live should not henceforth live unto themselves, but unto Him which died for them, and rose again." Building a background for his doctrine of reconciliation in this passage, Paul begins with the love of Christ which eventuated in His death for all which in turn resulted in the death of all (v. 14). There can be no doubt that substitution is in view here just as it is in Matthew 20:28 and Mark 10:45 where Christ is said to give His life a "ransom for many."[98] Morris puts it this way: "One died, not many. But the death of that one means that the many died. If language has meaning this surely signified that the death of the One took the place of the death of the many."[99] "... He died that death which is the death of all."[100]

The verses under consideration (2 Cor. 5:14, 15) provide strong argument for the universality of the atonement. Making the word "all" in these verses refer to the elect only, which is what the limited redemptionist is forced to do, leads to a meaningless interpretation. What would happen to the *elect* in verse 15 who did not "live"?

Walvoord's summarization of these verses is pertinent. "This concept of the universality of the provision of reconciliation is borne out in the context, in which reconciliation is discussed. In 2 Corinthians 5:14, emphasis is given to the fact that all were dead spiritually. The three instances of 'all' in 2 Corinthians 5:14-15 seem to be universal. This is followed by the limited application indicated in the phrase 'they which live.' Hence, the passage reads: 'For the love of Christ constraineth us; because we thus judge, that one died for all [universal], therefore all [universal] died; and he died for all [universal],

---

98 *Huper* is so used with the clear meaning of *anti* in Philemon 13 and in the papyri. Compare R. C. H. Lenski, *The Interpretation of St. Paul's First and Second Epistle to the Corinthians* (Columbus: Wartburg Press, 1946), pp. 1029, 1030; and Richard Chenevix Trench, *Synonyms of the New Testament* (Grand Rapids: Wm. B. Eerdmans Publishing Co., 1953), pp. 310-313.
99 Leon Morris, *The Cross in the New Testament* (Grand Rapids: Wm. B. Eerdmans Publishing Co., 1965), p. 220.
100 Ibid., p. 239.

that they that live [restricted to elect] shall no longer live unto themselves, but unto him who for their sakes died and rose again' (2 Cor. 5:14-15). The word 'all' is used, then, in a universal sense in this passage, followed by the restricted application indicated in the phrase, 'they which live.' This is reinforced by the use of the word 'world,' referring to all men, in verse 19."[101]

Those determined to make Scripture conform to the five-point Calvinistic mold must, out of necessity, reduce the "all" here, as elsewhere, to "some" or the "elect." John Owen, for example, insists that both "alls" in verse 14 are of equal extent. Owen says Paul does "not say, that 'Christ died for all that were dead,' but only, that 'all were dead which Christ died for': which proves no more but this, that all they whom Christ died for, were dead, with that kind of death, of which he speaks. The extent of the words, is to be taken from the first *all* and not the latter. The apostle affirms, so many to be dead, as Christ died for, not that Christ died for so many as were dead."[102] Without doubt, this is a typical strict Calvinistic explanation of this clear passage. No wonder someone exclaimed, "The Calvinistic efforts to limit this word to 'all the elect' constitute one of the saddest chapters in exegesis. The Scriptures shine with the 'all' of universality, but Calvinists do not see it. Their one effort is to find something that would justify them to reduce 'all' to 'some.'"[103]

If we omit the great emphasis in Scripture upon the necessity of faith and overlook in this very passage the clear distinction between the "all" for whom Christ died and "they which live," the Calvinistic charge of universalism against those who believe "all" here means every individual would be valid. Such a charge lacks validity, however, since Paul is speaking of the provision of Christ and not the securing of salvation.

Titus 2:11: "For the grace of God that bringeth salvation *hath appeared to all men.*"

---

101 John F. Walvoord, "Reconciliation," *Bibliotheca Sacra*, CXX (January-March, 1963), p. 10.
102 John Owen, *The Works of John Owen*, p. 465.
103 Lenski, *The Interpretation of St. Paul's First and Second Epistle to the Corinthians*, p. 1029.

Hebrews 2:9: "... That He by the grace of God should taste *death for every man*."

First Timothy 4:10: "... We trust in the living God, who is the *Saviour of all men*, specially of those that believe."

Second Peter 3:9: "The Lord is ... not willing that any should perish, but that *all should come* to repentance."

Limited redemptionist explanation of the unlimited passages

Those who are strict Calvinists, and therefore believe in limited atonement, are not unaware of the passages of Scripture which seem to teach an unlimited redemption. Neither have they failed to offer some explanations of them, even though their explanations are usually rather brief and superficial.

That host of passages including the words "all," "whosoever," and "world" is frequently dismissed in the following manner: "One reason for the use of these expressions was to correct the false notion that salvation was for the Jews alone. Such phrases as 'the world,' 'all men,' 'all nations' and 'every creature' were used by the New Testament writers to emphatically correct this mistake. These expressions are intended to show that Christ died for all men without *distinction* (i.e., He died for Jews and Gentiles alike) but they are not intended to indicate that Christ died for all men without *exception* (i.e., He did not die for the purpose of saving each and every lost sinner)."[104]

We must agree with this last observation and do so gladly. Christ did not die to save every lost sinner, and if He did, He was defeated; for they are not all saved. His death, however, did *make possible* the salvation of every lost sinner, to make them all redeemable, and that is saying something quite different from what Arminians and strict Calvinists say.

Even though Steele does not cite any references where these universal and all-inclusive phrases sometimes refer to the distinction between Jews and

---

104 Steele and Thomas, *The Five Points of Calvinism Defined, Defended, Documented*, p. 46.

Gentiles, this is no doubt sometimes true. However, it is equally true that this sweeping "removal" of the intention of these broad and unlimited words regarding the atonement simply does not answer the problem.

This explanation on the part of limited redemptionists does not fit all the passages. What Jew-Gentile distinction was John trying to remove in his Gospel (John 1:29; 3:16)? There is nothing in the context which would warrant saying John was trying to remove such a distinction.

One must certainly strain contexts to find such a purpose in the mind of Paul in his exhortation to Timothy (1 Tim. 2:3-6), to Titus (Titus 2:11), or in the mind of Peter (2 Pet. 3:9). Even if such an intention to remove distinction between Jew and Gentile would be granted in these and similar passages, this still does not prove that those among the Jews and Gentiles for whom Christ died were all of the elect.

Furthermore, what are we to do with such a broad term as "ungodly" in Romans 5:6, the "lost" in Luke 19:10, or the phrase "every man" in Hebrews 2:9? It would have been very easy for the writers of these passages to limit and confine the scope of Christ's death had that been the Spirit's intention. One must perform mental and theological gymnastics to confine these statements to the elect. The elect are not the only "ungodly" ones (Rom. 5:6) or "lost" ones (Luke 19:10), nor do the elect constitute the totality of mankind (Heb. 2:9); and yet the Son is said to have died for all the ungodly, all the lost and all mankind.

Limited redemptionists have another way of interpreting these universal passages. They do it by saying there are instances in Scripture where these words (i.e., "all," "world," etc.) do not mean one hundred percent of everyone and everything. For example, Hodge cites Luke 2:1 as an example and says, "When it is said that 'a decree went out from Caesar Augustus that all the world should be taxed' (Luke 2:1), no man understands that the term 'all the world' is to be taken absolutely."[105]

---

[105] Hodge, *The Atonement*, p. 424.

Or take this example: "When Jesus predicted: 'Ye shall be hated of all men for my name's sake' (Matt. 10:22), He surely did not mean that His disciples would be hated by every single man, woman, and child in the world, but only that worldly people, constituting the great majority of men, would hate them."[106] The same writer goes on to say: "And when the Pharisees commented on Jesus' great popularity after the resurrection of Lazarus: 'Behold, the world is gone after him' (John 12:19), they were obviously using the term 'world' in a much restricted sense."[107]

Now there is certainly no question about the fact that these words are sometimes used in a restricted sense. The question, however, is not related to the possibility of such restrictions as obviously exist in certain cases. The question is, "*Is it scripturally and logically sound always to restrict every usage of the words 'all,' 'whosoever,' and 'world' when they occur in a salvation context?*" This is precisely what the limited redemptionist always does and must do. There may not be a single exception if the limited viewpoint is to stand. The basis for this restriction rests upon the fact that in some instances, which are unrelated to the work of Christ on the cross, the words are thus restricted. But is this a valid reason for always restricting them in salvation passages? We say no, and we say it emphatically. Chafer has observed how strange some of these passages sound when translated as the limited redemptionist must interpret them. "'God so loved the elect, that He gave His only begotten Son, that whosoever [of the elect] believeth in Him should not perish, but have everlasting life.' 2 Corinthians 5:19 would read: 'God was in Christ, reconciling the elect unto Himself.' Hebrews 2:9 would read: 'He tasted death for every man of those who comprise the company of the elect.' 1 John 2:2 would read: 'He is the propitiation for our [the elect] sins: and not for ours only, but also for the sins of those who comprise the world of elect

---

106 Kuiper, *For Whom Did Christ Die?* p. 28.
107 Ibid.

people.' John 1:29 would read: 'Behold the Lamb of God, which taketh away the sin of the elect.'"[108]

Strange words these are! The only way in which these expressions can be so interpreted is by forcing the Scripture into a strict Calvinistic mold. But the Scripture will not thus be browbeaten. Instead of Scripture referring to the elect as the "world," which would be necessary to the limited viewpoint, it is emphatic in distinguishing the elect from the world. Is not this what Christ meant when He said, "I have chosen you out of the world, therefore the world hateth you" (John 15:19)?

Added to the impossibility of this restricting the word "world" to the world of the elect (the Scripture seems clearly to distinguish the elect from the world) are the absurdities and self-contradictions of such an interpretation.

Let us follow through with the limited view and interpretation of the word "world" in such a simple and familiar passage as John 3:16. If "world" means the elect only, then it would follow that he "of the elect" that believeth may be saved and he "of the elect" that believeth not is condemned (cf. John 3:18). This absurdity would contradict the most basic point of Calvinism, namely, that God has elected from eternity past certain individuals and that they alone will be saved. We have never heard of elect people being damned, and yet that is precisely what the limited interpretation leads to in John 3:16-18 when the limited concept is followed through.

The problem with the limited redemptionist is that, instead of accepting the testimony of Scripture of an atonement which was provisional for all and dependent for the bestowal of in benefits upon personal appropriation by faith, he insists that the mass of universal passages must be forced into agreement with the few limited ones.

Equally strange are the interpretations given to Hebrews 2:9 and 1 Timothy 4:10 by the limited redemptionists. Contemporary limited

---

108 Chafer, *Systematic Theology*, III, p. 203, 204.

redemptionists usually quote John Calvin or John Owen on these verses; therefore, the views of these men will be given.

Concerning the phrase, "that he by the grace of God should taste death for every man," in Hebrews 2:9, Calvin says: "By saying *for every man*, he means not only that he might be an example to others… but he means that Christ died for us, and that by taking upon him what was due to us, he redeemed us from the curse of death."[109] Thus, Calvin evidently assumed this reference to be confined to the elect by his use of the word "us." He did not seek to explain how this could be so in this passage. John Owen, his editor, did explain this more fully in a footnote: "'For every man,' *huper pantos*, that is, 'man,' mentioned in verse 6; and 'man' there means all the faithful, to whom God in Noah restored the dominion lost in Adam; but this dominion was not renewed to man as a fallen being, but as made righteous by faith."[110]

In his own work, Owen said of this verse: "'Every man'… is put for 'all men' by an enallage of number, the singular for the plural, for all men; that is, all those many sons which God by his death intended to bring unto glory, verse 10; those sanctified by him, whom he calls his brethren, verses 11, 12 and children given him by God, verse 13; whom by death he delivers from the fear of death, verses 14, 15; even all the seed of Abraham, verse 16.'"[111]

This is the kind of explanation which would be expected, but it simply does not solve the problem. In the first place, there is nothing in the context of this passage nor in that of Psalm 8, from which it is being quoted, to warrant saying that "man" in verse 6 means "all the faithful." Furthermore, the very fact that the writer has been dealing with the universality of the subjection in verse 8 supports the universality of the provision of redemption in verse 9. Added to this is the change from the general to the particular in the passage. The tasting of death was for every man (v. 9) but the bringing of many sons

---

109 John Calvin, *Commentaries on the Epistle of Paul the Apostle to the Hebrews,* trans and ed. John Owen (Grand Rapids: Wm. B. Eerdmans Publishing Co., 1948), p. 61.
110 Ibid.
111 Owen, *The Works of John Owen*, Vol. XII quoted by Kuiper, *For Whom Did Christ Die?* pp. 28, 29.

unto glory (v. 10) only relates to those sanctified or set apart through faith (v. 11). Therefore, the "brethren" and "they who are sanctified" constitute a group from among the ones for whom He tasted death. This is the only natural way to explain the change from the universal to the particular.

Alford's comment relating to the singular instead of the plural here is pertinent: "If it be asked, why *pantos* rather than *panton*, we may safely say that the singular brings out, far more strongly than the plural would, the applicability of Christ's death *to each individual man*..."[112] In the same vein, Robertson says: "The author ... puts Christ's death in behalf of (*huper*), and so instead of, every man as the motive for his incarnation and death on the cross."[113]

About the phrase in 1 Timothy 4:10, "...who is the Saviour of all men, specially of those that believe," Calvin said, "...for the word *soter* is here a general term, and denotes one who defends and preserves. He means that the kindness of God extends to all men."[114] Acknowledging that the term "Saviour" refers primarily to God the Father, Owen attempts, therefore, to remove the universal nature of this passage. He says: "Is it not the living God in whom we trust that is the Saviour here mentioned?"[115] He also argues from the fact that the word "mediator" is not used.[116]

No doubt, the reference here is to God the Father since He is spoken of in the context (vv. 4, 5), though it is not impossible that the Son is here being called "the living God" since He is also mentioned in the nearer context (v. 6). Granting the limited view the benefit of the doubt, this passage still insists on a universal work and a particular work. Nicole put it this way: "The *prima facie'* of *malista* certainly is that all men share in some degree in that salvation which the *pistoi* enjoy in the highest degree... The statement is more

---

112 Henry Alford, *The Greek Testament* (Boston: Lee and Shepard Publishers, 1874), IV, p. 41.
113 Archibald Thomas Robertson, *Word Pictures in the New Testament* (Nashville: Broadman Press, 1932), V, p. 346.
114 John Calvin, *Commentaries on the Epistles to Timothy, Titus, and Philemon*, trans. William Pringle (Grand Rapids: Wm. B. Eerdmans Publishing Co., 1948), p. 112.
115 Owen, *The Works of John Owen*, V, p. 268.
116 Ibid.

unreservedly universalist in tone than chap. 2.4 and Tit. 2.11; and perhaps must be qualified by saying that while God is potentially Saviour of all, He is actually Saviour of the *pistoi*."[117]

What Did Christ's Death Accomplish?

"It is finished" (John 19:30). Of the seven last sayings of Christ, this one provides us with the Lord's own testimony of the completeness and sufficiency of His death.

The name of Michelangelo is no doubt familiar to most people. Michelangelo was the great sculptor, designer, painter and architect. The story is told that he was temperamental and that it took him many years to complete some of his works. Knowledge about Michelangelo's world-famous statues of Moses and David has spread far and wide. What many people may not know, however, is that in Florence, Italy, an entire hall is filled with his *unfinished* sculptural works. Great though he was, he left more work unfinished than finished.

Jesus Christ left no unfinished works. The night before Calvary's experience He said, "I have finished the work which Thou gavest Me to do" (John 17:4). On the cross in His dying moments there fell from His parched lips the same cry of completion and absolute fulfillment, "It is finished" (John 19:30).

What was finished? Surely Jesus did not need to inform God or man that His physical life was about to end. That was so obvious it did not need to be stated. It is equally true that the suffering, ridicule and blasphemy which He endured at the hands of men were ended. In fact, never again would He be nailed to a cross and endure the torments of hell, the weight of sin and the turned back of His Father. That and much more was all finished and never to be repeated.

---

[117] W. Robertson Nicole, *The Expositor's Greek Testament* (Grand Rapids: Wm. B. Eerdmans Publishing Co., 1956), IV, p. 125.

Yet there must be more involved in Christ's cry than these. Robertson calls the words of Christ, "A cry of victory in the hour of defeat..."[118] The word translated "it is finished" means to bring something to its desired end, and the form of the word used here by our Lord means it was finished in the past, it is now finished, and it will remain finished in the future. The eternal plan of God for the salvation of men had now been enacted in time with the fruits of it extending into eternity future.

This announcement of victory in the hour of seeming defeat stands out in bold contrast to the oft-repeated sacrifices of the old economy in pre-cross days. No more is there any need for bloody animal sacrifices to be offered continually for priest and people, for now the supreme sacrifice had been offered to which all the others pointed. Christ as priest and sacrifice offered Himself once and for all, and His sacrifice need never be repeated. "It is finished."

There are three great words which sum up the totality of the completed work of Christ on the cross: redemption, propitiation, and reconciliation. It is our purpose here to examine each of these doctrines in relation to the extent of the atonement. Biblical usage of these terms in relation to the death of Christ reveals that they are used of a select and limited group and also of the work of Christ for the whole world. The fact that sometimes both the limited and unlimited concepts appear in the same passage of Scripture is even more significant.

Redemption

The doctrine of redemption fills the pages of both Old and New Testaments. Though various words are used in Scripture to convey the idea of redemption, the basic meaning remains the same–freedom by the payment of a price.

Several key passages deserve our attention in an attempt to understand the biblical extent of the redemption provided by Christ on the cross.

---

118 Robertson, *Word Pictures in the New Testament*, V, p. 304.

Second Peter 2:1: "But there were false prophets also among the people, even as there shall be *false teachers* among you, who privily *shall bring in damnable heresies, even denying the Lord that bought them,* and bring upon themselves swift destruction." The word translated "bought" is from the Greek word *agorazo* which means "to purchase" or "acquire by the paying of a ransom or price." In its classical usage, the word was used of the purchase of slaves in the slave market. Here this great redeeming work of Christ extends even to false teachers who deny the Lord and thus are never saved. Interestingly, this same word is used in speaking of believers who are said to be purchased by Christ's death (1 Cor. 6:20; 7:23). Two things are of extreme importance in the 2 Peter passage. One is that the purchase price of redemption was paid by the Lord for even the false prophets and teachers, although they quite obviously never accept it. The other important feature is that these for whom the purchase price was paid are heretics of the vilest sort, since they deny the only possible basis of salvation–the substitutionary atonement of Christ. They bring to the people "damnable heresies." The word translated "damnable" really means "destructive" and "…speaks of the loss of everything that makes human existence worthwhile."[119] These heretics not only bring to the people these destructive heresies but, Peter adds, they "bring upon themselves swift destruction." This is the same word translated *damnable* earlier in the verse. In other words, these individuals, whoever they are, deny the substitutionary nature of Christ's death and thus endure eternal separation from God, yet they are the very ones for whom Christ paid the purchase price. "Having been bought by the Master, they were His, and their lives should have been lived to His glory, and it is only against this background that their sin can be seen in all its vileness. There is also probably a contrast between their faithlessness and the love of Christ who paid such a price in love for them."[120]

---

[119] Kenneth Wuest, *In These Last Days* (Grand Rapids: Wm. B. Eerdmans Publishing Co., 1954), p. 47.
[120] Morris, *The Apostolic Preaching of the Cross*, p. 51.

One is reminded of another cry of the Savior while on the cross: "Father, forgive them; for they know not what they do" (Luke 23:34). To the honest observer, it seems as though the implications of this cry are self-evident. Either the prayer was answered or it was not. If it was not, serious question is brought to bear upon the Person of the Savior. If it was answered, then in accord with the rest of Scripture, it means Christ's death provided the basis of forgiveness even for those who rejected Him and crucified Him. The only other alternative would be to say that all of Christ's rejecters who were putting Him to death were elect people, and that seems hardly possible.

Galatians 3:13: "Christ hath *redeemed us* from the curse of the law…" A slightly different word is used here for "redeem." It is the same word as found in 2 Peter 2:1 attached to the prepositional prefix meaning "out." Thus, the work of redemption is here extended to the saved, since Paul includes himself, in contrast to the 2 Peter passage where it is extended to all, including the non-elect.

The additional factor here, however, is the prefixed preposition "out" to the word "redeem" which makes the meaning of the word a bit different. After the purchase price was paid for a slave, the owner would take the slave out of the marketplace. Paying the purchase price and removing the slave were two distinct acts. Thus, when Paul uses this word in relation to himself and other believers, he is saying that Christ paid the price demanded, and there is additional deliverance from the bondage and servitude of sin for the one who accepts the payment. This is not said to be true of all men; but in this context, it is related only to the believer, whereas the simple word *agorazo* is used by Peter in 2:1 to apply to all men, even those who reject its efficacy. There is a third important word in the original language, translated "redeem" in our English New Testaments, which is not used of all men indiscriminately but only of believers. This is the word *lutro* and implies that the purchased one who is taken from the slave market is ransomed or released and set free. Peter uses this word in a context related to the believer's service in 1 Peter 1:18, and Paul also uses it in relation to Christ's sacrifice for men in 1 Timothy 2:6. The believing sinner is no longer a slave in bondage to sin and Satan, but because of the acceptance of the purchased redemption, he is now delivered from sin's binding fetters and, even more, is released so that he now can become a voluntary bond-slave of Christ, the new Master.

The conclusion to be drawn from the New Testament usage of these three words for "redeem" is that the payment of the purchase price extends to all men (2 Pet. 2:1) but that the deliverance (Gal. 3:13) and release for service (1 Pet. 1:18, 19) are only for those who accept the payment.

Those who are determined to hold to a limited redemption at all costs find passages such as 2 Peter 2:1 most difficult to explain.

Calvin glosses over the problem in his discussion of this passage by simply emphasizing the necessity of the believer to live a life in accord with the high cost of redemption.[121] Owen attempts an explanation in a footnote to Calvin's treatment. He tries to remove the problem by removing the force of the word "bought." "… They denied Christ as their sovereign, as they rendered no obedience to him, though they may have professed to believe in him as a Saviour."[122]

The fact is, the word which is here translated "bought" does not mean "sovereign." As we have before noted, it is one of the three great words in the New Testament often translated "redeem." And that is precisely what it means. Thayer indicates that the word means "to buy."[123] It cannot be avoided that Peter is here saying, in words unmistakably clear, Christ paid the ransom price even for those who deny Him.

Hodge makes a less serious attempt to answer the problem when he simply includes the reference along with others such as John 3:14-17; 1 John

---

121 John Calvin, *Commentaries on the Catholic Epistles*, trans. and ed. John Owen (Grand Rapids: Wm. B. Eerdmans Publishing Co., 1948), p. 393.

122 Ibid., footnote No 2.

123 John Henry Thayer, *A Greek-English Lexicon of the New Testament* (New York: American Book Co., 1889), p. 8.

2:2; 1 Timothy 2:3, 4 and says: "In all these and the like cases the words *all* and *all men* evidently mean Jew and Gentile."[124]

Some even argue that, since the name of Christ is not mentioned here but the word "Lord" or "master" is used instead, the reference is actually being made to God the Father.[125] Whatever difference this makes is difficult to understand. Of course, God the Father was involved in redemption since He "sent" the Son. About all Gill has to offer on the passage is not an exegesis of it but rather a rejection of the clear teaching of the words. Without any attempt to explain the meaning of the words, Gill simply says: "Besides, if such as Christ has bought with His blood should be left to so deny Him as to bring upon themselves eternal destruction, Christ's purchase would be in vain, the ransom-price paid would be for naught—which can never be true."[126] Gill has forgotten, evidently, that the text does say that the Lord paid the purchase price whether it is believed or not. What the text does not say here or anywhere else is that the purchase price was paid for naught for those who reject it. That is an unwarranted conclusion drawn by those who refuse to allow Scripture to speak for itself.

At best, these explanations of an obvious and clear teaching of Scripture only serve to reveal the futility of imposing restrictions where Scripture does not place them. Walvoord's conclusion to the study of the doctrine of redemption in the Bible is in keeping with the teaching of Scripture, even though it may conflict with the viewpoint of extreme Calvinists. "The study of redemption in Christ in the New Testament reveals a clear teaching that Christ by act of substitution in His death on the cross paid the ransom price and redeemed the enslaved *sinner* from his sinful position before God. Christ's death constituted an act of purchase in which the *sinner* is removed from his former bondage in sin by payment of the ransom price [italics mine]."[127]

---

124   Hodge, *The Atonement*, p. 426.
125   John Gill, *The Doctrine of Particular Redemption*, p. 29.
126   Ibid.
127   Walvoord, "Redemption," *Bibliogtheca Sacra*, CXIX (January-March, 1962), p. 11.

Propitiation

Based on the direct usage of the idea of propitiation in both the Old and new Testaments, "propitiation" means to "satisfy," "appease," or "placate." When used in relation to the atoning work of Christ, this very same idea is conveyed (Rom. 3:25; Heb. 2:17; 1 John 2:2; 4:10). "Propitiation presupposes the wrath and displeasure of God, and the purpose of propitiation is the removal of this displeasure. Very simply stated, the doctrine of propitiation means that Christ propitiated the wrath of God and rendered God propitious to his people."[128]

This in no way implies that the love of God is restrained or held back because of propitiation. It is not a matter of either propitiation or love on the part of God but rather it is His infinite love which provided the propitiation or satisfaction of His Person in Christ. Neither are we ever to understand that Christ's propitiatory sacrifice turned the wrath of God into love. That is, God must never be viewed as One Who became soft and easygoing and simply overlooked, because of some emotional stress, the true intensity of His hatred for sin. No! He poured out the full judgment of sin on Christ, Who bore it all. "It is one thing to say the wrathful God is made loving. That would be entirely false. It is another thing to say the wrathful God is loving. That is profoundly true. But it is also true that the wrath by which he is wrathful is propitiated through the cross."[129]

Pagan usage of the word *propitiation* relates it to the appeasing of a heathen god. "The uniform acceptation of the word in classical Greek, when applied to the Deity, is the means of appeasing God, or of averting His anger; and not a single instance to the contrary occurs in the whole Greek literature."[130] The necessity of appeasing a deity implies the wrath and anger of the offended deity.

---

[128] Murray, *Redemption–Accomplished and Applied*, p. 36.
[129] Ibid, pp. 37, 38.
[130] George Smeaton, *The Apostles' Doctrine of the Atonement* (Grand Rapids: Zondervan Publishing House, 1957), p. 455.

It is readily agreed that Old Testament usage of the word "propitiation" in the Septuagint does not involve satisfying the crude and unreasonable deities of heathen culture. The Old Testament concept of a righteous but offended God Who is satisfied by a propitiation includes not only His wrath but also His everlasting love, and this makes the difference. Jehovah's wrath in the Old Testament, as well as in the New Testament for that matter, is His holy reaction to sin (Job 21:20; Ezek. 16:38; Jer. 6:11; 2 Chron. 28:11-13; 2 Kings 13:3; Neh. 13:18). The difference between the concept of propitiation in pre-biblical heathenism and in the Old Testament is not to be found in the fact or nature of it but rather in the character of the one who is propitiated. The God of the Bible is holy, just, and righteous altogether and not vengeful as the heathen gods were represented to be. "The Bible writers have nothing to do with pagan conceptions of a capricious and vindictive deity inflicting arbitrary punishments on offending worshippers, who must then bribe him back to a good mood by the appropriate offerings."[131]

Though pagan ideas of wrathful deities are foreign to the Scriptures, this does not mean, as the modern biblical critic asserts, that there is no concept of wrath and satisfaction found in the Bible. "In view of the abundant evidence in the Old Testament describing God as a deity who must bring judgment upon the sinner, a serious question may be raised as to whether the attempts of modern writers to eliminate the idea of the wrath of God entirely from the Old Testament is a justifiable procedure. It is more accurate to conclude that the doctrine of the righteousness of God is coupled with the love and mercy of God in the Old Testament. The harmony established between these attributes by the doctrine of satisfaction for sin is embodied in propitiation."[132]

We have been attempting to show that there is a difference in the concept of propitiation in the Old Testament from that in pre-biblical

---

[131] Morris, *The Apostolic Preaching of the Cross*, p. 129.
[132] John F. Walvoord, "Propitiation," *Bibliotheca Sacra*, CXIX (April-June, 1962), p. 99.

paganism. That difference, it has been noted, lies in the fact that the God to be satisfied in the Old Testament is not only a God of wrath but also a God of love, righteousness, and mercy. There is another difference which separates the biblical concept of propitiation from that of heathenism. The God of the Scriptures not only demands total and complete satisfaction from the offender but also has, in and through His infinite love, provided mankind with such a propitiation–His Son, Jesus Christ, the righteous One.

The most important text of Scripture dealing with propitiation and the extent of the atonement is given by John: "My little children, these things write I unto you, that ye sin not. And if any man sin, we have an advocate with the Father, Jesus Christ the righteous: And He is the *propitiation for our sins*: and not for ours only, but *also for the sins of the whole world*" (1 John 2:1, 2; emphasis added).

One finds it hard to imagine how John could have been any clearer in stating the universal aspect of the atonement than he was in this passage. The normal, unbiased approach to this text evidences the fact that the propitiation was not only "for our sins" but also "for the sins of the whole world." When it is remembered that propitiation in the biblical context involves God's wrath and vicarious substitution, the extending of this to the "whole world" provides strong argument for an unlimited atonement.[133] The intensity of the argument here is not lessened by the fact that the last phrase of the verse ought to read "but also for the whole world" rather than "but also for the sins of the whole world." The words "the sins of" in this latter phrase were added by the translators for clarification.[134] The fact of the universal extent remains, however.

That this book was written to Christians and that the writer is concerned in the immediate context with sinning Christians does not militate against

---

133 We need not be concerned here with contemporary denials of substitution in propitiation. Usually these revolve around the unfounded and unbiblical idea that God's love makes substitution for sin unnecessary. Limited redemptionists agree that propitiation includes substitution and therefore our purpose will be to study the extent of the substitution in this text.

134 This ellipsis is a very common occurrence according to the Greek scholar Alford, *The Greek Testament*, IV, p. 433.

the universality of the propitiation in verse 2. Writers of Scripture must be allowed to widen their messages beyond those Christians to whom they addressed themselves. This is done frequently in Scripture as the writers in the clearest language possible extend their meanings to others. Furthermore, the very context in 1 John is filled with contrasts between the saved and the unsaved, between the ones obeying God's commandments and walking in the light and the ones without the love of God in them, denying Jesus Christ.

Some limited redemptionists insist that propitiation in Scripture has nothing to do with the redemptive or atoning work of Christ's sacrifice for sin. They relate the work of Christ in propitiation to the work associated with the mercy seat of the Old Testament (Lev. 16:14). There is some justification for this since both in the Septuagint and in Hebrews 9:5, the word for propitiation is used for mercy seat. The mercy seat in the Old Testament was that place where the high priest came on the Day of Atonement and sprinkled the blood which had been shed on the altar. Thus, it is argued, Christ's death fulfilled the type, and His death was for His people only, just as the blood sprinkled on the mercy seat was for Israel only.

When the above argument is used to dissociate propitiation from Christ's substitutionary work in redemption, two weaknesses are evident. First of all, propitiation is related to redemption in Scripture. In 1 John 4:10, the same writer associates God's love with the giving of His Son "… to be the propitiation for our sins." Also, in Romans 3:24, 25, Paul clearly connects redemption in Christ Jesus with "propitiation through faith in His blood." The scriptural usage of the word for propitiation and its cognates demonstrates that Christ was not only the place of propitiation (mercy seat) but also the very sacrifice itself. Secondly, it must be remembered that even if it be granted that 1 John 2:2 refers back to the mercy seat in the Tabernacle, the blood sprinkled there was for "the people" and surely not all those represented were of the number of the elect remnant. In order for this attempt in associating propitiation with the mercy seat alone to be valid as an argument against the universality of the atonement, one would need to assume that the high priest was only offering the sacrifice for elect Israelites. This is a most untenable position unless one is prepared to make every Jew thus being represented an elect, or saved, Jew. It is doubtful that anyone would wish to go to that extreme.

All attempts to restrict the extent of the atonement in this passage are futile. To make the first phrase, "for our sins," and the last phrase, "for the whole world," both refer to the elect reduces John's clear statement to a redundancy. Notice how meaningless the passage becomes if the limited concept is applied: "And he is the propitiation for our sins [sin of the elect]: and not for ours only, but also for the whole world [world of the elect]." Neither is the difficulty alleviated when the phrase "our sins" is made to refer to the sins of elect Jews and "sins of the whole world" made to refer to sins of elect Gentiles.[135] John knew the words for "Jews" and "Gentiles" and could have used them had that been his intention. Paul did not hesitate to use those words when describing the universality of guilt (Rom. 3:9).

Pink does what most limited redemptionists do in dealing with the word "world" here. He arbitrarily limits it to the elect. Yet when the same word occurs in a text dealing with man's sin, he broadens its meaning. "'*Kosmos*' is used of the whole race: Rom. 3:19, etc."[136]

Westcott's comment on the extent of the propitiation in this passage is helpful: "But for all alike Christ's propitiation is valid. The propitiation extends as far as the need of it (l.c.) through all place and all time. Comp. iv.14 (John iv.42; xii.32; xvii.22-24)."[137] A.T. Robertson's comment is equally appropriate: "At any rate, the propitiation by Christ provides for salvation for all (Heb. 2:9) if they will only be reconciled with God (II Cor. 5:19-21)."[138]

---

135 Pink, *The Sovereignty of God*, pp. 315-318.
136 Ibid., p. 312.
137 B.F. Westcott, *The Epistles of St. John* (Grand Rapids: Wm. B. Eerdmans Publishing Co., 1952), p. 45.
138 Robertson, *Word Pictures in the New Testament*, VI, p. 210.

It is indeed interesting to note how those who believe in limited atonement deal with this clear passage. One such writer put it this way: "What, then, does he mean when he calls it a propitiation for the whole world? He intimates that it was not for him and for those to whom he wrote alone, but for the redeemed of every period, place, and people–that is, prospectively and retrospectively. The apostle connects the intercession and propitiation in such a way as to show that Christ's work is applicable to all the redeemed who then lived, or had ever lived, or should ever live, wherever found in the nations of the earth, and in whatever. This is the point of the distinction; it is not the distinction elsewhere expressed between Jew and Gentile."[139]

This kind of explanation fits into the limited viewpoint very well, but whether it fits the biblical meaning of the words involved is another matter entirely. One questions the right of the interpreter to make the word "world" mean the "redeemed." Such arbitrary and forced meanings will not tolerate the searchlight of an honest inquiry.

Murray admits that no text in Scripture presents more plausible support for the doctrine of universal atonement than 1 John 2:1, 2. "It must be said that the language John uses here would fit in perfectly with the doctrine of universal atonement if Scripture elsewhere demonstrated that to be the biblical doctrine."[140] After making this admission, Murray proceeds to argue that since other Scripture teaches a limited atonement, therefore, this one must be so interpreted also. He presents a threefold argument to explain John's universal statement. First, he says John is setting forth the "scope" of Jesus' propitiation; that is, it was not limited in its virtue and efficacy to the immediate disciples. Second, John desired to emphasize the "exclusiveness" of Jesus as a propitiation. No one else but Jesus could be the propitiation. Third, John needed to remind his readers of the "perpetuity" of Christ's propitiation.

---

139 Smeaton, *The Apostles Doctrine of the Atonement*, p. 460.
140 Murray, *Redemption–Accomplished and Applied*, p. 82.

That is to say, the propitiation which Jesus made endures forever and never loses its efficacy.[141]

Murray has here performed an excellent service in describing the nature of the work of Christ in propitiation. The only problem is that John was not dealing with the nature of that work but with the *extent* of it. Murray has not dealt with the problem which his view of the atonement faces in this passage.

This explanation given by Murray seems to be the best the limited redemptionist can offer. Calvin refuses to discuss the problem and simply insists that "… the design of John was no other than to make this benefit common to the whole church."[142] Hodge's explanation is even less definitive because he groups the passage together with the other references to "all" and to "world" and evidently sees no special problem.[143]

John Owen, however, devotes much space to this verse. His view may be summarized best in his own words: "…That as by the world in other places, men living in the world are denoted, so by the whole world in this can nothing be understood, but men living throughout the whole world, in all the parts and regions thereof (in opposition to the inhabitants of any one nation, place, or country as such)…"[144]

This explanation by Owen should demonstrate that limited redemptionists simply will not allow writers of Scripture to mean "world" when they say, "world," even when they generalize and particularize in the same passage. One looks in vain for contextual evidence for such limitations.

Reconciliation

This is basically a New Testament doctrine with little contribution coming from the Old Testament or the Septuagint. Even in the New Testament, the specific word for reconciliation used in relation to the death

---

141 Ibid., p. 83.
142 Calvin, *Commentaries on the Catholic Epistles*, p. 173.
143 Hodge, *The Atonement*, p. 424.
144 Owen, *The Works of John Owen*, V, p. 440.

of Christ occurs in only a few passages (i.e., Rom. 5:10ff; 2 Cor. 5:18-20; Col. 1:20ff). Of course, the concept of reconciliation pervades many portions of the New Testament even where the word does not occur. It is believed by some to be the basic idea of the atonement and the best New Testament word to describe the purpose of the atonement.[145]

The basic Greek word for reconciliation is *katallasso* and it means "*to change, exchange* (esp. of money); hence, of persons, *to change* from enmity to friendship, *to reconcile.*"[146] On the basis of this meaning, Johnson defines reconciliation in relation to the atonement as "... a finished work of God by which man is brought from an attitude and position of enmity with God to an attitude and position of amity and peace with God by means of the removal of the enmity through the cross. To be effective it must, of course, be received in faith (cf. Rom. 5:10; 2 Cor. 5:20)."[147]

Among those who have studied the doctrine of reconciliation there has been little difference as to the meaning of the term in biblical usage. However, there have been a number of views as to who is reconciled–God, man or both–even among evangelical theologians.[148] A great deal of this difference of opinion arises because of a confusion of terms. If the biblical terms are employed with the meaning which they have in the Bible, the difficulty is lessened considerably. Those who speak of God as reconciled usually mean God's attitude is changed toward the sinner because of the death of Christ, but this is described in the Bible as propitiation, not reconciliation. The fact is that Scripture nowhere states that God is ever

---

145 Morris, *The Apostolic Preaching of the Cross*, p. 186 citing T. H. Hughes and Vincent Taylor.
146 G. Abbott-Smith, *A Manual Greek Lexicon of the New Testament* (New York: Charles Scribner's Sons, 1956), p. 236.
147 S. Lewis Johnson, "From Enmity to Amity," *Bibliotheca Sacra*, CXIX (April-June, 1962), p. 144.
148 Shedd, *Dogmatic Theology*, II, pp. 395-397, holds that God is reconciled. Hodge, *Systematic Theology*, II, p. 514, believes God and man are reconciled. A. H. Strong, *Systematic Theology*, p. 886, on the other hand, insists that man alone is reconciled. Likewise Owen, *The Works of John Owen*, V pp. 356-359, Calvin's interpreter and champion of limited atonement, views reconciliation as related to God and man. He speaks especially of God being reconciled, and thus he cannot accept unlimited atonement because God's wrath rests upon some and this would mean God is not reconciled to all. Owen failed to recognize that Scripture never speaks of God as reconciled.

reconciled (changed). On the contrary, the abundant testimony of Scripture is that man is reconciled to God (Rom. 5:10; 2 Cor. 5:18).

No doubt, it should be emphasized that the reconciling work of God is related in Scripture to the death of Christ and not to His incarnation. Contemporary liberal and neo-orthodox writers, in keeping with their denial of the vicarious and substitutionary nature of Christ's death, place emphasis upon His incarnation and life as God's means of displaying His love and, thus, of reconciliation. No one would deny the necessity of the Incarnation to the reconciling cross-work of Christ, yet according to Scripture, it was His death which brought about the reconciliation. In the greatest passage on reconciliation as it related to man, the death of Christ is mentioned frequently (Rom. 5:6-10). No wonder it could be said that "…The greatest passage which says that God was in Christ reconciling says in the same breath that it was by Christ being made sin for us. The reconciliation is attached to Christ's death, and to that as an expiation."[149]

A crucial passage on reconciliation, which relates to the extent of the reconciling work of Christ, is found in 2 Corinthians 5:18-20: "… God, who hath *reconciled us* to Himself by Jesus Christ… was in Christ, *reconciling the world* unto Himself…" Reconciliation as it is used here refers to the change which God wrought in the world of men through the death of His Son. The apostle here declares this reconciliation to extend to the redeemed, "us," and to the mass of mankind, "the world." The change or reconciliation of the apostle and the believers to whom he wrote produces in the reconciled one a responsibility in the ministry of reconciliation (v. 18). The basis for this ministry of reconciliation rests in the fact that God has altered, changed, or reconciled the world in relation to Himself (v. 19) and for that reason, we are ambassadors for Christ, beseeching men to be reconciled to God (v. 20).

This passage is very similar to Romans 5:10, 11: "*For if when we were enemies we were reconciled to God through the death of His Son, much more,*

---

149 P. T. Forsyth, *The Cruciality of the Cross* (New York: Hodder & Stoughton, n.d.), p. 68.

having been reconciled, we shall be saved by His life. And not only that, but we also rejoice in God through our Lord Jesus Christ, through whom we have now received the reconciliation." (Romans 5:10–11, NKJV) . (The Authorized Version, unfortunately, has "atonement" instead of "reconciliation.") It is obvious from both of these passages that reconciliation must be personally received to be effective. The reconciling work of Christ was done before anyone would or could respond to it. In the Corinthians text, God is said to have "reconciled the world" and "reconciled us to Himself by Jesus Christ." And in the Romans passage, "we were reconciled to God by the death of His Son" while we were enemies and the accomplished reconciliation must be "received" to be effective.

From the grammatical standpoint, it is important to note the verbs used in 2 Corinthians 5:18, 19. When speaking of the believer's reconciliation, Paul uses the aorist tense, which denotes an act that is finished (v.18). On the other hand, when speaking of the reconciliation of the world, he uses the present tense, indicating the continuous process (v. 19). Evidently, the apostle was in this way stressing the fact of the believers' reconciliation as an accomplished thing, both objectively and subjectively, since they had received Christ, and thus, His reconciling work by faith (cf. Rom. 5:10). The case is much different, though, as far as unbelieving mankind in general is concerned. True, according to the aorist tense used in verses 14 and 15, Christ died for all in an objective sense. Yet Paul, by his use of the present participle in verse 19, *"reconciling* the world unto Himself, *not imputing* their trespasses unto them," is highlighting the fact that while the reconciling took place historically, it is likewise ongoing in a sense, as men believe and thus appropriate the objective historical reconciliation by means of faith. Further emphasis upon this twofold aspect of reconciliation is found when Paul speaks of the ministry of reconciliation as "given" to each believer (v. 18) and the word of reconciliation as "committed" to us (v. 19). In both cases the aorist tense is used, which stresses the past fact of reconciliation as the basis of the ambassador's message (v. 20). The reason we can preach the message of reconciliation to a lost world, and in fact the very basis of that message, is the final and all-inclusive work which Christ accomplished on the cross.

Lenski's summarization of these verses is the result of careful and accurate exegesis:

> What does Paul say? That what God has finished for him and for his helpers (aorist *katallazantos*) he is still busy with (durative present participles) in regard to the world, namely the individuals in it; that in steadily working at this reconciling and not reckoning to men their transgressions God employed Paul and his helpers in the ministry which he gave them with the word of reconciliation that he deposited with them. This work began when Christ died, when "God was in Christ," when he wrought the objective reconciliation "through Christ" (v. 18). That objective reconciliation includes the whole world. But it must be brought to the world, to be made a personal possession by faith, a personal, individual reconciliation by means of the ministry of the reconciliation and the word of the reconciliation.[150]

Of course, the limited redemptionists must again impose restrictions or limitations upon the death of Christ for "all" in 2 Corinthians 5:14 and 15 as they must on the reconciliation of the "world" in verse 19. John Gill, for example, who refers to his view as that of particular redemption, has this to say of verses 14 and 15: "Let it be observed that in the supposition, 'if one died for all,' the word 'men' is not used. It is not 'all men,' but simply 'all.' All whom? It may be supplied from other Scriptures, 'all His people' whom Christ came to save…"[151]

This explanation completely ignores the plain and obvious fact of the contrast between the "us" and "we" of verse 14 and the "all" of verses 14 and 15. Also, it fails to account for the phrase "they which live" in verse 15. The

---
150 Lenski, *The Interpretation of St. Paul's First and Second Epistle to the Corinthians*, p. 1045.
151 Gill, *The Doctrine of Particular Redemption*, p. 22.

omission of the word "men" in the text is a common practice in Greek, especially in a case such as this where the ones constrained by the love of Christ are most assuredly men.

John Owen interprets "world" in verse 19 as the world of the elect. To do so, he says: "They who are called the *world*, verse 19, are termed 'us'; verse 18…by the *world* here can be meant none but the elect believers."[152] Or again he says, "The *world* here then is only the world of blessed pardoned believers, who are made the righteousness of God in Christ."[153]

Steele and Thomas dismiss this passage very quickly by associating it with other verses containing similar words and saying Christ died for all without distinction but not for all without exception.[154] Murray and Hodge do not even deal with the passage when seeking to answer the objection to their limited view.

Now these explanations surely fit the strict Calvinistic view of the atonement; there is no doubt about that. There are doubts, though, that these attempts of arbitrary limitation fit the context and content of Scripture.

Another passage of Scripture which expands and confirms this twofold aspect of reconciliation is found in Colossians 1:20-22: "And, having made peace through the blood of His cross, by Him to reconcile all things unto Himself; by him, I say, whether they be things in earth, or things in heaven. And you, that were sometimes alienated and enemies in your mind by wicked works, yet now hath he reconciled In the body of His flesh through death, to present you holy and unblameable and unreproveable in His sight."

It seems rather clear from these verses that there was a universal provision of reconciliation as well as an individual application of that reconciliation with both aspects finding their origin in the death of Christ. There is mention of the reconciliation of "all things" (v. 20) and the personal reconciliation of

---

152 Owen, *The Works of John Owen*, V, p. 451.
153 Ibid., p. 452.
154 Steele and Thomas, *The Five Points of Calvinism Defended, Documented*, p. 46.

the individual (v. 21). This individual reconciliation, it should be noted, is related to those who were "alienated and enemies" of God.

Walvoord states,

> It should be clear from this passage, as well as from the others, that the act of reconciliation in the death of Christ does not in itself affect reconciliation for the individual, but rather that it is provisional and makes possible the reconciliation of the individual. The natural state of the unsaved continues unchanged even after the death of Christ until such time that the reconciling work is made effective in him when he believes.[155]

A question may be raised as to the necessity of the reconciliation of the "things in earth, or things in heaven" (v. 20). The answer lies in the extent of the curse of sin brought on the universe by Adam's transgression and the race's participation in it. According to Romans 8:22, "the whole creation groaneth and travaileth" and is affected by the curse of God because of sin. Seemingly the earth, which was created perfect by God, was brought down to the level of fallen man when man fell. That curse will be lifted one day when the Lord restores it to its original status in the kingdom reign.

How Should We Then Live?

In Harmony with Christ's Finished Work

Since the cross of Christ is so terribly important, it behooves us to be sure we never forget all that Christ accomplished on the cross. The cross work of Christ is indispensable for one to become a child of God and to live like one.

---

[155] Walvoord, "Reconciliation," *Bibliotheca Sacra*, CXX (January-March, 1963), p. 8.

As Forgiven People

Why, we might ask, was Christ's cross necessary? The reason is because we all sinned in Adam according to the Bible. "For as in Adam all die, even so in Christ shall all be made alive" (1 Cor. 15:22). In other words, we all have fallen short of God's glory and only He can forgive when we accept Him as our Savior and Lord.

Walking with Christ

The Lord Jesus Christ paid it all and washed His children, making them white as snow (Isaiah 1:18). For whom did Christ die? Was it only for those who believe? No, "For God so loved the world, that He gave His only begotten son, that whosoever believeth in Him should not perish, but have everlasting life" (John 3:16). We believers need to walk with Christ and let our lights shine for Him. That's how we should then live.

PART 4

CHRIST'S CROWN

OUTLINE

I. **Introduction: Frequently Asked Questions about the Last Days**

    A. Are there any indications that Christ may return soon?

    B. Is the U.S. mentioned in prophecy?

    C. What kingdom did Jesus say was "at hand"?

    D. Is Christ on the throne of David now?

    E. How is Jesus going to return?

    F. What is meant by the coming Great Tribulation?

    G. Will anyone who has rejected Christ before the Rapture be saved during the Tribulation?

    H. Who will be the Antichrist?

    I. Is the Antichrist alive now?

    J. Is there going to be a one-world government?

    K. Is there going to be a one-world church?

    L. What is the battle of Armageddon?

    M. Is there a future Millennium?

    N. What will heaven be like?

    O. Will we know each other in heaven?

    P. What happens to Christians at death?

    Q. What is the Great White Trone Judgment?

    R. Will the unsaved suffer eternally?

    S. What is Preterism?

II. Evangelicals and the Last Days
    A. Evangelicals and Fundamentalists
    B. The Historical Setting
    C. A Call to Consider
    D. Digging Deeper

III. Evangelical Agreement on Things to Come
    A. The Immortality of the Soul
    B. The Intermediate State
    C. The Future Bodily Resurrection
    D. The Future Divine Judgment
    E. The Future Return of Christ
    F. The Eternal State
    G. Digging Deeper

IV. How Evangelicals Differ over Things to Come
    A. Premillennialism
        1. Differences among premillennialists
        2. The church to be raptured before the Tribulation begins
        3. The church to go through the Tribulation
        4. The church to go through the first half of the Tribulation
        5. The Prewrath rapture of the church
        6. Only spiritual believers to be raptured before the Tribulation begins
    B. Amillennialism
    C. Postmillennialism
        1. Rise and development
        2. Differences among postmillennialists
        3. Summary of the Three Eschatologies
    D. Why the Variant Views of Things to Come?
        1. Interpreting Scripture
        2. Importance of the issue
        3. Methods of interpretation

   a. The Literal or Normal Method
   b. The Spiritualizing or Allegorizing Method

V. Are You Ready for Christ's Return?
  A. A Coming One-World Church
  B. A Coming One-World Government
  C. How Should We Respond?

CHRIST'S CROWN

Introduction: Frequently Asked Questions about the Last Days

Though written over 200 years ago, John Newton's "Amazing Grace" has not lost its ability to touch chords deep within us:

> Amazing grace!
> How sweet the sound,
> That saved a wretch like me!
> I once was lost,
> But now am found
> Was blind, but now I see.

Something about the melody and the words is *immediately* interesting, appealing, and evocative. Regardless of whether the song reflects our sentiments and experience, it stirs the hearts of men and women around the world.

And yet the song takes on a deeper and more powerful meaning when we learn that the man who wrote the song, Newton, spent ten years of his life in the African slave trade. Trafficking in men and treating them in ways that a good man wouldn't treat his dog, John Newton truly was a man who had done wretched things. In short, he was exactly the kind of man to clearly display God's amazing grace.

God transformed Newton, "chief among sinners," into a preacher of the gospel–and Newton never got over the wonder of that divine transaction. And it was that sense of wonder that led him to pen the words to "Amazing

Grace," setting them to the tune of a popular bar song with which he was all too familiar. Knowing the background–the story behind the story, if you please–increases our appreciation for the song.

Just as something about "Amazing Grace" moves people, so also something about Bible prophecy is inherently intriguing. From the Bible, we know that God is intimately involved not only in the moment-by-moment existence of the universe, but also in the affairs of humanity. Yet prophecy speaks of much more than this. Using vivid language and mysterious imagery, it speaks in great detail of coming times of unprecedented and dramatic destruction, devastation, and deliverance. It at once warns and encourages us about things to come–and enjoins us to watch expectantly for their inevitable fulfillment.

And so, we are drawn to books and sermons which address prophetic issues such as, "How do we understand prophecy?" "Is the destruction prophesied in Scripture the result of atomic warfare, or Ebola-like disease, or both?" or, "Who is the Antichrist?" The prophetic portions of the Word of God are as interesting as tomorrow's newspaper, and far more accurate. So of course, we want to know more.

This section (Part 4) is about prophecy, and prophecy is a vitally important subject. You are to be commended for taking the time to dig deeper into it. Prophecy is as timeless as God's settled Word and is as current as today's news. Every tick of the clock brings God's prophecies closer to fulfillment. Even the most cursory glance reveals that the events prophesied in the Bible are taking shape. We see this, know the time is short, and want to know the answers to questions such as, "Are we the terminal generation?" or "Is the U.S. mentioned in prophecy?"

These are some of the questions–and good ones–that this book is committed to answering. The book is an invitation to go deeper, to delve into the issues behind these intriguing questions. Armed with this background, you can understand and appreciate prophecy much more.

Many people would rather avoid prophecy altogether. Some keep their distance because they don't know how to distinguish between people who treat the text with integrity and those who are just as adamant that Gorbachev's birthmark is the mark of the beast. This section is addressing "hot" questions carefully and textually, while at the same time giving you a crucial foundation for understanding prophecy and evaluating prophetic teaching.

Others prefer to stay on the surface of prophecy. To them it seems that for every two Christians there are three positions on the same prophetic issue. Despairing that anything can be known for sure, they dismiss prophecy, saying, "The big idea is that God wins. The rest is detail." Well, God certainly does win. But if that were all the attention God wanted us to pay to prophecy, it doesn't make much sense that He allotted more than a quarter of the Bible to communicate what He could have communicated in two words, "God wins."

With great care and conviction, evangelicals have set forth their particular views on God's program for the future. Much time and effort has been spent, and is still being spent, in defense of specific details of end-time events. It seems that as soon as a particular view is presented and defended, it is countered and answered by arguments from an opposing side.

Those classified as evangelical (conservative, orthodox, or fundamental) have a great deal in common as they embrace the historic Christian faith. Yet they battle fiercely with each other over things to come. While they stand united when it comes to the great historic truths of the Christian faith, they are sorely divided in their understanding of God's plan for the future. Why? This section will take you deeper in order to answer this urgent question.

For a long time, I have sensed the need to set forth the differences among evangelicals over things to come in the hope that the study would serve to ease tensions and strengthen ties among Bible believers. Evangelicals simply have too much in common to lose to the opposition because of our differences in eschatology.

This section sets forth the major differences among evangelicals in their interpretation of unfulfilled prophecy. I have made every effort to be objective and fair in presenting the different evangelical views. It may be hard for some to admit, but it is still true: no particular scheme of end-time events is without its problems. Helpful suggestions are made in this section for further reading and study in each of the various views.

My purpose here is not to defend my particular view of eschatology. I will answer frequently asked questions about the last days from my own point of view, which is pretribulational and premillennial. However, in the rest of Part 4, I will not critique the other positions on things to come but instead will set them out as fairly as I know how.

Since this is, at least in part, a study of what evangelicals believe, it is presented on the premise that the Bible, in its entirety, is the inerrant Word of God. The Scriptures are viewed as the basis and guide for all doctrinal beliefs, including those concerning the future program of God.

May the One around whom all unfulfilled prophecy revolves, the Lord Jesus Christ, be exalted in these pages and in the heart and life of the reader as we begin by looking at the commonly discussed issues.

Are there any indications that Christ may return soon?

Yes. There are a number of events taking place which indicate God is setting the stage for all that will transpire after Christ returns for His own. Perhaps the reconstitution of Israel as a nation and the computer age are among the greatest indications.

I mention Israel because it is clear from Scripture that in the end times God is dealing with Israel and the nations. Yet from the destruction wrought by Titus in the first century to 1948, the nation of Israel did not exist. So her existence today as a nation seems to indicate that the stage is being set. By the same token, it is entirely possible that the nation of Israel could be wiped off of the map tomorrow. But if this happened, and I pray that it won't, then God would have to start over again regathering Israel as a nation.

I mention computers because computer technology, its convergence with television, and its integration into the economy make it more possible than ever before for one person to control the economy, the media, and information itself. The Scripture is clear that in the Tribulation, one (unspeakably evil) person will exercise this kind of control. His name will be "Antichrist."

Is the U.S. mentioned in prophecy?

Not directly, so we don't know what her involvement will be in the Tribulation and the battle of Armageddon. There are a number of possible reasons for this absence. Some think the U.S. is not mentioned in Scripture because she will no longer exist as a nation, either through war or plague or some other calamity.

Others believe that the U.S. will be part of the revived Roman Empire which will be headed by the Antichrist. It is also worth noting that while specific geographical locations and peoples are given for the Northern and Southern powers, they are not given for the Eastern force nor the revived Roman Empire. If the U.S. is a part of the Antichrist's confederation, then that means she may eventually turn against her historically, Israel.

What kingdom did Jesus say was "at hand"?

Jesus, along with John the Baptist, the twelve apostles, and the seventy whom He sent out in pairs preached the very same message. It was a bona fide offer of the Davidic, earthly, messianic kingdom. The contingency of the offer was that the nation needed to repent for the kingdom to be established. They did not repent. The kingdom "at hand" in Jesus' day is not now a reality in any sense, but it will be when He sits on David's throne in Jerusalem and rules the world with a rod of iron at His second advent. I'll discuss this in more detail in question 4, but at the end of the Tribulation, the Jewish people will turn to their Messiah, looking toward Him whom they have pierced (Zech. 12:10), and so be saved. Then, during the Millennium, the kingdom that was "at hand" will be on earth.

Is Christ on the throne of David now?

No. He is at the right hand of His Father's throne. Interestingly enough, David's throne is never pictured as being in heaven but always on earth as a physical, literal, earthly throne. David ruled over an actual geographical area, and so will David's son and the focal point of David's dynasty, the Lord Jesus.

From the right hand of the Father, Jesus is currently interceding on our behalf with the Father and preparing dwelling places for us. But in the Millennium, the Lord Jesus will rule from the literal, physical throne of David in Jerusalem. He will rule over all the earth from there in a time of unprecedented peace and prosperity.

How is Jesus going to return?

First, He will come in the clouds of heaven and gather His own who are alive on the earth. Believers who have died since the Day of Pentecost will be raised from the dead, and together these will all go to be forever with the Lord. This is the Rapture. Following this coming of Christ, the Great Tribulation will take place on earth. After this, those who were raptured and raised when Christ came in the clouds will return with Him and He will establish His kingdom on earth. This is the Second Coming.

Some scholars lump the Rapture and the Second Coming together. Here's why I believe they are distinct events. While the Rapture is described as something which brings peace and comfort, and believers should anticipate with longing, the Second Coming is "after the Tribulation of those days," following on the heels of the great outpouring of God's wrath. In the Rapture, Christ comes to the air. In the Second Coming, Christ comes to the earth. After the Rapture, believers appear before the judgment seat of Christ and will be with the Lord forever. After the Second Coming, Christ judges the nations and Israel and then rules from the throne of David in Jerusalem over the world. At the Rapture, Christ comes *for* His saints. At the Second Coming, Christ comes *with* His saints.

A close comparison of John 14:1-3, 1 Thessalonians 4:13-18, and 1 Corinthians 15:51, 52 with Matthew 25 and Revelation 19 will, I believe, demonstrate that the Rapture and the Second Coming are separate events.

What is meant by the coming Great Tribulation?

This is a future seven-year period when God's wrath will be poured out on the earth as never before. It is the seventieth week of Daniel 9:24-27. Many students of prophecy refer only to the second half of this period as the "Great tribulation." I have no quarrel with them, but the first half of the Tribulation is going to involve great tribulation while the second half, if anything, is going to involve even greater tribulation. I think it is important to recognize that the entire seven-year period is going to be an unprecedented outpouring of God's wrath.

The Tribulation will begin when Israel signs a treaty with the Antichrist, who undertakes to guarantee Israel's peace. Thereafter, the devastating seal judgments are visited upon the earth. Around the midpoint of the Tribulation, the trumpet judgments devastate the earth and then shortly before the Second Coming, the bowl judgments are poured out upon the earth. The effects of these judgments are lingering and compounding, and things on the earth dramatically and progressively deteriorate. The Tribulation ends with the Second Coming of Christ, who defeats Satan and the armies of the world at Armageddon and ushers in a millennial kingdom of peace, prosperity, and righteousness.[156]

Will anyone who has rejected Christ before the Rapture be saved during the Tribulation?

Probably not. The apostle Paul declares in 2 Thessalonians 2:9-12:

> "Even him, whose coming is after the working of Satan with all power and signs and lying wonders, And with all deceivableness of unrighteousness in them that perish; because they received not the love of the truth, that they might be saved. And for this cause God shall send them strong delusion, that they should believe a lie: That they all might be damned who believed not the truth, but had pleasure in unrighteousness."

In other words, it appears that God will allow them to be supernaturally blinded by Satan. This just underscores the importance for the lost who have heard the gospel to trust Christ right now. Not only is there no guarantee about tomorrow, but this passage seems to indicate that there is a guarantee that there will be no tomorrow if they make a conscious decision to reject the claims of Christ and the Rapture occurs.

Nevertheless, those who have not been confronted with the gospel and therefore have never said "no" to Christ, very likely will have the opportunity to become Christians. I believe that millions upon millions will.

Who will be the Antichrist?

We do not know who he is, but we are told about his character and his conduct. Because of the importance of this question, I'm going to take some time to develop it.

The Antichrist, whose signing of a covenant with Israel will commence the Tribulation, is *the* major human character of that time.

John describes him as "a beast" in Revelation 3:1-15. Not only will

---
156 See Revelation 15–16 for bowl judgments.

his character be beastly, but so will his appearance. In Daniel 7:8, he is described as the "little horn" on the fourth beast, which symbolizes "a fourth kingdom upon earth" (Dan. 7:23), namely some form of a revived Roman Empire. This revived Roman Empire may only share geographical boundaries with the old Roman Empire or it might be something much more than that.

The Antichrist and his false prophet will promote a system of their own and exalt it above all other forms of worship–both true and false (Dan. 11:36). He will feel the freedom to abolish and change religions as it suits his purposes (2 Thess. 2:4). The false prophet will "cause that as many as would not worship the image of the beast should be killed" (Rev. 13:15). While compelling the world to worship him, the Antichrist himself will worship Satan, the destroyer and bringer of death.

He will be particularly opposed to the worship of the one true God (Dan. 11:36). God declares that such men are accursed, and the fate of the Antichrist bears this out.

The general course of his quest runs like this: the revived Roman Empire will become the strongest power in the world, and the Antichrist will become the ruler of this empire. He will set himself against God and will persecute the Jewish people and those who refuse to receive "the mark of the beast" (Rev. 13). Jesus and His legions will defeat the Antichrist in the final battle of the war of Armageddon (Rev. 19:11-19). The Antichrist and the false prophet will be captured alive after this battle and thrown into the lake of fire (Rev. 19:20).

The Antichrist will not simply be handed the control of this revived Roman Empire (also called the Western Confederacy or fourth kingdom by some scholars)–he will have to seize the power. This Western Confederacy will initially be a confederation of ten kings. These ten kings will be in place and will reign before the advent of the Antichrist. When the Antichrist comes forward, he will meet and overcome initial opposition from three of the kings. He will then gain ascendancy over the remaining seven kings. We see an account of this in both Daniel and Revelation:

> "After this I saw in the night visions, and behold a fourth beast, dreadful and terrible, and strong exceedingly; and it had great iron teeth: it devoured and brake in pieces, and stamped the residue with the feet of it: and it was diverse from all the beasts that were before it; and it had ten horns. I considered the horns, and, behold, there came up among them another little horn, before whom there were three of the first horns plucked up by the roots: and, behold, in this horn were eyes like the eyes of man, and a mouth speaking great things… Thus he said, The fourth beast shall be the fourth kingdom upon earth, which shall be diverse from all kingdoms, and shall devour the whole earth, and shall tread it down, and break it in pieces. And the ten horns out of this kingdom are ten kings that shall arise: and another shall rise after them; and he shall be diverse from the first, and he shall subdue three kings. And he shall speak great words against the most High, and shall wear out the saints of the most High, and think to change times and laws: and they shall be given into his hand until a time and times and the dividing of time" (Dan. 7:7-8,23-25; cf. Rev. 13:1; 17:3, 7, 12, 16).

Thus, his rise to power will be all the more remarkable in that it will be accomplished without a large power base.

Is the Antichrist alive now?

He certainly could be, but we do not know for sure. The first event which will conclusively reveal the identity of the Antichrist is described in Daniel 9:26, 27:

> "And after threescore and two weeks shall Messiah be cut off, but not for himself: and the people of the prince that shall come shall destroy the city and the sanctuary; and the end thereof shall

be with a flood, and unto the end of the war desolations are determined. And he shall confirm the covenant with many for one week: and in the midst of the week he shall cause the sacrifice and the oblation to cease, and for the overspreading of abominations he shall make it desolate, even until the consummation, and that determined shall be poured upon the desolate."

The person who signs the covenant with Israel guaranteeing her peace will be none other than the Antichrist. And the signing of the treaty launches the seven-year Tribulation.

Is there going to be a one-world government?

Yes, it appears there will be. It seems to be in existence during the Tribulation and is described in Revelation 18. But the term "one-world government" may convey the wrong impression. It's not as if the Antichrist is going to rule over every single square foot of territory on earth. It is probably more accurate to say that the government headed by the Antichrist will be the one superpower in existence during the Tribulation.

The power of the Antichrist will be vast. He will be the head of what I believe will be the revived Roman Empire, consisting of at least ten nations. It will be the economic, military, and religious force on the planet. No nation or group of nations will be able to attempt much of anything and succeed apart from the blessing of this revived empire. Perhaps the greatest tribute to this is the fact that Israel will entrust its security to the Antichrist. She will not do this now with the U.S. but she will do this in the future with the Antichrist.

Yet we see throughout the Tribulation that the Antichrist is involved in one military conflict after another. Most prominent among the other governments mentioned during the Tribulation are the king of the North (which I believe will be Russia), the kings of the East (which I believe will be China, India, and other Asiatic countries), and the kings of the South (which I believe will be a pan-Arab coalition).

Is there going to be a one-world church?

Yes. There will be a one-world religion during the Great Tribulation. All who do not worship the Antichrist will not be able to survive. Revelation 17 describes this false religious system.

Even today, all around us we see the consolidation of Protestant religions through organizations like the National Council of Churches, the World Council of Churches, and the Consultation on Church Union. The leaders of these organizations, almost without exception, reject the cardinal doctrines of the faith.

But the important thing to note about the coming one-world religion is that it won't require every person on earth to believe the same things. It will be the embodiment of "tolerance," a religion of the least common denominator. As long as a religion or sect acknowledges the deity of the Antichrist, worships his image, and follows the leadership of the false prophet, the rest of what they believe will be tolerated.

What is the battle of Armageddon?

This is the last world war. It will be the final conflict in a series of battles between world powers over the city of Jerusalem and the land of Israel. It is therefore more of a campaign that rages through most of the last half of the Tribulation rather than one single battle.

Is there a future Millennium?

Yes. The Millennium will be a thousand-year period in which Christ will set up a kingdom and rule over the entire earth (Rev. 20:4). It will begin about seventy-five days after the end of the Tribulation (Dan. 12:12). This thousand-year period is explicitly mentioned six times in six verses

(Rev. 20:2-7).

The Millennium will serve at least two useful purposes in the program of God. One will be to fulfill His promises, especially the promises that He made to Abraham in Genesis 12:2, 3. There are three central features to this promise of God.

The first feature is that He would make a great nation of Abraham's progeny. The second feature is related to the first, and it is the promise to Abraham of a multitude of descendants (Gen. 15:5). To be sure, this promise has been fulfilled in part, since Abraham does have a multitude of descendants through his sons Ishmael and Isaac. But in the Millennium, he will have even more because people will be healthier and live longer (Isa. 35:6, 7; 65:20, 22, 23).

The third feature is that Israel will be given "everlasting possession" of the promised land, the boundaries of which are set forth in Genesis 15:18-21. The nation of Israel has yet to control this entire section of land.

What will heaven be like?

The thing that will make heaven heavenly is that we will be with the Lord Jesus. In heaven we will have new bodies, and not only will the old sinful nature be gone, but the curse and the effects which are now all around us will be fully and finally gone. Because of that, we will experience no more sorrow, sin, pain or death. But not only will we not experience them, we won't cause others to experience them either. We will be living the life that was intended for us, with the Savior who loves us, worshiping Him and joyfully giving thanks to Him for all that He has done in that beautiful place with streets of gold.

Will we know each other in heaven?

There is every reason to believe that we will know each other. One of the many joys of heaven, I suspect, will be heartwarming reunions with family and friends. I don't know what we'll look like. I don't know that we'll look the same as we do now, but we will be recognizable.

But I wonder if behind this question is a certain lack of understanding about how amazing the fellowship in heaven is going to be. We will be with the Lord Jesus. The "God-shaped" vacuum inside of all of us will be filled, and we will feel more complete and fulfilled than ever before. Not only that, but the fellowship that we will enjoy with the saints in heaven will be way beyond the richest experience of fellowship we've had on earth. So even if we won't be able to recognize others in heaven, it will take nothing away from the experience.

What happens to Christians at death?

They go immediately into the presence of the Lord where they will be forever. They will receive a glorified body at the time of the future resurrection.

This raises the question of whether we will have some sort of intermediate body for the period between when we die and when we are given new bodies. I tend to believe that the answer to this question is "yes." But the Scriptures simply do not address this issue. Yet the most important issue is not what form we are in during this intermediate time, but whom we are with. And during this time between death and resurrection, whatever our form, we will be in the glorious, comforting presence of the Lord.

At the Rapture, whether we are living on the earth or have just experienced resurrection at the instant of God's trumpet call, we will be given new bodies. The new bodies will be related to our old bodies in the same sense that a cornstalk issues forth from a corn seed. Our resurrection bodies will be free from sin, sickness, or death, and be like Jesus' body was after His resurrection.

What is the Great White Throne Judgment?

It is the final, dreaded judgment. All the unsaved of all ages will appear at this judgment. It is described in Revelation 20:11-15. Jesus sits upon this throne. And His presence is fearsome–so much so that heaven and earth flee from His presence. And with good reason, for all who appear before this throne will be condemned to spend eternity in conscious suffering in the lake of fire.

As each person appears before the Lord Jesus, a series of books is reviewed in which his or her deeds have been recorded. One book in particular stands out. It is the book of life. Because there is none righteous, no not one, every person who stands before Christ on that day will find that his works are inadequate and–having failed to trust Him–their names will not be found in the book of life.

Will the unsaved suffer eternally?

Yes. They will suffer in what the Bible calls "the lake of fire." Conscious, eternal torment awaits those who have not trusted Christ as their Savior. He Himself said those not rightly related to Him would "go away into everlasting punishment" (Matt. 25:46).

I believe that whatever heaven is, hell is the total opposite. Those who are ushered into heaven will dwell there forever. Conversely, those who are consigned to the lake of fire will be there forever. There are degrees of reward for those who dwell in heaven, and I believe there will be degrees of punishment for those in hell. I believe that Jesus lends credence to this as He sums up the parable of the faithful steward:

> "And that servant, which knew his lord's will, and prepared not himself, neither did according to his will, shall be beaten with many stripes. But he that knew not, and did commit things worthy of stripes, shall be beaten with few stripes. For unto

whomsoever much is given, of him shall be much required: and to whom men have committed much, of him they will ask the more" (Luke 12:47, 48).

What is Preterism?

Preterism comes from the Latin word *preter* or past. Today there are three kinds of Preterism–mild, moderate, and extreme. The *mild* view is the earliest form and holds that the book of Revelation, with the exception of the Second Coming, was all fulfilled in the first three hundred years of the Christian church. *Moderate* preterists believe chapters 4 through 19 of Revelation refer to the destruction of Jerusalem in A.D. 70. They hold, for example, that in the future there will still be a second coming of Christ and bodily resurrection of saved and unsaved. R. C. Sproul, Kenneth Gentry, and Gary DeMar hold this view. *Extreme* preterists believe that we are already living in the New Heavens and the New Earth, and are represented by such men as J. Stuart Russell, Max R. King, and John L. Bray.

All varieties of Preterism stand in stark contrast with what might be called "futurism." Futurism is the view held by premillennialists and dispensationalists who hold that everything from Revelation 6:1 to 22:21 is still future. This view is based on a consistent literal or normal interpretation of Scripture.

Evangelicals and the Last Days

Why another book about the future? That seems to be a fair question since the market has been flooded with material on prophecy in recent years. No new view of things to come will be set forth in these pages. Rather, my primary reason for this section is to compare and contrast the various eschatologies that already exist among evangelicals.

Evangelicals and Fundamentalists

A word of orientation and background will help us. Just as there are liberals and conservatives in the political world, similar segments exist in the religious world. There are also variations, of course, within these two groupings, both in politics and religion. For example, there are extreme liberals and moderate liberals, just as there are strong conservatives and moderate conservatives. Other descriptions abound also, such as right- and left-wing. We often set ourselves up as the standard of judgment. Too many times we define our own view as the center, the true one, and then assign others accordingly, left or right of us.

In 1909, two Christian laymen made possible the publication of a twelve-volume set called *The Fundamentals*.[157] Three million copies of this scholarly defense of the faith were circulated. This monumental work restated and clearly defined biblical, historic Christianity. The contributors were men of great faith and scholarship. The work was a defense of the faith against the attacks that had been and were being made upon it by secular philosophy, unbelieving science, and especially modern, liberal theology.

Five major doctrines and themes related to them were set forth in the twelve small volumes. The major doctrines were:

1. The inspiration and authority of Scripture
2. The Virgin Birth of Christ
3. The deity of Christ
4. The substitutionary atonement of Christ
5. The bodily resurrection of Christ and His second coming

A quick look at the list tells us that the two doctrines around which all the discussion revolved were the Person and work of Christ and the inspiration of the Bible.

---

157 *The Fundamentals–A Testimony to the Truth* (Chicago: Testimony Publishing Co., 1909).

On the basis of these fundamentals, the evangelicals (or the fundamentalists as they became known) and the liberals (or modernists as they were called then) were separated. The lines were clearly drawn. Those who embraced and defended these traditional doctrines of the faith were called fundamentalists and those who did not were called modernists.

Today other terms are sometimes used to designate these two groups. Modernists are now called liberals and fundamentalists are sometimes called evangelicals. Actually, the word evangelical is a biblical one and when used in its historic sense, describes those who believe with conviction the five fundamentals of the faith in addition to other cardinal doctrines.[158]

As is the case with most words, "evangelical" and "evangelicalism" have been given new meanings and need to be explained, but so do the words "fundamental" and "fundamentalism." They, too, are sometimes used today to represent more than belief in the five fundamentals of the faith. Descriptive words like these have overtones or connotations that are undesirable to some who are otherwise content with the designation.

When used in this volume, the term "evangelical" refers to one who accepts the great cardinal doctrines of the faith. Some who do so are, of course, more vociferous in their defense of those fundamentals than others. Because of this, there are differences regarding associations which Christians have with each other, depending on how important those differences are perceived to be. The term "evangelical," however, designates one who is orthodox in his beliefs, in contrast to one who is unorthodox.

This section deals with only one of the five fundamentals presented above. While all who are legitimately called evangelical or fundamental believe all five, and more besides, there are considerable differences in the ranks over how to understand some of the details concerning the second coming of Christ.

---

158 See the author's *NeoEvangelicalism Today* (Schaumburg, IL: Regular Baptist Press, 1978) for a description of a rather new variation called NeoEvangelicalism within which there are those who deny the total inerrancy of Scripture.

He will return! Evangelicals agree fully on that. On the question of what specifics will be associated with His return, what the exact order of events will be, and what sequence of time in which they will come to pass, however, there is little agreement.

The Historical Setting

Many Christians consider all the "fuss" about the future unnecessary. They view the discussion of any order of end-time events as inconsequential and a waste of time and effort. As far as they are concerned, it is more important that we spread the gospel than it is to debate what they consider to be trivialities about how events will unfold in the future.

On the other hand, theologians and many Christian leaders hold tenaciously to particular views of future happenings. Denominations, mission agencies, schools, parachurch ministries and other Christian organizations, as well as individuals, are divided over God's plan for the future. Much time and effort is spent in defense of the various views. Why? Prophecy is in the proverbial ring, to draw from the sport of boxing. I doubt that many would deny that. But the question remains, Why? We are going to try to find out why in this study.

Viewed from the perspective of a casual onlooker, the evangelical world is splintered over the order of things to come. The body of Christ is truly fractured over future events. What is more, the divisions have existed for a long time. Since the third century of the Christian era, the controversy has raged. It has always been serious, but in the last seventy-five years the conflict has increased to the point of crisis.

A notable theologian with special interest in the subject of prophecy and future events made this observation regarding the renewed interest in the question of future events:

> The events of the last quarter of a century or more have had tremendous impact on the thinking of the scholarly world. In

philosophy there has been a trend toward realism and increasing interest in ultimate values and ethics. In science, the moral significance of scientific knowledge and the growing realization that physical science is a part of world life and meaning have emerged. In theology there has been what amounts to a similar revolution, particularly in the study of prophecy.[159]

There are three major belief systems regarding God's program for the future. Equally dedicated, sincere, and godly men have contended for these three end-times scenarios. *Premillennialism* is the view that Christ will return and institute a kingdom of perfect peace and righteousness on earth that will last for one thousand years. After this reign of true peace, eternity begins. *Amillennialism* is the view that when Christ returns, eternity begins with no prior thousand-year (millennial) reign on earth. The *postmillennial* view (though out of favor for some time, is again gaining popularity) has it that through the church's influence, the world will be Christianized before Christ returns. Immediately following His return, eternity begins. These views will be explained further in Section IV.

Whatever else may be said of these views, one thing is sure. They cannot all be right. The views cancel each other out. I suspect that a good number of Christians would not be disappointed if all three systems were cancelled out and the tug-of-war among believers over prophecy would cease. No doubt many would like to call for a moratorium on the prophecy debate. For them, that would indeed be the coming of kingdom bliss.

Regrettably, the prophecy war probably will not stop. But a better understanding of the reasons for the conflict will surely lessen the tension. The differences will probably prevail until the Lord Himself comes and fulfills His Word. So, let us not engage in wishful thinking. We must face the facts and evaluate the situation as it is. The time has come for us to take a long,

---

[159] John F. Walvoord, *The Millennial Kingdom* (Findlay, OH: Dunham Publishing Company, 1959), p. 3.

careful look at the various views and their relation to God's Word. It is also essential that we see the importance of unfulfilled prophecy in relationship to other areas of the Bible's teaching. Last-days views, like all other theological issues, are never held in isolation.

Wrongly, the three views of the future defined above have often been set forth as primarily the result of one's interpretation of the references to the "thousand years" in Revelation 20:1-7. This is far too simplistic an answer. Instead of one's interpretation of this phrase determining his millennial view, it is really the other way around. One's millennial system arrived at on other biblical grounds determines how Revelation 20:1-7 will be interpreted.

Scriptural teaching of the Millennium or kingdom is by no means confined to specific kingdom terminology. One who could not be classified as a particular friend of evangelicalism made this point with real force:

> For the concept of the Kingdom of God involves in a real sense the total message of the Bible. Not only does it loom large in the teaching, it is to be found in one form or another through the length and breadth of the Bible… Old Testament and New Testament thus stand together as the two acts of a single drama. Act 1 points to its conclusion in Act 2 and without it the play is an incomplete unsatisfying thing. But Act 2 must be read in light of Act 1 else its meaning would be missed. Where the play is organically one, the Bible is one book. Had we to give that book a title, we might with justice call it, "The Book of the Coming Kingdom of God."[160]

A Call to Consider

It is hoped that this section will contribute to the reduction of the warfare among evangelicals over the understanding of unfulfilled prophecies. I have not written to stir up more controversy or to enlarge the battle over

---
160 John Bright, *The Kingdom of God* (Nashville: Abingdon, 1953), p. 1, 7, 197.

end-time events. I am convinced there is a good deal of misunderstanding and misrepresentation in the furor over the future.

No doubt much of this is because of insufficient information or misdirected zeal, and maybe some of each.

What is said here will surely not solve all the problems, eliminate all the differences, or bring about a cessation of the war over end-time events among evangelicals. We want to provide evangelicals with a better understanding of their own views and why Christians differ over these matters. With this understanding, I hope there will also come a deeper commitment to the Lord Jesus Christ, the living Word of God, and the Bible, the written Word of God. When this occurs, there will be a deeper love for the people of God regardless of their understanding of things to come.

Several positive reasons, therefore, prompt me to write about prophecy. First, I want to set forth the various views held by evangelicals with regard to the future. Second, the reasons for these differences need to be explored and explained. Third, I want to alert the Christian public concerning the intensity of the battle over the Bible's teaching about events to come and offer a suggested solution. Most clergymen and church leaders are well aware of the conflict, but many lay people need more information. They have a right to know why the people of God, who agree on other essentials or fundamentals of the faith, differ so widely and battle so tenaciously over prophecy. Why fight over future events? What makes this doctrine so different from the others over which Christians disagree? These are basic questions of this study.

Fourth, I want to suggest that evangelicals begin to practice in their use of prophecy what they preach in their doctrine of the family of God. It is time that we behave like brothers and sisters in the heavenly family. Each child in the household of faith is needed, and we must never forget that the exercise of Christian love is just as essential in eschatology as it is in every other area of God's truth and Christian living.

If what I have said in these pages makes even the smallest contribution toward easing the tensions over events to come, it will have been well worth the effort.

Digging Deeper

The original twelve-volume set of *The Fundamentals* first published in 1909 consisted of articles contributed by recognized biblical scholars such as Benjamin B. Warfield, Melvin Grove Kyle, and H. C. G. Moule. The authors came from a wide spectrum of background and expertise–Episcopal bishops, attorneys, theologians, and Egyptologists. Almost all the articles defended the inspiration and authority of the Bible and some aspect of the Person and work of Christ. Of the ninety articles included in the twelve small volumes, only one dealt specifically with the return of Christ to the earth. In that article entitled, "The Coming of Christ," Charles R. Erdman of Princeton Theological Seminary argued that the return of Christ was indeed a fundamental of the historic Christian faith. In his defense of this cardinal doctrine, Erdman insisted Christ's return would be personal and glorious. He was quick to point out the fallacies of the liberal or modernistic view. Christ's promised coming again, he argued, was not to be confused with His spiritual presence among believers, the coming of the Holy Spirit on Pentecost, providential events of history, or the believer's death.

Interestingly, in the article, Erdman, an amillennialist, did not belabor his differences with opposing premillennial and postmillennial views. Rather, his guns were leveled at the theological liberals of his day and their rejection of the Bible as God's infallible Word. For those who wish to examine firsthand the basic content of these volumes as well as the manner in which the conflict was waged, see the two-volume presentation of the original twelve volumes by Charles Feinberg.[161]

---

161 Charles Feinberg. *The Fundamentals: The Famous Sourcebook of Foundational Biblical Truths.* (Grand Rapids: Kregel, 1958).

Others may want to dig deeper into the present state of affairs in the evangelical/fundamentalist discussions. For this, see "History and Development" in my NeoEvangelicalism. Also see Edward Dobson's *In Search of Unity* and Ernest Pickering's response in "Should Fundamentalists and Evangelicals Seek Closer Ties?".[162]

Evangelical Agreement on Things to Come

From Genesis to Revelation, the Bible is filled with prophecy. It has been said that one-fourth of the books of the Bible are prophetic in nature and one-fifth of the actual text of Scripture was prophetic when it was written.[163] Whether or not these percentages are altogether accurate is debatable. However, it must be admitted that Scripture abounds with prophecy and that much of what has been predicted has already come to pass.[164]

Perhaps the best examples of fulfilled prophecies are those related to the Lord Jesus Christ. More than three hundred prophecies were fulfilled at the first advent of Christ.[165]

There are, to be sure, a significant number of predictions made in the Bible that have not yet come to pass. These are the chief concern of this section regardless of which view one takes of the order of future events or the manner in which they are to be fulfilled. All who accept the Bible as God's infallible Word agree that they have not yet been fulfilled but will be in the future.

The order in which the major unfulfilled prophecies are presented is not significant. No particular emphasis is intended by the presentation and it

---

162 Ernest Pickering. "Should Fundamentalists and Evangelicals Seek Closer Ties?" *Baptist Bulletin* (March, 1986), 9-38.
163 Lewis Sperry Chafer, *Systematic Theology* (Dallas, Dallas Seminary Press, 1947), IV, 256.
164 A work by a well-known and greatly respected premillennial writer dealing with all the significant prophecies of Scripture in the order in which they appear in the Bible is *Prophecy Knowledge Handbook* by John F. Walvoord (Wheaton, IL: Victor Books, 1990).
165 Charles C. Ryrie, *The Bible and Tomorrow's News* (Wheaton, IL: Scripture Press Publications, Inc., 1969), 58-59.

is not my purpose to defend any particular scheme of prophecy by the order. Evangelicals agree there is unfulfilled prophecy and that is what needs to be emphasized here. Those who love the Lord and His Word have little argument with each other about the certainty of these future events. What they do argue about though (and sometimes in very unchristian ways) is the *order* in which these things will be fulfilled, the time sequence. Indeed, orthodox Christians argue tenaciously over events to come and do not hesitate to part company because of differences over end-time events.

Our primary concern in this section will not be over areas of difference but with those prophecies of Scripture that all evangelicals agree have not yet been fulfilled. In other words, we first want to know what the major unfulfilled prophecies are–the events still to come–that evangelicals do not fight over. Therefore, what major prophecies are accepted by most evangelicals?

The Immortality of the Soul

Belief in the immortality of the soul implies an eternal state of some kind. (More will be said about the eternal state later in this section.) "Immortality means the eternal, continuous, conscious existence of the soul after the death of the body."[166] Strictly speaking, this doctrine does not by itself demand that there be a resurrected body. Evangelicals do believe, however, that there will be a resurrection of the body. (There will be more on this later also.) Evangelicals concur that both Old and New Testaments teach clearly the immortality of man's soul. Without doubt, the resurrection of Christ is positive proof of life beyond the grave.

The Intermediate State

"By the intermediate state is meant that realm or condition in which souls exist between death and the resurrection."[167] Evangelicals do differ over

---
166 Loraine Boettner, *Immortality* (Philadelphia: Presbyterian and Reformed Publishing Co., 1962), 59.
167 Ibid., 91.

the nature of the believer's existence in the intermediate state, but there is a general consensus that there is such a state. They believe the intermediate state for the believer is a time of conscious existence, a state of rest, happiness, and freedom from sin and pain, in the very presence of Christ. For the unbeliever, it is a state of temporary suffering to be followed by the judgment and eternal separation from God in the lake of fire.

The Future Bodily Resurrection

From the beginning of the Christian era, belief in future divine judgment was generally associated with belief in the certainty of the future resurrection of all people; the dead will be raised so that they might be judged. The Apostles' Creed, the earliest apostolic testimony about Christ, refers to the judgment when it states that "Christ shall come to judge the quick [living] and the dead," but not everyone agreed that this statement meant there would be a resurrection.

When Jesus was on earth, some believed in the future resurrection of all people while others did not. The Pharisees accepted the doctrine, but the Sadducees rejected it (Matt. 22:23; Acts 23:8). Their differences over the resurrection did not, of course, keep them from joining together in their opposition to the Savior. They were perfectly willing to overlook their otherwise rigidly held views so they could form a united front against Christ.

When Paul preached the doctrine of the resurrection on Mars Hill, he was met with mocking and scoffing (Acts 17:32). There were others in New Testament times who either doubted the doctrine or regarded the resurrection as purely spiritual (1 Cor. 15:12; 2 Tim. 2:18).

Evangelicals base their view of future resurrection upon the clear teaching of Scripture. They see implications and direct teaching of this doctrine in the Old Testament (Ps. 49:15; 73:24-25; Prov. 23:14; Job. 19:25-27; Isa. 26:19; Dan. 12:2).

In the New Testament, there is more teaching about the future resurrection of the dead. Jesus Himself argued for the resurrection in opposition to the Sadducees (Matt. 22:23-33). As He did so, He paralleled what He said with what the Old Testament declared (Ex. 3:6). In this way, He appealed to the Old Testament to defend His own teaching.

On another occasion in reply to His critics, Jesus clearly set forth the doctrine of future resurrection from the dead. He said, "… the hour is coming, in the which all that are in the graves shall hear his voice, and shall come forth; they that have done good, unto the resurrection of life; and they that have done evil, unto the resurrection of damnation" (John 5:28-29).

Repeatedly, Jesus promised, "I will raise him up at the last day," to those who belonged to Him (John 6:39-40, 44, 54). He claimed to be "the resurrection and the life" (John 11:24-25).

On the basis of these and other passages of Scripture, there is common agreement among evangelicals–all the dead will be raised at God's appointed time in the future. Again, regardless of other differences, all who name the name of Christ in truth can repeat the Apostles' Creed without a tongue-in-cheek attitude when it says, "I believe in the Resurrection of the body."

The Future Divine Judgment

Non-evangelicals find it impossible to reconcile the doctrine of divine judgment with their concept of God, which is understandable since they reject so much of what the Bible says about Him. But evangelicals accept the authority of the Bible as well as the God of the Bible and therefore they believe in divine judgment ahead.

Any concept of God as heavenly Father that compares him only to a lenient, permissive, earthly father is not true to the biblical presentation of Him. Indeed, He is loving, gracious, and merciful; He is not a tyrant who rejoices in His judgment and punishment of sin. But God is also righteous and just, and His love moved Him to make provision for sin in His Son.

Rejection of Christ His Son means rejection of the only acceptable remedy for sin. Righteous wrath awaits all who reject God's Son as personal Savior.

Those who accept the Bible as God's word acknowledge that all men, as well as Satan and the wicked angels, will one day stand before the God of the Bible in judgment. Conflict does not exist among evangelicals over this prophecy. The question among evangelicals is not, "Will God bring all to judgment?" They all agree that He will. This broad area of agreement is what we want to explore.

The agreement among evangelicals about the certainty of future divine judgment is not marred by their differences over the order of events. Their high view of God and His Word brings them all to the conclusion that divine judgment is ahead. True, God does judge sin in the present, but Scripture makes it clear that these judgments of God experienced in the here and now are not final.

John's record of the revelation given to him by God makes it clear that all the unregenerate will one day appear before God in judgment:

> "And I saw a great white throne, and Him that sat on it, from whose face the earth and the heaven fled away; and there was found no place for them. And I saw the dead, small and great, stand before God; and the books were opened: and another book was opened, which is the book of life: and the dead were judged out of those things which were written in the books, according to their works. And the sea gave up the dead which were in it; and death and hell delivered up the dead which were in them: and they were judged every man according to their works. And death and hell were cast into the lake of fire. This is the second death. And whosoever was not found written in the book of life was cast into the lake of fire" (Rev. 20:11-15).

Scripture is equally clear in its prophecy of the certainty of all believers standing personally and individually before God to give an account to Him. The apostle Paul reminded the Christians in Corinth and Rome of this. To the Corinthians he wrote: "Every man's work shall be made manifest: for the day shall declare it, because it shall be revealed by fire; and the fire shall try every man's work of what sort it is. If any man's work abide which he hath built thereupon, he shall receive a reward. If any man's work shall be burned, he shall suffer loss: but he himself shall be saved; yet so as by fire" (1 Cor. 3:13-15).

In his second letter to the same people he wrote, "For we must all appear before the judgment seat of Christ; that every one may receive the things done in the body, according to that he hath done, whether it be good or bad" (2 Cor. 5:10).

The Roman Christians were given the very same teaching. "But why dost thou judge thy brother? or why dost thou set at nought thy brother? for we shall all stand before the judgment seat of Christ. For it is written, As I live, saith the Lord, every knee shall bow to Me, and every tongue shall confess to God. So then every one of us shall give account of himself to God" (Rom. 14:10-12).

Final judgment also awaits the devil and his demons. The everlasting fire of hell was prepared for the devil and his angels (Matt. 25:41). In his vision, John was able to see "the devil that deceived them was cast into the lake of fire and brimstone, where the beast and the false prophet are" (Rev. 20:10). There he is to be tormented day and night forever and ever.

Peter and Jude, both directed by the Holy Spirit, tell us of wicked angels being reserved in chains until the day of their final judgment (2 Pet. 2:4; Jude 6).

Regardless of denominational affiliation or lack thereof, and in spite of whether one believes there will be one final judgment or whether there will be a number of different judgments separated by time, all evangelicals believe in future divine judgment. They take the words of the psalmist seriously and even literally and, therefore, as yet unfulfilled when he said, "… for He cometh, for He cometh to judge the earth: He shall judge the world with righteousness, and the people with His truth" (Ps. 96:13).

The Future Return of Christ

The Old Testament prophets did not distinguish between the time of Christ's coming as a babe in Bethlehem's manger and His coming the second time in power and great glory. However, their prophecies concerning Christ's coming are understood differently by evangelicals. Some see all the Old Testament prophecies of Christ's coming as already fulfilled in His first advent. Others believe a significant number of the prophecies await future fulfillment when He comes the second time.

Nevertheless, all Bible believers do agree that in the New Testament we have clear prophecy of Christ coming to the earth again. Jesus and the writers of the New Testament agree; His first coming will be followed by a second one.

Those who witnessed Christ's ascension heard the angelic messengers say, "Ye men of Galilee, why stand ye gazing up into heaven? this same Jesus, which is taken up from you into heaven, shall so come in like manner as ye have seen him go into heaven" (Acts 1:11).

Long before He returned to the Father, Jesus taught His followers that He would come again. As He sat on the Mount of Olives, He told His disciples about the future. They were warned of difficult times ahead and were assured of their Lord's return:

> "For then shall be great tribulation, such as was not since the beginning of the world to this time, no, nor ever shall be. And except those days should be shortened, there should no flesh be saved: but for the elect's sake those days shall be shortened. Then if any man shall say unto you, Lo, here is Christ, or there; believe it not. For there shall arise false Christs, and false prophets, and shall shew great signs and wonders; insomuch that, if it were possible, they shall deceive the very elect. Behold, I have told you before. Wherefore if they shall say unto you, Behold, he is in the desert; go not forth: behold, he is in the secret chambers; believe it not. For as the lightning cometh

out of the east, and shineth even unto the west; so shall also the coming of the Son of man be" (Matt. 24:21-27).

In what has come to be called Christ's Upper Room Discourse, Jesus brought comfort to His disciples by announcing that He would come again for them. They had been told, but they did not want to think about His death, and in order to encourage them Jesus said, "I will come again, and receive you unto Myself" (John 14:3).

Even the last book in the Bible holds out the promise of Christ's second coming. John, in a vision, saw Christ whose name is called "The Word of God" coming from heaven to earth along with the armies of heaven (Rev. 19:11-16).

It makes no difference whether they embrace the amillennial, postmillennial, or premillennial scheme, evangelicals all agree that the predictions of Christ's future return have not yet been realized. Will Christ come first in the air for all His children (1 Thess. 4:13-18)? Is this "coming" to be distinguished from His "coming" to the earth (Rev. 19:11-16)? Evangelicals have different answers to such questions, but they all agree that Christ is coming to the earth again just as surely as He came the first time.

What have we discovered thus far in our study? We have seen that despite differences over details, evangelicals agree on several major issues regarding prophecy of things to come. They all agree that mankind lives on after death and that heaven as well as hell will be occupied by humans. There will be a new heaven and a new earth in the future. All of God's creatures will face Him in judgment. The dead, small and great, will be raised to spend eternity either with God in heaven or with the devil in hell. Christ is coming back to this earth again and His future coming will be just as literal as when He came as a babe in Bethlehem's manger.

We evangelicals have so much in common and some of these major areas of agreement have been explored. The great fundamentals of the faith bind us together in the family of God and set us apart from those who reject the inspiration and authority of the Bible. One of these fundamentals is the doctrine of the future bodily return of Christ. Fellowship in the things of the Lord that we hold in common should characterize our lives, not fights over details of unfulfilled prophecy.

The Eternal State

Evangelicals all believe heaven and hell are real places and human beings will dwell forever in one or the other. The Bible plainly says both exist and will be occupied by humans throughout eternity.

Critical biblical scholarship tells us we can no longer believe the pre-Copernican view of the universe. Science, we are told, has disproved belief in a three-decker universe, which was a common belief around the time the Bible was being written. Modern science insists that the sun, not the earth, is the center of our galaxy. Therefore, "up" is no longer really up for earth dwellers, and "down" is no longer down.

Such views were bound to make an impact upon theological thinking sooner or later, and so they did. Rudolf Bultmann expressed his unbelief in the Bible's view of heaven and hell this way:

> Man's knowledge and mastery of the world have advanced to such an extent that through science and technology it is no longer possible for anyone seriously to hold a New Testament view of the world–in fact, there is no one who does… No one who is old enough to think for himself supposes that God lives in a local heaven. There is no longer any heaven in the traditional sense of the word. The same applies to hell in the sense of any mythical underworld beneath our feet. And if this is so, we can no longer accept the story of Christ's descent into hell or His Ascension into Heaven as literally true. We can no longer look for the return of the Son of Man on the clouds of heaven or hope that the faithful will meet in the air (1 Thess. 4:15ff).[168]

---

168 Rudolf Bultmann, *Kerygma and Myth* (London: SPCK, 1954), 4.

In the opinion of many modern scientists, truth does not exist outside the scientific realm. The supernatural, the miraculous, is denied by unbelieving scientists and consequently by much of modern theology as well.

In response to the contention that we can no longer accept the Bible's teaching that heaven and hell are real places and remain intellectually honest, Lesley Woodson made this observation: "What is so often overlooked is that there are different truth dimensions and truth in one of these dimensions need not be denied by truth in another. Their natures are not the same. Thus one can be intellectually honest while embracing both the Copernican view of the physical world and a three-decker view of the metaphysical world at one and the same time."[169]

Time will not go on forever! This is another point of agreement among Bible believers. Eternity is as much a certainty for evangelicals as time is now a present reality. While the Bible does clearly teach eternity, when time ends and eternity begins is another question. God's people do not dispute that there is a future world out there, and no believing student of the Scripture accepts the notion that death ends it all.

True biblical teaching regarding heaven and hell is often neglected today. Heaven and hell are also frequently misrepresented. Modern man often uses the biblical terminology but invests it with new meaning. For example, experiences of a hard life are sometimes described as "hell on earth" and the person who is deprived of the essential things, or simply the good things of life, is "going through hell." Ron Devillier gave this description of hell:

> "Hell is where the poor are trapped in the ghetto of indifference. It is the high school campus where some persons are socially crippled because they do not fit. It is the back section of a psychiatric ward of a charity hospital where the bruised ones that did not get enough love are hidden. It is a small village in Vietnam where people lay in the streets, victims of a stray bomb. It is a dingy jail

---

[169] Lesley H. Woodson, *Hell and Salvation* (Old Tappan, NJ: Fleming H. Revell Co., 1973), 24.

downtown where frightened human beings cower. It is a small town high school where a teenage girl returns from a home for unwed mothers after giving birth to her child. It is a street of charred buildings, broken windows, and looted stores–the aftermath of a riot–kindled by frustration, hopelessness, and rage."[170]

Devillier may have a biblical view of hell, but his words in this instance do not reveal it. To be sure, those who go through the experiences he described are, no doubt, having the nearest thing to "hell on earth," but the Bible tells us that there is a hell far worse than anything possible on this earth. No misfortune and poverty, and all that goes with them, even begin to compare with the horrors and torments of hell. Those who reject the Lord Jesus Christ as their personal Savior will go to a place of eternal torment that the Bible calls the "lake of fire."

Because the Bible teaches it, evangelicals believe in an eternal existence for man, either in heaven or hell. Prophecy concerning man's existence in these two abodes, and the bliss or torment to be encountered there, are rarely disputed by evangelicals. They accept Scripture's clear teaching on these issues at face value.

Concerning heaven, Jesus said, "I go to prepare a place for you" (John 14:2). He told the disciples plainly that He wanted them with Him in this place He would prepare and that he would receive them there.

Hell, Jesus taught, was also a real place promising eternal torment for the devil and his angels, as well as for the sons and daughters of Adam who rejected Him and His sacrifice for their sins. He called it a place of "damnation" where "the fire is not quenched" (Matt. 23:33; Mark 9:48). There is an abundance of other Scripture teaching the same thing in addition, of course, to what Jesus said about heaven and hell as eternal abodes.

Evangelicals agree, too, that there will be a new heaven and a new earth in the future. The prophet Isaiah wrote of these. He recorded Jehovah's

---

170 Ron Devillier, *Real* (Spring, 1972).

answer to the prayer of the believing remnant. In part, the answer was, "For, behold, I create new heavens and a new earth: and the former shall not be remembered, nor come into mind" (Isa. 65:17). "For as the new heavens and the new earth, which I will make, shall remain before me, saith the LORD, so shall your seed and your name remain" (Isa. 66:22).

In New Testament times, Peter was still predicting judgment upon the present heavens and earth (2 Pet. 3:7). He also said, "The heavens shall pass away with a great noise, and the elements shall melt with fervent heat, the earth also and the works that are therein shall be burned up" (v. 10). But he prophesied further, "we… look for new heavens and a new earth, wherein dwelleth righteousness" (v. 13). John in his apocalyptic vision saw Christ on a throne and from his "face the earth and the heaven fled away" (Rev. 20:11). Also, the beloved disciple "saw a new heaven and a new earth" (Rev. 21:1).

The present heavens and earth have not yet been "destroyed." Prophecy stating that they will awaits future fulfillment and so does the prophecy of the creation of the new heaven and the new earth. Bible believers do not differ over such things. They agree that the eternal state has not yet begun.

In another section we will present the different evangelical viewpoints with regard to how and in what order these future happenings will take place. There are a number of variations in the sequence and details accompanying these major unfulfilled prophecies. Study of these will get us close to the actual battle, which to our shame is sometimes fierce, with rancor and often without regard for the rules of Christian ethics.

Digging Deeper

Those who believe in a future resurrection and a final judgment generally agree that there is a state of existence between this life and the resurrection, but not on the conditions surrounding that intermediate state. The doctrine of purgatory advanced by the Roman Catholic Church is rejected by evangelical protestants because they do not believe it has any biblical support. It was not until the middle of the fifteenth century that the Latin branch of the church denounced a common view within ancient Judaism. The idea was that believers were in a semiconscious state between death and resurrection. Soul sleep between death and resurrection is embraced by Jehovah's Witnesses and Seventh-Day Adventists, but this is rejected by mainline evangelicalism.

Evangelicals differ most over whether or not there is an intermediate body for the believer in the intermediate state. The major passage of Scripture dealing with this matter is 2 Corinthians 5:1-3. For further study on this question, I recommend two excellent sources. Loraine Boettner's *Immortality* has a good section on the intermediate state.[171] A scholarly defense of the belief in an intermediate body for believers is also found in Greg Enos' Th.D. Dissertation, "To Die Is Gain: The Christian's Intermediate State."[172]

Another area in which the reader may want to dig deeper is the current controversy among evangelicals over the eternal destiny of the unsaved. "Biblical universalism" or "qualified universalism" describes the moderate belief between the view of eternal torment for the unregenerate and universalism. Some evangelicals are seeking to defend the view that God assigns an irrevocable and definite death to those who have not responded to the gospel. They believe the "fire" of hell does not torment eternally. Rather, it consumes the wicked. In other words, they are advocating that it is the death that is everlasting punishment rather than the torment.

For further study on this and other related issues, see the extended article by Roger Nicole, Neal Punt, Clark Pinnock, Kenneth Kantzer, and

---

171   Loraine Boettner. *Immortality* (Philadelphia: The Presbyterian and Reformed Publishing Co, 1962).
172   Greg Enos. "To Die Is Gain: The Christian's Intermediate State." (Dallas: Dallas Theological Seminary, 1989).

David Wells, entitled "Universalism: Will Everyone Be Saved?"[173] and Jon E. Braun's book *Whatever Happened to Hell?*.[174]

How Evangelicals Differ Over Things to Come

We have noted that three major evangelical systems of thought–premillennialism, amillennialism, and postmillennialism–offer explanations of God's plan of procedure for the future. Since the adherents of each view are evangelical, they accept biblical authority and seek to be true to the meaning of God's Word. Dedicated men and women who love the Lord and His Word hold these views and their honesty and sincerity should not be questioned. But all three systems cannot fully represent the biblical teaching because they are so different and in conflict with each other.

Each millennial system has a different picture of what will take place when Christ returns to the earth. Will Christ return after the church has Christianized the world? Will He establish an earthly kingdom and reign for one thousand years on David's throne in Jerusalem? Or will the eternal state be ushered in at His second coming?

Other sharp distinctions exist between the major interpretations of things to come but these questions are at the basis of all: Will Christ institute the Davidic kingdom on earth? Will the church succeed in Christianizing society before Christ returns? Will He usher in the eternal state when He comes again?

The three systems of thought need to be presented along with important variations that are true of each one. Little will be said for or against them. Our purpose here is simply to expose the reader to the different views of unfulfilled prophecy as held by evangelicals.

---

[173] Roger Nicole, Neal Punt, Clark Pinnock, Kenneth Kantzer, David Wells. "Universalism: Will Everyone Be Saved?". *Christianity Today* (March 20, 1987).

[174] Jon E. Braun. *Whatever Happened to Hell?* (Nashville: Thomas Nelson Publishers, 1979).

Non-evangelicals or non-conservatives of all religious varieties usually have such a weak view of the Bible and its authority that they find no difficulty dealing with prophecy the way they deal with most of the Bible–reject it, and treat it as myth or as pure symbolism without any literal meaning. In short, they do not take Scripture seriously.

An example of the liberal view will show the contrast with evangelical belief. C. H. Dodd in his book *The Parables of the Kingdom* made famous the phrase "realized eschatology." In general, all non-evangelicals agree with Dodd in his view of the unfulfilled prophecies: "The eschaton has moved from the future to the present, from the sphere of expectation into that of realized experience."[175]

According to his view, all eschatology–the doctrine of future things–was fulfilled at the Incarnation of Christ. Dodd arrives at his view by a process of wholesale discrediting of Scripture. With apparent ease, he calls much of the Bible fraudulent. What is not fraudulent, he either explains away or distorts to fit his presuppositions and even goes so far as to say that Christ was simply mistaken in some of His prophecies. In other words, the Lord Jesus Christ was wrong.

But among those who accept the divine authority of Holy Scripture and who do, therefore, take it seriously, three totally different views about the future program of God for mankind and the world persist. The distinctions between these systems of belief are by no means imaginary or unimportant. To the contrary, there are far-reaching consequences associated with each of the views. These views will now be presented in the order they arose and developed in the history of the church.

Premillennialism

The word "millennium" comes from the Latin words *mille* meaning thousand and *annus* meaning year. Though not found in the Bible, the Greek

---

175 C. H. Dodd, *The Parables of the Kingdom* (New York: Charles Scribner Sons, 1961), 50.

equivalent of millennium appears six times in Revelation 20. The word refers to a designated period of time. Belief in such a period of time has been called chiliasm or millenarianism. The prefix "*pre-*" before the word "millennium" means before. Thus, premillennialism describes the belief that Christ will return before the millennium and, in fact, will establish it when He returns to the earth.

The future 1000-year millennium will be characterized by righteousness (Isa. 60:21), holiness (Isa. 52:10), truth (Ps. 45:4) and the fullness of the Holy Spirit of God (Joel 2:28-29). Christ will rule and reign from His throne in Jerusalem over the whole world. Satan will be bound in the abyss for the entire period (Rev. 20:1-6). During that time, all war will cease (Isa. 9:4-7), and there will be joy (Isa. 9:3-4), peace (Isa. 65:25), holiness (Isa. 1:26-27), glory (Isa. 24:23), comfort (Isa. 12:1-2), perfect justice (Isa. 9:7), the lifting of the curse imposed because of sin, the removal of sickness (Isa. 33:24), healing of the deformed (Isa. 29:17-19), great economic prosperity (Isa. 25:1-2), unified worship of God (Isa. 45:23), and the visible manifestation of the very presence of God Himself (Ezek. 34:27-28).

Charles Ryrie, a distinguished defender of the premillennial system of thought defined it this way:

> In general, the premillennial system may be characterized as follows: Premillennialists believe that theirs is the historic faith of the church holding to a literal interpretation of the Scriptures. They believe that the promises made to Abraham and David are unconditional and have had or will have a literal fulfillment. In no sense have these promises made to Israel been abrogated or fulfilled by the Church which is a distinct body in this age having promises and a destiny different from Israel's. At the close of this age, premillennialists believe that Christ will return for His church meeting her in the air (this is not the Second Coming of Christ), which event called the rapture or translation, will usher in a seven-year period of Tribulation on the earth. After this

the Lord will return to the earth (this is the Second Coming of Christ), to establish His kingdom on the earth for one thousand years during which time the promises to Israel will be fulfilled.[176]

It is generally agreed by students of the early church that premillennialism was the view held by many in the post-apostolic age. The fact that it is the oldest of the three millennial views is seldom debated, but age of course, does not necessarily mean accuracy. The view prevailed and was virtually unchallenged until the time of Origen (185–254 AD) and his allegorical or nonliteral method of interpretation of Scripture. The basic reason for the three millennial views is the method used by each system in its interpretation of those passages of Scripture dealing with unfulfilled prophecy. More will be said about this later.

Premillennialism went into something of an eclipse from the time of Origen to about 1830, which was the beginning of the time of the prophetic Bible conferences, when premillennialism was revived. During the intervening years, amillennialism (to be studied later) was the prevailing system of belief.

Differences among premillennialists

Premillennialists all agree that when Christ returns to the earth, He will institute the kingdom promised to David. Christ's second coming in power and great glory is not followed immediately by the eternal state. Instead, the one-thousand-year earthly rule of Christ begins at that time. Old Testament promises to Israel will then be fulfilled, and the covenants God made with Abraham (Gen. 12) and David (2 Sam. 7) will then be realized.

Is there going to be, in the future, a seven-year period of unprecedented tribulation that will be the outpouring of God's wrath upon the world? Will this be what Jeremiah called "the time of Jacob's trouble" (Jer. 30:7), a time of divine judgment unlike any other? Did Jesus refer to this time when He

---

176 Charles C. Ryrie, *The Basis of the Premillennial Faith* (New York: Loizeaux Brothers, 1953), 12.

told His disciples there would be a "great tribulation, such as was not since the beginning of the world until this time, no, nor ever shall be" (Matt. 24:21)? Premillennialists are in general agreement in answering "yes" to these questions.

Will the church, the body of Christ, be called upon to go through the seven-year period of tribulation? Premillennialists do not all agree on the order in which some of the future events will transpire and give different answers to this question. For example, there are at least four different views of the relation of the church, which is Christ's body, to the coming tribulation.

The church to be raptured before the Tribulation begins

Some believe the entire church will be raptured, caught up to be with the Lord, before any part of the future seven-year Tribulation begins. Those who hold this view are called pretribulationists.

The future seven-year period of unprecedented tribulation will be characterized by global wars, famine, death, anarchy, hail, and fire mixed with blood burning up one-third of the trees and all green grass, whole mountains burning with fire, one-third of the seas becoming blood, water resources becoming bitter as gall, darkness in the skies during the daylight hours, plagues of scorpions and painful sores, death of all sea life, sun scorching humans with fire, earthquakes, and catastrophic earth and heaven revolutions (cf. Rev. 6–16).

John F. Walvoord, a widely-recognized authority and spokesman for premillennial pretribulationalism, defined the position this way:

> The pretribulational interpretation regards the coming of the Lord and the translation of the church as preceding immediately the fulfillment of Daniel's prophecy of a final seven-year period before the second advent. Based on a literal interpretation of Daniel's prophecy, it is held that there has been no fulfillment of Daniel 9:27 in history and that therefore it prophesies a future

period, familiarly called "the tribulation." The seven years of Daniel, bringing to a close the program of Israel prior to the second advent, will, therefore, be fulfilled between the translation of the church and the second advent of Christ to establish His kingdom on earth. At the translation, before the seven years, Christ will return to meet the church in the air; at the second advent after the seven years, it is held that Christ will return with His church from heaven to establish His millennial reign on earth.[177]

Despite many similarities, pretribulationists find a definite distinction in Scripture between God's program with Israel and His program with the church. They also see a difference between Christ's coming *for* His own and His coming *with* His own. The coming *for* His own they call the "Rapture"; Christ's coming *with* His own to the earth is called the "Second Coming." At least one thousand years for the earthly reign of Christ and seven years of tribulation on the earth come between the Rapture and the Second Coming in this view.

Pretribulationists are also dispensationalists. A dispensationalist sees a clear distinction in the Bible between God's program with the nation Israel and His program with the church. Most dispensationalists believe the church began on the Day of Pentecost as a distinct entity from Israel. According to this view, God has dealt differently with His people at different times.

It is generally agreed that a dispensation is "a distinguishable economy in the outworking of God's purpose."[178] The dispensational system of biblical interpretation may be described this way:

> Dispensationalism views the world as a household run by God. In this household-world, God is dispensing or administering its affairs according to His own will and in various stages of revelation in the process of time. These various stages mark off the distinguishably different economies in the outworking of His total

---

[177] John F. Walvoord, *The Rapture Question* (Findlay, OH: Dunham Publishing Co., 1957), 49.
[178] Charles C. Ryrie, *Dispensationalism Today* (Chicago: Moody Press, 1965), 29.

purpose and these economies are the dispensations. The understanding of God's differing economies is essential to a proper interpretation of His revelation with those various economies.[179]

Basic to the pretribulational view is belief in Christ's imminent return, that He could come at any time. In other words, there are no prophecies awaiting fulfillment before His return in the air for His own. Among premillennial pretribulationists, there is general agreement on the order of major events in the future. A listing of these will be helpful in understanding the view:

1. Increase in apostasy as this age draws to a close (1 Tim. 4:1-3; 2 Tim. 3:1-5)

2. Resurrection of the dead in Christ, or those saved in this age, accompanied by the translation of the living saints and the rapture of both groups (1 Cor. 15:20-24, 35-50; 1 Thess. 4:13-18)

3. The seven-year Tribulation on earth (Rev. 6–16)

4. Those resurrected and translated earlier are with the Lord in heaven. The judgment seat of Christ (1 Cor. 3:12-15) and the marriage of the Lamb take place (Rev. 19:7) while the Tribulation judgments are poured out on earth.

5. The Battle of Armageddon and the end of the Tribulation

6. Christ comes with His own to the earth (Rev. 19:11-16). When Christ comes, Israel will be regathered and judged (Matt. 24:37–25:46). The Gentile nations will also be judged (Matt. 25:31-46).

7. The millennial reign of Christ begins. It will be one thousand years in length (Rev. 20:1-6). Before it begins, however, Satan is bound in the bottomless pit (Rev. 20:1). After the one-thousand-year reign, Satan will be loosed for a little season (Rev. 20:7). He will deceive the nations and lead a revolt against God, be defeated by

---

[179] Ibid., 31.

Christ, and then cast into the lake of fire where he will remain forever (Rev. 20:10).

8. The Great White Throne Judgment (Rev. 20:11-15) occurs at which all the unsaved of all the ages appear and are afterward cast into the lake of fire.

9. Creation of a new heaven and a new earth (Rev. 21:1)

10. Eternity (Rev. 22:1-6).

The Church to go through the Tribulation

Some who insist they are premillennial have raised serious questions about the belief that the church will escape the future, seven-year Tribulation. They do not believe the church will be raptured or caught up to meet the Lord in the air before the Tribulation begins on earth. Rather, it is their contention that the church must pass through the period called "the time of Jacob's distress" in Scripture, or future seven-year Tribulation on earth. They insist God will protect or preserve His own through this time. This view is called posttribulationism.

Alexander Reese, an advocate of the view, gave this definition of premillennial posttribulationism. "The Church of Christ will not be removed from the earth until the advent of Christ at the very end of the present Age: the Rapture and the Appearing take place at the same crisis; hence, Christians of that generation will be exposed to the final affliction under Antichrist."[180]

Considerable differences exist among evangelicals who are posttribulational. Those who do not subscribe to premillennialism believe the Tribulation began with the early church.[181] Some even say it began with Adam.[182] But

---

[180] Alexander Reese, *The Approaching Advent of Christ* (London: Marshall, Morgan & Scott, Ltd., 1959), 18.

[181] George L. Rose. *Tribulation Till Translation* (Glendale, CA: Rose Publishing Co., 1943), 68-69.

[182] George H. Fromow, *Will the Church Pass Through the Great Tribulation?* (London: The Sovereign Grace Advent Testimony, n.d.), 1.

posttribulationists who are premillennial take Scripture that speaks of great tribulation (Jer. 30:7; Dan. 12:1; Matt. 24:21) as unfulfilled and yet to be fulfilled in the future.[183]

As can be seen from Reese's definition above, the premillennial posttribulationists' position makes little distinction between Christ's coming for His own in the Rapture and His coming to the earth with His own to establish the kingdom. Distinction between God's program for Israel and His program for the church is even less marked, and the hope that Christ could come at any time is either denied or redefined.

Posttribulationists are not dispensational[184] and they do not generally present a detailed order of future events. We may safely say, however, that they all believe the church will go through the coming Tribulation. Christ's coming *for* His own and coming *with* His own will be at the same time and a general resurrection and general judgment of all men and evil angels will occur before the eternal state begins.

The Church to go through the first half of the Tribulation

There are also some premillennialists who believe the church will pass through half of the future Tribulation. The last half of the seventieth week mentioned in Daniel 9:24-27 is seen to be far more severe than the first half. This view has the church raptured in the middle of the week or in the middle of the Tribulation and is known as the midtribulational view. It is a relatively new explanation of the relation of the church to the coming Tribulation. Midtribulationists do not usually use the term midtribulation to refer to themselves. They consider themselves pretribulational since they do believe Christ will return to rapture His own before what they call the

---

183 George E. Ladd, *Blessed Hope* (Grand Rapids: Eerdmans, 1956), 72-77; and Robert H. Gundry, *The Church and the Tribulation* (Grand Rapids: Zondervan, 1973).

184 An exception to this is R. H. Gundry in his *The Church and the Tribulation,* 12-28.

great Tribulation or the last half of Daniel's seventieth week.[185]

Gleason L. Archer, who holds the position, gave this description of the view:

> Between the competing views of the pretribulation and the post-tribulation rapture stands a mediating option, the theory of the mid-seventieth week rapture. Some refer to it as the midtribulation rapture as though the sudden deliverance of the Church were to take place after the first three and a half years of the final seven before the return of Christ to establish His kingdom on earth. But if the great tribulation is regarded as commencing with the outpouring of the wrath of God on the world as described in Revelation 16–18, then it is hardly accurate to describe the mid-week view as a midtribulation theory, for it is really a form of pretribulation rapturism which limits the time interval climatic world suffering to the final three and a half years prior to the battle of Armageddon. To me, this approach seems to offer fewer problems than either of the other views.[186]

To a certain extent, the divine programs with Israel and the church seem to overlap in this viewpoint. This is because the church participates in at least part of the Tribulation called "the time of Jacob's trouble" and the seventieth week of Daniel, but not the most severe judgments of the period.

As can be noted in the Premillennial Midtribulational Rapture, the order of events for the future is basically the same in the midtribulation view as in the pretribulational position.

The Prewrath Rapture of the Church

This view, though similar to the midtribulational view, is also different in some ways. The similarity is that it also sees the church in the first part of Daniel's seventieth week (Dan. 9:24-27). Neither of the views has the church

---
185 Norman B. Harrison, *The End* (Minneapolis: The Harrison Service, 1941), 118.
186 Gleason L. Archer, "Jesus is Coming Again: Midtribulation," *Christian Life* (May, 1974), 21.

raptured before that "week" of seven years begins.

The prewrath view is different from the midtribulational view in that it does not have the rapture exactly in the middle of the week. Midtribulationism places the rapture with the sounding of the seventh trumpet (Rev. 11), while prewrath rapturism places it with the sounding of the first trumpet and at the same time as the Second Coming which is before the Day of the Lord begins.

The prewrath rapture view is currently a minority view. It has been embraced and popularized by Marvin Rosenthal who was the executive director of the Friends of Israel Ministries for sixteen years. He and this organization staunchly defended the pretribulational rapture view until his change. He is no longer a part of the Friends of Israel Ministries. Rosenthal's book *The Prewrath Rapture of the Church* sets forth the view and its defense.[187]

In brief, it may be said that the view is built on the basic assumption that the seal judgments (Rev. 6) do not represent the wrath of God. The divine wrath begins with the trumpet judgments introduced by cataclysmic disturbances. Also, the view places the church within the Olivet Discourse as given by Jesus in Matthew 24 and 25.

Rosenthal does have the entire church involved in the rapture. The rapture takes place eighteen months before the seven-year Tribulation comes to an end. The Second Coming is initiated by the rapture which brings God's wrath on earth dwellers. This will all culminate at the Battle of Armageddon and will be followed by the millennial reign of Christ.

The prewrath rapture view is different from the normal premillennial view in that it does not consistently distinguish between God's program with Israel and His program with the church. In addition to this difference, this view also has the church in Israel's seventieth week and does not hold to the doctrine of imminency.

---

187 Marvin Rosenthal, *The Prewrath Rapture of the Church* (Nashville: Thomas Nelson, 1990).

Only spiritual believers to be raptured before the Tribulation begins

The major difference between this view and the pretribulational view is the number of believers who will be raptured when Christ returns. Partial rapturism is the name of this interpretation.

A contemporary exponent of the view presented three purposes for the future Tribulation. It is to be a time of trouble for Israel and a means of destroying the wicked.

> Finally, we would note that the purpose of the tribulation is also to be the testing of lukewarm shallow Laodicean Christians who will be left behind at the coming of Christ. No doubt multitudes who expected to be raptured will be disappointed because like the foolish virgins, they were not watchful. Tribulation is then for the purpose of trying the faith of these who profess to be Christians but who really never repented or are living in disobedience to the will of God.[188]

According to partial rapturism, only those Christians who are ready for the Lord are raptured when He comes. One is made ready for that great event by living a spiritual life and being watchful for Christ's return. Believers reveal their readiness by looking for the Lord while those who are not living spiritual lives will not be prepared and raptured along with the spiritual Christians. They will be left to go through at least some of the Tribulation so that they will be made ready to meet their Lord.

The Premillennial Pretribulation Partial Rapture View holds that the order of future events in this position is the same as that of the pretribulation order given earlier except that some Christians remain to go into the Tribulation for purposes of cleansing.

---

188 Ray Brubaker, "The Purpose of the Tribulation," *Radar News* (December, 1968), 6.

Amillennialism

The prefix "*a-*" means "no." Amillennialism is the view that does not hold to a future literal reign of Christ on earth for a thousand years in fulfillment of the Old Testament promises of God.

One of its advocates, J. G. Voss, has defined it this way:

> Amillennialism is that view of the last things which holds the Bible does not predict a "millennium" or period of world-wide peace and righteousness on this earth before the end of the world. Amillennialism teaches that there will be a parallel in contemporaneous development of good and evil–God's Kingdom and Satan's kingdom–in this world which will continue until the second coming of Christ. At the second coming of Christ, the resurrection and judgment will take place, followed by the eternal order of things–the absolute, perfect kingdom of God, in which there will be no sin, suffering, nor death.[189]

Jay Adams, who embraces the amillennial interpretation, calls the term amillennialism an unhappy one. He does not believe it really describes the position accurately:

> *Amillennialism* is not only a misnomer because it is negative, but the distinction which it makes is a false one. No amillennialist denies that the Bible teaches a millennium. But the word *amillennialism* means no millennium. The issue is not whether Revelation 20 teaches a millennium. All amillennialists believe it does... The true difference between amillennialism and the other systems involves two things: 1. The nature of the millennium. 2. The chronological position of the millennium in the economy of God. The word *amillennialism* fails to draw either of these distinctions. Instead it expresses the belief which no conservative holds–that there is no millennium. The term cannot be defended and certainly should be

---

[189] J. G. Voss, *Blue Banner Faith and Life* (January–March, 1951) cited from Loraine Boettner, *The Millennium* (Nutley, NJ: The Presbyterian and Reformed Publishing Co., 1964), 109.

abandoned. Amillennialists simply are not amillennialists.[190]

A new term is suggested by Adams to refer to the position that he embraces and that has been known historically as amillennialism:

> Accurately speaking the biblical system may be distinguished from the other systems as *realized millennialism*. Whereas both pre and postmillennialists look forward to a future unrealized millennium, realized millennialists contend that the millennium is a present reality. This chronological difference necessarily involves the *nature* of the period. If the millennium is a present reality, it is most certainly of the non-utopian type. Both of the other systems maintain that the millennium is future exactly *because* they cannot conceive of its nature as identical with the recent church age. Both wrongly look for an earthly utopia apart from that fiery purging which alone will bring what the Bible calls "the new earth." They anticipate a golden age prior to the judgment of all men. Adherents to *realized* millennialism, on the other hand, maintain that such a belief confounds the millennium with the eternal state described in the last two chapters of Revelation; 2 Peter 3:12-14; Isaiah 65:17, and other prophecies. While *realized* millennialists believe there is a future golden age, they teach that it follows the millennial period. It will not come until the old earth has "fled away" (Rev. 20:11).[191]

Perhaps the term "realized millennialism" is a better description of the position traditionally known as amillennialism, but be that as it may, the fact still remains that this interpretation does not allow for a future earthly kingdom with Christ ruling from David's throne in Jerusalem. In that way, it is distinct from premillennialism and postmillennialism.

All amillennialists reject dispensationalism. They believe it is a rather recent human invention foisted upon the Scriptures. In place of dispensational

---

190 Jay Adams, *The Time Is at Hand* (Nutley, NJ: The Presbyterian and Reformed Publishing Co., 1966), 8.
191 Ibid., 9.

theology, amillennialists, and postmillennialists for that matter, have traditionally substituted what is known as covenant theology.[192] "It represents the whole of Scripture as being covered by two covenants: (1) the covenant of works; (2) the covenant of grace."[193]

The covenant of works was an agreement between God and Adam where God promised life for obedience or death for disobedience. Adam and mankind in him failed. In order to save man from the penalty of his disobedience, the covenant of grace became operative. This is the agreement between the offended God and the offending elect sinner in which God promises salvation through Christ. A covenant of redemption, or the agreement in eternity past between the Father, Son, and Holy Spirit as to each one's part in the redemptive plan of God, is also usually included in the system. See the Theological Covenants for the relation of these to each other.

The covenants in covenant theology–redemption, works, grace–must not be confused with the covenants such as the Abrahamic and Davidic stressed by dispensationalists. In covenant theology, these biblical covenants are subservient to the covenant of grace. Dispensationalism, on the other hand, places primary emphasis upon the biblical covenants. In other words, covenant theology and dispensationalism are built upon entirely different foundations. The former understands the Bible on the basis of the covenant of grace and the latter, to be discussed later, interprets it more from the perspective of the Abrahamic, Davidic, Palestinian, and New covenants. See the Four Biblical Covenants for their relation to each other.

Amillennialism is not without division in its ranks. The division comes over the exact way to interpret Scripture verses that seem to describe

---

[192] For a presentation and defense of covenant theology from the perspective of an advocate, see L. Berkhof, *Systematic Theology* (Grand Rapids: Wm. B. Eerdmans, 1968), 262-304. For a critique of covenant theology from the perspective of a dispensational opponent, see Charles Ryrie, *Dispensationalism Today* (Chicago: Moody Press, 1965), 177-191.

[193] George N. M. Collins, "Covenant Theology," *Baker's Dictionary of Theology* (Grand Rapids: Baker Book House, 1960), 144.

a millennium. Some follow Augustine (354-430 AD) and see the millennium as being fulfilled now on earth.

Others, following B. B. Warfield's lead, believe the promises of a millennium are being fulfilled in heaven now. This is the more contemporary view.

Both groups agree that Christ will come again literally and bodily. When He comes a second time, He will not institute a kingdom on earth but instead will usher in the eternal state.

Regardless of whether the church is viewed as the kingdom on earth or whether the kingdom promises are being fulfilled in heaven now, the future order of events is the same in amillennialism. Either way, there is no future nation of Israel. God's promises to His people were conditional, and since the conditions were not met, they have been abrogated or, according to some amillennialists, transferred and are now being fulfilled by the church.

The future order of events embraced by most evangelical amillennialists is:

1. Worsening conditions in the world before the Second Coming
2. The Second Coming of Christ accompanied by the general resurrection and general judgment followed by
3. Eternity

Conclusive evidence for widespread amillennialism in the first two centuries of the Christian church seems to be lacking. With the rise of the allegorical interpretation of Scripture in the third century, amillennialism came into existence and flourished.

Augustine seems to be the first theologian of any stature to embrace the amillennial system of theology. He argued that the church was the kingdom on earth. The hermeneutic he employed was the allegorical and nonliteral method of interpretation applied to prophecy. He systematized and applied to prophecy the hermeneutical (interpretational) method supplied by Origen before him. The allegorical or spiritualizing method of interpretation is the method that uses the normal or literal method as a vehicle to get to a deeper, more profound meaning, after which the literal method and meaning are discarded.

Evangelicals, however, who embrace the amillennial view of things to come employ a less-than-literal method of interpretation only in certain unfulfilled prophecies. More will be said about the interpretation of Scripture in the next section because nothing is more basic to the understanding of prophecy.

The Roman Catholic Church fully embraced the Augustinian variety of amillennialism from the very beginning. The Protestant Reformers did the same. Their chief interest, however, was not with prophecy and future, final events. Salvation by faith alone and the authority of the Bible alone were the primary concerns of the Reformers and they seldom or never discussed eschatology.

Amillennialism continued to flourish until the time of Daniel Whitby (1638–1726) and the rise of postmillennialism. For some time, the postmillennial view prevailed and amillennialism was in abeyance. When World War II shattered postmillennialism's optimistic outlook, amillennialism came back into prominence again, but in a slightly different version.

The Augustinian tradition that said the church was the kingdom on earth was rejected. In its place came the view that the millennium is distinct from the church after all. Christ's kingdom was said to be heavenly, not earthly. The kingdom promises in the Bible were said to be fulfilled in the state of blessedness of the saints in heaven and Christ's position at the right hand of the Father. In other words, Christ's present position was seen as the fulfillment of the kingdom promises in the Old Testament. This is the most common variety of amillennialism held by evangelicals today.

Postmillennialism

According to this system, Christ will return after society has been Christianized by the church. In this view, the church is not the kingdom, but it will, through the spread of the gospel, build it. The prefix *"post-"* before millennial means that Christ will come *after* a kingdom has been established. The one thousand years of Revelation 20, or the millennium, are not taken literally.

The Baptist theologian Augustus Hopkins Strong subscribed to postmillennialism and describes it this way: "Scripture foretells a period called in the language of prophecy 'a thousand years' when Satan shall be restrained and the saints shall reign with Christ on the earth. The comparison of the passages bearing on this subject leads us to the conclusion that this millennial blessedness and dominion is prior to the second advent."[194]

Loraine Boettner, a more contemporary postmillennial theologian, defines the system in these words:

> Postmillennialism is that view of last things which holds that the kingdom of God is now being extended in the world through the preaching of the gospel and the saving work of the Holy Spirit, that the world eventually will be Christianized, and that the return of Christ will occur at the close of a long period of righteousness and peace commonly called *the millennium*... It should be added that on postmillennial principles the second coming of Christ will be followed immediately by the general resurrection, the general judgment, and the introduction of heaven and hell in their fullness.[195]

Actually, evangelical postmillennialism differs from evangelical amillennialism primarily in its belief in the final triumph of good over evil before

---

[194] Augustus Hopkins Strong, *Systematic Theology* (Philadelphia: American Baptist Publication Society, 1907), III, 1010-1011.

[195] Loraine Boettner, *The Millennium* (Philadelphia: Presbyterian & Reformed Publishing Co., 1964), 4, 14.

Christ returns. Some postmillennialists believe the entire church or interadvent age is the millennium. Others believe the Christianizing of society will come gradually and be fully realized at a time in the remote future but before the return of Christ. For the postmillennialists, Christ's coming closes this age and is followed by the eternal state. As we have seen, this is also believed by amillennialists.

Rise and development

There were variations in the mid-seventeenth century as a result of the reaction against humanism and liberal theology, but until the World Wars, postmillennialism was a most important and influential millennial view. The near demise of postmillennialism came with the collapse of utopian dreams in the two World Wars. Today, it is a growing minority view among evangelicals. Another factor in its decline is that postmillennialism found it almost impossible to stem the tide toward liberal theology. The nonliteral method of prophetic interpretation that both postmillennialism and amillennialism rest on leaves the door wide open, hermeneutically at least, for the same kind of interpretation to be applied to other biblical matters, such as the deity of Christ and the authority of the Bible as well.

Differences among postmillennialists

Evangelical postmillennialism as defined above needs to be distinguished from the liberal theological view that teaches that a kingdom of God, or utopia, would be created on earth through human achievement and betterment.

A new kind of postmillennialism, different from both the earlier liberal and evangelical varieties, is gaining popularity and respect today. The new postmillennialism differs drastically from the old liberal utopian belief in the future through the successful advances of science and technology and coupled with belief in the universal fatherhood of God and brotherhood of man.

The current expression of postmillennialism is not exactly like the older variety expressed by evangelicals such as Augustus Hopkins Strong and Loraine Boettner. The older view held a special optimism for the final stage of earth's history and argued for a future utopian age brought about by the universal spread and acceptance of the gospel. By contrast, contemporary postmillennialism[196] believes the kingdom already exists in fulfillment of Old Testament prophecies and is coexisting with the present age rather than the special period at the close of the church age.

The new postmillennialism is aligned closely with theonomy reconstructionism.[197]

The word comes from two Greek words—*theos* (God) and *uomos* (law). "The word is now being used to designate a new idea gaining ground in some circles, particularly those emphasizing Reformed doctrine that the governments of the world today should be guided in their judicial decision by all the legislation of the Old Testament and in particular, should assess the Old Testament penalties for any infraction of those laws, whether civil or religious."[198]

In his book *Theonomy in Christian Ethics* Greg Bahnsen argues at great length, appealing especially to Matthew 5:17-18, that the Mosaic law constitutes a continuing norm for all mankind. The duty of the civil magistrate is

---

196 Principal sources of information for this are The Chalcedon Foundation and *The Journal of Christian Reconstruction*. Some significant publications promoting it are Greg L. Bahnsen, *Theonomy in Christian Ethics*; Rousas J. Rushdoony, *The Institutes of Biblical Law* (Phillipsburg, NJ: Presbyterian and Reformed Publishing Co., 1988); and *God's Plan for Victory* (Fairfax, VA: Thoburn Press, 1977).

197 See this author's articles in *Bibliotheca Sacra* (January–March 1986, April–June 1986 and July–September 1986) on "Theonomy and Dispensationalism." Also see Thomas D. Ice, "An Evaluation of Theonomic Neopostmillennialism" in *Bibliotheca Sacra* (July–September 1988). An outstanding exception is John Jefferson Davis' work—*Christ's Victorious Kingdom—Postmillennialism Reconsidered* (Baker Book House, 1986). Davis is postmillennial but he does not embrace the theonomy-reconstructionist viewpoint.

198 R. Laird Harris, "Theonomy in Christian Ethics" *Covenant Seminary Review* 5 (f979), 1.

to enforce it–both its precepts and its penalties. "*Every* single stroke of the law must be seen by the Christian as applicable to *this* very age between the advents of Christ."[199] Bahnsen makes no apology in insisting that civil authorities today should be pressured by the church to carry out the death penalty for such things as idolatry, witchcraft, murder, adultery, incorrigibility in children, apostasy, sorcery, false pretensions to prophecy, blasphemy, homosexuality, and Sabbath breaking.[200]

Though the new postmillennialism-theonomy package has roots in reformed and amillennial theology, it is being criticized by some in that tradition. Premillennialism rejects it as well.

Summary of the Three Eschatologies

We have set forth the three millennial views and their major variations as held by evangelicals. These were presented in broad outline. The most basic issue that divides the views is the method of hermeneutics or interpretation used when seeking to understand prophecy. The picture is confusing with three different millennial viewpoints and what makes it even more difficult and complex are the variations within each of the millennial views.

Matters can be simplified if we keep some basics in mind. First, with regard to the millennium, some evangelicals believe the kingdom promises in the Bible have been fulfilled and when Christ returns, the eternal state will begin. Others believe Christ will come again after society has been Christianized. Still others believe the kingdom promises have not been fulfilled but will be when Christ returns and establishes the one-thousand-year kingdom on earth before the eternal state begins. In this latter view, the church is in no sense the recipient of promises given to Israel.

---

199 Greg Bahnsen, *Theonomy in Christian Ethics* (Phillipsburg, NJ: Presbyterian and Reformed Publishing Co., 1977), 82.
200 Ibid., 427, 439, 445, 466ff.

Second, regarding the future seven-year Tribulation, some evangelicals do not believe there is a literal future seven-year Tribulation at all. For them the Tribulation is now. Among those who do believe in such a time, some believe the church will be protected while it goes through the Tribulation. Others believe the entire church will be raptured before any part of the Tribulation begins, while some believe that only spiritual believers will be raptured before the Tribulation starts. Still others hold that the church will experience only the first half of the coming Tribulation.

The question of why these differences over unfulfilled prophecy exist among evangelicals will now be explored. It is no secret that the differences are real, but the reasons they exist are not necessarily widely known.

Why the Variant Views of Things to Come?

Interpreting Scripture

Though they all embrace the Bible's inspiration and authority, evangelicals who defend a particular view of events to come do not all understand Scripture in the same way. They understand it differently because they use different methods of interpreting some of the unfulfilled prophecies of Scripture. This is the most basic reason for the differences between *pre-*, *a-*, and *post*millennialism. It also has much to do with the differences over the relation of the church to the coming Great Tribulation.

The science and art of biblical interpretation is called "hermeneutics," and it is easy to see that a method of interpretation, a system of hermeneutics, is most important to the understanding of God's Word.[201] Without it, the Bible is a closed book, which is true of all literature. Whenever we read anything, we unconsciously follow certain rules of interpretation so that we may understand the material. Without even thinking about it, the reader often asks the question, "What does this mean?" while reading a piece of literature.

---

[201] Bernard Ramm, *Protestant Biblical Interpretation* (Boston: W. A. Wilde Co., 1950), 1.

The interpretation of Scripture is one of several crucial matters related to the total doctrine of Scripture. A brief review of these related matters will help us put things in focus before we discuss the bearing that interpretation has on the differences over things to come.

The meaning of the interpretation of Scripture is related to the revelation, inspiration, authority, and canonicity of the same Scriptures.

Revelation, in reference to Scripture, means the act of God whereby He made Himself and His will known to man. God gave the revelation; man received it. God revealed His Word to many human penmen over about 1500 years. The earliest and simplest revelation is just as true, just as inspired, as the later revelation. It is the amount of information about Himself and about all He has made known which has progressed. Therefore, in order to know what God has said about Himself, or any subject, the whole needs to be examined. The later revelation never changes or corrects the earlier recipients or locations, for example, from Israel to the church or from earth to heaven.

Inspiration has to do with the recording of the revelation. When we speak of the inspiration of the Bible as Paul did in 2 Timothy 3:16-17, we are referring to God's work of guiding and controlling the human writers of Scripture in the very choice of the words used in the original manuscripts. The result of this divine work upon the fallible, human writer was the recording of God's message without error or omission in all its parts.

Because the revelation recorded in the Bible without error came from God, it is of course divinely authoritative. It bears the very *authority* of the One who gave it.

The God who gave His Word also preserved it for us. From the very time the revelation was given and recorded, it was accepted by God's people as His Word. We call the human recognition of God's Word by His people the *canonization* of Scripture.

My purpose in presenting this brief background in the doctrine of Scripture has been to distinguish the science of biblical interpretation from the other facets of the doctrine and to show its relation to them. Historically, evangelicals have had little difference over the revelation, inspiration, authority, and canonicity of Scripture,[202] but they have not ever agreed on a method of interpretation to be followed uniformly throughout the Bible. Nor is there agreement on how the doctrine of progressive revelation affects one's hermeneutics. There is also considerable difference among evangelicals over the relation of the Old Testament to the New and how the use of the Old in the New relates to the question of biblical interpretation.[203]

Is there a single method of interpretation to be used throughout Scripture, or do some parts of the Bible require a different method? How does the way the New Testament uses the Old affect one's eschatology, or view of things to come? Such issues greatly divide evangelicals and the result is much fighting.

Importance of the Issue

When it comes to the understanding of prophecy or events to come, the most important questions are, How is it to be interpreted? What does this prophetic Scripture mean? Representative spokesmen of each of the various evangelical views of things to come candidly admit that this is indeed the important issue. All must agree–although some are more reluctant to admit it than others–that they disagree about events to come because they interpret the prophecies differently.

Here are a few admissions which illustrate my point. Oswald T. Allis put the issue bluntly. His book *Prophecy and the Church* was intended to show what he felt was error in premillennial dispensationalism and to defend his own view of amillennialism. He said: "Old Testament prophecies if literally

---

[202] For a discussion of differences some evangelicals want to make between inspiration and inerrancy, see Harold Lindsell's *The Battle for the Bible* (Grand Rapids: The Zondervan Corporation, 1976) and his *The Bible in the Balance* (Grand Rapids: The Zondervan Corporation, 1979). Also see *Inerrancy* edited by Norman L. Geisler (Zondervan, 1979).

[203] I recommend the following for study in this area. Roy B. Zuck, *Basic Bible Interpretation* (Wheaton, IL: Victor Booksk, 1991) and Elliott Johnson, *Expository Hermeneutics: An Introduction* (Grand Rapids: Zondervan, 1990).

interpreted cannot be regarded as having been yet fulfilled or as being capable of fulfillment in the present age. It is consequently assumed by premillennialists that they will be so fulfilled during the Millennium when Satan will be bound and the saints will reign with Christ."[204]

A more contemporary amillennial writer reflected the same view in these words:

> One very basic conflict between different millennial groups is their hermeneutics–the manner in which they interpret the Bible. In fact, this difference is what divides equally conservative men into different camps with reference to the Millennium. This fact is acknowledged frequently by all millennial schools of thought. Each of the millennial views has been held by conservative, scholarly men who were devoted to the correct interpretation of the Bible and all have looked on the Scriptures as being divinely inspired and as the Christian's only rule of faith and life.[205]

In Jay Adams' book, *The Time Is at Hand*, he also revealed the importance of the interpretation of unfulfilled prophecy:

> In this transition from pre to posttribulationalism, some have gone further and are beginning to test the foundations of premillennialism itself in the process, doubts about fundamental presuppositions have arisen. Having rejected the unbiblical principle of exclusively literal interpretation of Old Testament prophecy, many no longer look upon the so-called "nation Israel" as God's chosen people. They cannot agree to a "Jewish millennium" fully equipped with rebuilt Temple and restored sacrificial system. They find no indication of a utopian-type millennium anywhere upon the pages of the New Testament.[206]

---

204 Oswald T. Allis, *Prophecy and the Church* (Philadelphia: Presbyterian and Reformed Publishing Co., 1945), 238.
205 William E. Cox, *Amillennialism Today* (Philadelphia: Presbyterian & Reformed Pub. Co., 1966), 13.
206 Jay Adams, *The Time Is at Hand* (Nutley, NJ: Presbyterian and Reformed Publishing Co., 1966), 13.

Loraine Boettner, evangelical postmillennial theologian, expressed his awareness of the crucial importance of one's method of interpretation. He agrees the basic reason for different views of things to come has to do with principles of biblical interpretation:

> That believing Christians through the ages using the same Bible and acknowledging it to be authoritative, have arrived at quite different conclusions appears to be due to different methods of interpretation. Premillennialists place strong emphasis on literal interpretation and pride themselves on taking Scripture just as it is written. Post and amillennialists, on the other hand, mindful of the fact that much of both the Old and New Testament unquestionably is given in figurative or symbolic language have no objection on principle against figurative interpretation and readily accept that if the evidence indicates that it is preferable.[207]

But amillennialists and postmillennialists are not alone in acknowledging the importance of biblical interpretation for the understanding of things to come; premillennialists also agree wholeheartedly. Their writings on the future are filled with emphatic statements on this point.

The Theocratic Kingdom of Our Lord Jesus the Christ is a classic three-volume set in defense of premillennialism. In it, George N. H. Peters states his view of the importance of a proper method of interpretation:

> The literal, grammatical interpretation of the Scriptures must (connected with the figurative topical [sic] or rhetorical) be absorbed in order to attain a correct understanding of this kingdom. Its import is of such weight and the consequences of its adoption of such moment, the tendency it possesses of leading to the truth and the vindicating Scriptures of such value that we cannot pass it by without some explanations and reflections.[208]

---

[207] Loraine Boettner, *The Millennium* (Philadelphia: Presbyterian & Reformed Publishing. Co., 1964), 82.

[208] George N. H. Peters, *The Theocratic Kingdom of Our Lord Jesus the Christ* (Grand Rapids: Kregel Publications, 1957), 47.

A contemporary spokesman for premillennialism voiced the same understanding of the importance of the interpretation of prophecy. "There is a growing realization in the theological world that the crux of the Millennial issue is the question of method of interpreting Scripture. Premillenarians follow the so-called 'grammatical-historical' literal interpretation while amilleniarians use a spiritualizing method."[209]

It is an accepted fact; nobody debates the issue. The method of interpretation one uses is crucial to the understanding of what is read. This is no less true of prophetic Scripture than of any other literature.

Methods of interpretation

Two methods of interpreting the Bible are prominent today. Other methods have been suggested in the history of the church,[210] but the literal, or normal, and the spiritualizing, or allegorical method, have been and still are the two most prominent and important methods.

The Literal or Normal Method

Premillennial Christians usually pride themselves in their belief in the literal interpretation of all Scripture. They are frequently described by friends and foes as "literalists." They are sometimes called "wooden literalists," which implies they do not allow for types and symbols in their understanding of Scripture. That criticism does not seem to square, however, with the fact that premillennial writers have contributed much to the understanding of these areas of biblical study.

By a literal interpretation of Scripture, premillennialists mean a straight interpretation. To them, the Bible is to be interpreted just like all other literature. "The literal interpretation as applied to any document is that view which

---

209 John F. Walvoord, *The Millennial Kingdom* (Findlay, OH: Dunham Publishing Co., 1959), 59.
210 See Milton S. Terry, *Biblical Hermeneutics* (Grand Rapids: Zondervan Publishing House, 1959), 163-74 for other methods.

adopts as the sense of a sentence, the meaning of that sentence in usual, or normal conversation or writing."[211] "To interpret literally means nothing more or less than to interpret in terms of normal usual designation."[212]

Premillennialists are agreed in accepting the above as an accurate definition and description of their method of interpreting the whole Bible.

The literal method of interpreting Scripture is also called the grammatical-historical method. This designation emphasizes that the meaning of Scripture is determined both by the grammatical and the historical considerations.

Premillennialists, especially dispensational premillennialists, have not failed to support their use of the literal, normal, or grammatical-historical interpretation of Scripture. Many reasons are often given by them in defense of their position,[213] but there seem to be three crucial reasons:

> Philosophically, the purpose of language itself seems to require literal interpretation. Language was given by God for the purpose of being able to communicate with man…If God be the originator of language and if the chief purpose of originating it was to convey His message to man, then it must follow that He, being all wise and all loving, originated sufficient language to convey all that was in His heart to tell men… The second reason why dispensationalists believe in the literal principle is a Biblical one. It is simply this: The prophecies of the Old Testament concerning the first coming of Christ–His birth, His rearing, His ministry, His death, resurrection–were *all* fulfilled literally. There is no nonliteral fulfillment of these prophecies in the New Testament… A third reason is a logical one. If one does not use the plain, normal, or literal method of interpretation, all objectivity is lost. What check would there be in the variety of interpreta-

---

211 Bernard Ramm, *Protestant Biblical Interpretation* (Boston: W. A. Wilde, Co., 1950), 53.
212 Ibid., 64.
213 Examples of these may be found in J. Dwight Pentecost, *Things to Come* (Findlay, OH: Dunham Publishing Co., 1958), 9-15; and Paul Lee Tan, *The Interpretation of Prophecy* (Winona Lake, IN: B. M. H. Books, Inc., 1974), 29-39.

tions which man's imagination could produce if there was not an objective standard which the literal principle provides?[214]

Premillennialists insist the New Testament's use of the Old Testament substantiates the literal method. In support of this, reference is often made to the many Old Testament prophecies that were fulfilled literally in the New Testament. Why, premillennialists argue, should we expect unfulfilled prophecies to be fulfilled any differently?

Appeal is also made to Jesus' method of interpreting the Old Testament. It seems clear from His example that He used a normal, literal, historical-grammatical method. His interpretation of Scripture was always in harmony with the grammatical and historical meaning. Jesus frequently interpreted one passage of Scripture by appealing to another passage to add further clarification to the meaning (i.e., Matt. 19:3-8 and Deut. 24:1; cf. Matt. 12:1-7 and Hosea 6:6).

The Spiritualizing or Allegorizing Method

According to proponents of this view, it is simply impossible to apply the literal method of interpretation to all of Scripture. Amillennialists and postmillennialists insist on this and, especially in prophetic portions, employ a less than literal method at times.

Oswald T. Allis, for example, believes a thoroughly literal interpretation of Scripture is impossible.[215] He gives three reasons for his belief:

> (1) The language of the Bible often contains figures of speech. This is especially true of its poetry… (2) The great theme of the Bible is God and His redemptive dealing with mankind. God is a spirit; the most precious teachings of the Bible are spiritual and these spiritual and heavenly realities are often set forth under the form of earthly objects and human relationships… We

---

214 Charles C. Ryrie, *Dispensationalism Today* (Chicago: Moody Press, 1965), 87-88.
215 Allis, op. cit., 17.

should remember the saying of the apostle that spiritual things are "spiritually discerned"... (3) The fact that the Old Testament is both preliminary and preparatory to the New Testament is too obvious to require proof.[216]

Premillennialists have not failed to respond to these objections.[217] No matter which view one takes, however, it must be admitted that not until the third century A.D. and the Alexandrian school of theology was there any serious opposition to the literal method. Teachers in this school–Clement of Alexandria and Origin–used a method of interpretation that made all Scripture an allegory. In the fifth century, Augustine led a rejection of this movement. He did not completely reject the allegorical method, but taught that only prophecy needs to be allegorized or spiritualized. Much of biblical truth was salvaged by Augustine's efforts. Yet he and many of his followers, including the great Reformers, continued to use the allegorical method in their interpretation of some unfulfilled prophecy.

Luther, Calvin, and others of the Reformers stressed the need for the literal sense of Scripture and a grammatical-historical approach. They also stressed the literal meanings in arriving at their view of salvation by faith alone and the inspiration and sole authority of the Bible. But they did not apply those principles to their interpretation of *all* unfulfilled prophecy.

In addition, those who reject the spiritualizing approach argue further that the spiritualizing, or allegorizing, method of biblical interpretation did not arise out of a desire to understand Scripture. Instead, it owes its birth to heathen philosophy. "The allegorical system that arose among the pagan Greeks was copied by the Alexandrian Jews and was next adopted by the Christian church, and dominated the church to the Reformation."[218] The allegorical or spiritualizing method of interpretation may be defined as "the

---

216 Ibid., 17-18.
217 Pentecost, op. cit., 14-15.
218 Ramm, op. cit., 23.

method of interpreting the literary text that regards the literal sense as the vehicle for a secondary, more spiritual and more profound sense."[219]

Premillennialists believe such a method for seeking to understand the meaning of any part of Scripture has serious dangers. They question such a method. What is the basic authority in interpretation–the Scriptures or the mind of the interpreter? They do not feel that the allegorical method really involves interpretation of Scripture. How can the conclusions of the interpreter who uses this method be tested?

Do not all evangelical expositors of the Bible use the literal, historical-grammatical method? Could anybody possibly be evangelical if he did not apply this method to the biblical teaching about Christ, salvation, and sin? These are questions literalists ask of allegoricalists. They believe evangelicalism results only by following the literal method. Premillennialists are convinced that the system of hermeneutics they use is a tremendous safeguard against liberal theology.

All evangelicals do use the literal method for their understanding of most of the Bible, but some, namely those of amillennial and postmillennial persuasion, think it best to use a less-than-literal hermeneutic, often with unfulfilled prophecy. It is at this point that the evangelical world is divided over things to come and this is what puts prophecy in the middle of the debate. Premillennialists cannot understand why their Christian brothers and sisters insist on using a different method of interpretation with some unfulfilled prophecy but not with all of it. They wonder, "On what grounds is the less-than-literal approach to be restricted to only some themes of unfulfilled prophecy?"

To summarize the differences between the two schools of thought, this may be said: all evangelicals use the literal method in their interpretation of the Bible.

Some evangelicals believe this same method is to be used with *all* Scripture; these are the premillennialists. Other evangelicals believe that while the literal method is to be used of Scripture in general, it is not necessarily to

---

219 Ibid., 21.

be used with all unfulfilled prophetic portions. Some of the biblical prophecies (i.e., those concerning the first advent of Christ) are to be understood literally and in fact were fulfilled literally,[220] but many prophecies related to the future coming again of Christ must be understood in a less-than-literal way.

Are You Ready for Christ's Return?

There is no question about it, the Bible predicts a number of things about mankind's last days on earth. Christians may not agree on how to interpret these prophecies, but there can be no doubt that the Bible records them.

As we have seen in this survey of last days, the Bible is more specific and clear about some future events than it is about others. Those who believe the Bible cannot deny that Jesus promised He would come to earth again, that the dead would be raised and judged, and that there is a heaven to gain and a hell to shun. The question that many are asking is this: How shall we then live? Does what the Bible says about these major end-time events make any difference to us? So what?

The Bible anticipates both a one-world church and a one-world government in the last days. There are certainly signs and forerunners of both in the news today. According to the Bible, both will be in existence before Christ returns and rights all wrongs and brings perfect peace and justice to the world.

A Coming One-World Church

Religionists began the drive to build a world church long ago. The history, theology, and goals of such organizations as the Federal Council of Christian Churches (1908), the National Council of Churches (1950), the World Council of Churches (1948), and the Consultation on Church Union (1960) bear abundant testimony to this fact.[221]

---

220 See Meno J. Brunk, *Fulfilled Prophecies* (Krockette, KY: Rod & Staff Publications, Inc., 1971).
221 See my *Church Union–A Layman's Guide* (Des Plaines, IL: Regular Baptist Press, 1971) for a fuller explanation of the coming one-world church and the coming world government.

The modern ecumenical movement has its roots in liberal theology with its denial of the essentials of the historic orthodox Christian faith. Liberal theology, to take one more step backward, was born in and grew out of the man-centered philosophies of the Renaissance (1453–1690) and periods which followed.

What is the goal of the contemporary liberal ecumenical movement among churches? Many in the movement have denied any desire to build a world church, a one-world religion. Despite all the past and present protestations, the clear goal seems to be the creation of one church for one world. Everything else must take second place to the dream of ecumenists—bringing all religions of the world under one organizational structure, one religious umbrella. This does seem to be preparing the way for what is described in Revelation 17.

The initial goal to build a world church remains intact today. A number of religious leaders from around the world gathered in San Francisco, all seeking to sign a charter of the United Religions. Episcopal Bishop William Swing was quoted in the *San Francisco Chronicle* on June 20, 1996, as saying: "I am convinced that the time is ripe for a global initiative to call the world's religions together… The whole world must get on board" to make this a reality, he said so long ago.

Konrad Raiser, the general secretary of the World Council of Churches, called for a council to settle doctrinal differences beginning in the year 2000. This universal council would have as its goal the resolving of the issues dividing the church.[222]

The United Religions Initiative (URI) is another ecumenical bid for a one-world church. This 800-member body started in 2000 and is a world-peace initiative of various religious organizations.[223]

---

222 Ecumenical News International
223 https://en.wikipedia.org/wiki/United_Religions_Initiative. Internet; accessed June 1, 2018.

A Coming One-World Government

Paralleling the goal of building a world church and closely associated with it has been the dream of a world government. This has always been true. Some years ago, a staff member of the Foundation for Economic Education put it this way:

> Influential churchmen and theologians operating through official church agencies and organizations have strained to the task of molding the Protestant churches into a politically potent Great Church for the Great Society. Their joint efforts have not been for the attainment of Christian unity for its own sake; it has been unity–for the sake–of power.[224]

The idea of a one-world government is heralded as the only way to "save" the world. Our planet, we are told, has no hope without global participation. As Nobel Prize winning economist Jan Tinbregen put it: "Mankind's problems can no longer be solved by national governments. What is needed is a world government. This can best be achieved by strengthening the United Nations system."

There are other harbingers of a future one-world government. An example of this is former Soviet dictator Mikhail Gorbachev's book, *The Search for a New Beginning: Developing a New Civilization*, which is a blueprint for such a government and was discussed at the five-day meeting in San Francisco with world and political leaders some years ago.

There are many efforts toward a one-world government, all of which seem clearly to be preparations for what is described in Revelation 18.

How Should We Respond?

We cannot be sure of the development nor the nature of the coming one-world church or one-world government. We can be sure though, that Jesus is coming again. The human writers of the New Testament and the early

---

[224] Kenneth W. Ingersalson, compiler, *Your Church–Their Target* (Arlington, VA: Better Books Publisher, 1966)

Christians believed He could come in their lifetimes. We should believe that too. If we really do believe it, our way of living will be affected.

I have on my desk a favorite small motto which reads, "Perhaps Today." This is a reminder that Jesus could come to take His own to be with Him at any time. Because this is true, each of us who claims Jesus as our substitute for sin should be ready to appear before Him any moment. We need to keep short accounts with God. Unconfessed sin should not weigh us down. Broken fellowship with God and others needs to be restored. The hope we Christians have ought to be shared with others by our lives and by our lips. Indeed, God wants us to be light and salt in this dark and corrupt world.

Imagine you just got word that some people who are very important to you are coming to your house. Your friends are not sure of the exact time of their arrival, but they assured you it would be soon. This news comes to you and your family as a complete shock. It has been fifteen years since you last saw these folks. Your two youngest children have never even seen them or their children. As the time draws near, what would you do to be ready for the visit? Special cleaning–inside and out–would certainly be done. Plenty of food would be brought in–special delicacies and only the best of everything would be gathered. These are special people. You have been honored to be on their list of friends whom they want to visit. Above everything else, you want to be completely ready when they arrive.

God has sent us a letter in the Bible. He has promised that His Son would come again just as surely as He came the first time, hundreds of years after His coming had been predicted. He expects us to be ready for His coming. He has not told us exactly when He will come, but He did promise that He would come again. We are to live in an expectancy mode, anticipating, looking for Him to return at any time. It could be today! This day may, in fact, be the last day before Jesus comes again.

ANNOTATED BIBLIOGRAPHY

The following annotated bibliography has been divided into three categories–Beginner's Level, Intermediate Level, and the Advanced Level. In this way, the reader will be able to find those books which will meet his particular need. Please note that inclusion in this bibliography is not an endorsement, but rather a listing of books addressing the subject under which heading they are found.

Amillennialism

Beginner's Level
Adams, Jay. *The Time Is at Hand*. Philadelphia: Presbyterian and Reformed Publishing Co., 1974. 123 pp. Presentation of positive statement of the amillennial position as an orderly system.

Intermediate Level
Cox, William E. *Amillennialism Today*. Philadelphia: Presbyterian and Reformed Publishing Co., 1966. 143 pp. Presents the amillennial view of crucial doctrines related to eschatology

Advanced Level
Allis, O. T. *Prophecy and the Church*. Philadelphia: Presbyterian and Reformed Publishing Co., 1945. 339 pp. An examination and rejection of the dispensationalist claim that the church is a mystery. A claim that the Old Testament promises to Israel are fulfilled by the church.

Hamilton, Floyd E. *The Basis of Millennial Faith*. Grand Rapids: William B. Eerdmans Publishing Co., 1942. 160 pp. An attempt to present amillennialism as a system of belief and to show that it is orthodox.

Postmillennialism

Beginner's Level
Boettner, Loraine. *The Millennium*. Philadelphia: Presbyterian and Reformed Publishing Co., 1964. 380 pp. Postmillennialism, amillennialism, and premillennialism are presented. Author argues in favor of postmillennialism.

Intermediate Level
DeMar, Gary. *The Debate Over Christian Reconstruction*. Dominion Press, 1988. The author sets forth a defense of Christian reconstructionism and postmillennialism.

House, H. Wayne and Ice, Thomas. *Dominion Theology: Blessing or Curse?* Multnomah, 1988. This is a critique of Theonomy and contemporary postmillennialism from two dispensational premillennialists.

Kik, Jay M. *Matthew 24* and *Revelation 20*. Philadelphia: Presbyterian and Reformed Publishing Co., 1948, 1955 respectively, 97 pp. and 92 pp. respectively. In these two books the author argues for postmillennialism from these two crucial passages.

Advanced Level
Davis, John Jefferson. *Christ's Victorious Kingdom–Postmillennialism Reconsidered*. Baker, 1986. A scholarly defense of the system without embracing Theonomy and reconstructionism.

Premillennialism

Beginner's Level
Feinberg, Charles L. *Premillennialism or Amillennialism*. Wheaton, IL: Van Kampen Press, 1954. 154 pp. The systems are compared and contrasted with each other. Author argues for premillennialism.

Ryrie, Charles C. *The Basis of Premillennial Faith*. New York: Loizeaux Brothers, 1953. 160 pp. Well-outlined defense of premillennialism.

Intermediate Level
Pentecost, J. Dwight. *Things to Come*. Grand Rapids: Zondervan Publishing Co., 1958, 633 pp. Most complete presentation of premillennial, pretribulational eschatology. Presents opposing views with author's refutations.

Walvoord, John F. *The Millennial Kingdom*. Findlay, OH: Dunham Publishing Co., 1959. 373 pp. Comprehensive treatment of the millennial systems. Author builds case for premillennialism from Scripture and history.

Advanced Level
Clouse, Robert G., Ed. *The Meaning of the Millennium*. InterVarsity Press, 1977. 223 pp. Historic premillennialism, dispensational premillennialism, postmillennialism, and amillennialism are presented by advocates of these positions. Opponents then respond to each of the positions.

McClain, Alva J. *The Greatness of the Kingdom* (Chicago: Moody Press, 1968. 566 pp. Traces idea of mediatorial kingdom through the Bible. Places strong emphasis upon premillennialism. A classic.

Pentecost, J. Dwight. *Thy Kingdom Come*. Wheaton, IL: Victor Books, 1990, 360 pp. Traces God's rule from eternity past to eternity future. The author demonstrates that God's kingdom program is the outworking of His unconditional covenants.

Peters, George, N. H. *The Theocratic Kingdom*, 3 vols. Grand Rapids: Kregel, 2180 pp.

Midtribulationism

Beginner's Level
Archer, Gleason L. "Jesus Is Coming Again," *Christian Life*, May 1974, p. 21f.

Rosenthal, Marvin. *The Prewrath Rapture of the Church*. Nashville: Thomas Nelson, 1990. The view presented is more closely associated with the midtribulational view than with any of the other options. The author's major contention is that the seal judgments do not represent God's wrath, and the Rapture and Second Coming are not separate events.

Intermediate Level
Harrison, Norman B. *The End*. Minneapolis: Harrison Service, 1941. 239 pp. Defense for the Rapture in the middle of Daniel's seventieth week.

Partial Rapturism

Beginner's Level
Brubaker, Ray. *The Purpose of the Great Tribulation*. St. Petersburg, FL, 1968. 8 pp. Also other pamphlets. Viewing one of the purposes of the Tribulation as a means of testing lukewarm Christians, the author argues his case for partial rapturism.

Advanced Level
Lang, G. H. *The Revelation of Jesus Christ*. London: Oliphants, 1945. 420 pp. Most complete and comprehensive presentation of the partial Rapture position available.

Posttribulationism

Beginner's Level
Ladd, George E. *The Blessed Hope*. Grand Rapids: Zondervan Publishing Co., 1956. 167 pp. Defines the blessed hope not as deliverance from the Tribulation but preservation through it. A premillennial posttribulational defense.

Intermediate Level
Rees, Alexander. *The Approaching Advent of Christ*. London: Marshall, Morgan & Scott, n.d. 328 pp. A classic posttribulational polemic.

Advanced Level
Gundry, Robert H. *The Church and the Tribulation*. Grand Rapids: Zondervan Publishing Co., 1973. 224 pp. An exegetically based defense of premillennial posttribulationism. Author seeks to build his case by showing that passages often used in defense of pretribulationalism may also be used to support posttribulationism.

Payne, Jay Barton. *The Imminent Appearing of Christ*. Grand Rapids: William B. Eerdmans Publishing Co., 1962. 191 pp. Presents a new view of imminency that the author feels is in harmony with posttribulationism.

Pretribulationism

Beginner's Level
English, E. Schuyler, *Rethinking the Rapture.* Travelers Rest, SC: Southern Bible Book House, 1954. 123 pp. Brief and concise defense of pretribulationism.

Walvoord, John F. *The Rapture Question.* Grand Rapids: S Zondervan Publishing Company, 1957. 204 pp. The various views respecting the time of the Rapture and the participants in it are presented. Author sets forth arguments used in defense of the position and concludes by giving fifty arguments for pretribulationism.

Intermediate Level
Wood, Leon J. *Is the Rapture Next?* Grand Rapids: Zondervan Publishing Company, 1956. 120 pp. A solid defense of pretribulationism. Deals with crucial issues.

Advanced Level
Showers, Renald E. *Maranatha.* Bellmawr, NJ: Friends of Israel Gospel Ministry, Inc., 1995. This work is scholarly and is a thorough defense of the pretribulational view. Stress is upon the doctrine of imminency. It is the most extensive and definitive work to date setting forth the imminent hope of Christ's return for His own and refuting the prewrath view of Marvin Rosenthal.

Ice, Thomas and Demy, Timothy, editors. *When the Trumpet Sounds.* Eugene, OR: Harvest House Publishers, 1995. A wide gamut of issues is discussed, with an emphasis on alerting the reader to the urgency of the hour and the need for preparation in view of the imminent hope.

Antidispensationalism

Beginner's Level
Cox, William E. *An Examination of Dispensationalism.* Philadelphia: Presbyterian & Reformed Publishing Co., 1963. 61 pp. Author finds problems with dispensational beliefs and with early spokesmen of the view.

Intermediate Level
Bass, Clarence B. *Backgrounds to Dispensationalism.* Grand Rapids: William B. Eerdmans Publishing Co., 1960. 184 pp. An attempted refutation of the dispensational system by appealing to its recency and by showing flaws in one of the earliest spokesmen for the system.

Kraus, C. Norman. *Dispensationalism in America*. Richmond, VA: John Knox Press, 1958. 156 pp. Deals with the rise of dispensationalism and the relation of dispensationalism to premillennialism.

Advanced Level
Bahnsen, Greg L. and Gentry, Kenneth L. Jr. *House Divided: The Break-Up of Dispensational Theology*. Tyler, TX: Institute for Christian Economics, 1989. 411 pp. Authors seek to expose and explore differences among dispensationalists in an attempt to discredit the system.

Dispensationalism

Beginner's Level
Barndollar, Walker W. *The Validity of Dispensationalism*. Des Plaines, IL: Regular Baptist Press, 1964. 47 pp. Shows the logic and biblical base for dispensationalism.

Intermediate Level
Ryrie, Charles C. *Dispensationalism*. Chicago: Moody Press, 1995.
Chafer, Lewis Sperry. *Systematic Theology*, 4 volumes. Grand Rapids: Kregel Publications, 1993.

Willis, Wesley and Master, John, editors. *Issues in Dispensationalism*. Chicago: Moody Press, 1994. Some of the ramifications of progressive dispensationalism as it affects other doctrines are described and highlighted in this volume.

Advanced Level
Poythress, Vern S. *Understanding Dispensationalists*. Grand Rapids: Zondervan, 1987. This is a friendly evaluation and critique of dispensationalism by one who does not embrace the system.

Showers, Renald E. *There Really Is a Difference! A Comparison of Covenant and Dispensational Theology*. Bellmawr, NJ: Friends of Israel Gospel Ministry, Inc., 1990. Both systems are examined and evaluated. The author builds a case for dispensational theology.

Biblical Interpretation

Beginner's Level
Tan, Paul Lee. *The Interpretation of Prophecy*. Winona Lake, IN: BMH Books, Inc., 1974. 435 pp. A detailed defense for the literal interpretation of Prophecy.

Intermediate Level
Ramm, Bernard. *Protestant Biblical Interpretation*. Boston: W. A. Wilde Company, 1950. 197 pp. A standard text on the interpretation of Scripture in general.

Advanced Level
Johnson, Elliott. *Expository Hermeneutics: An Introduction.* Grand Rapids: Zondervan, 1990. The author described this excellent work in these words: "Hermeneutics is a discipline whose importance is recognized in the process of Bible study. All believers have the opportunity and responsibility to read and interpret their Bibles and hermeneutics helps to bring normative control to that study of the text. This normative control rests in a literal system of interpretation which includes principles of grammatical, historical, literary, and theological contexts of interpretation."

Zuck, Roy B. *Basic Bible Interpretation.* Wheaton, IL: Victor Books, 1991. This is a scholarly yet reader-friendly study of how to interpret the Bible. The work is true to its title. All the bases are covered in clear, understandable language. It is a gold mine of information and helps on how to understand the Bible. The literal and normal method of interpretation is championed.

Preterism

Beginner Level
Lahaye, Tim and Hindson, Ed., Eds. *Popular Encyclopedia of Bible Prophecy*. Eugene, OR: Harvest House, 2004

Sproul, R. C. *The Last Days According to Jesus.* Grand Rapids: Baker Book House, 1998.

Intermediate Level
Gentry, Kenneth L. "A Preterist View of Revelation," *Four Views on the Book of Revelation*, ed. Marvin Pate. Grand Rapids: Zondervan, 1998.

Lahaye, Tim and Ice, Thomas, eds. *The End Times Controversy*, Eugene, OR: Harvest House, 2003.

Advanced Level
Hitchcock, Mark. "The Stake in the Heart–A.D. 95 Date of Revelation," *The End Times Controversy*, Lahaye and Ice, eds. Eugene, OR: Harvest House, 2003.

Dispensational Publishing House is striving to become the go-to source for Bible-based materials from the dispensational perspective.

Our goal is to provide high-quality doctrinal and worldview resources that make dispensational theology accessible to people at all levels of understanding.

Visit our blog regularly to read informative articles from both known and new writers.

And please let us know how we can better serve you.

Dispensational Publishing House, Inc.
PO Box 3181
Taos, NM 87571

Call us toll free 844-321-4202

www.DispensationalPublishing.com

www.ingramcontent.com/pod-product-compliance
Lightning Source LLC
Chambersburg PA
CBHW071316110526
44591CB00010B/910